STEM
Gems

How 44 Women Shine in
Science, Technology,
Engineering and Mathematics,
And How You Can Too!

Stephanie Espy

ISBN: 978-0-9975337-0-5

Library of Congress Control Number (LCCN): 2016906534

Printed in the United States of America

Cover and interior design by Elaine Callahan/True You Brand Alchemy.

⊖This paper meets the requirements of ANSI/NISO Z39.48-1992 (Permanence of Paper)

TO MY DAUGHTER ZOË

Table of Contents

Acknowledgments

I first have to acknowledge God for His love, grace and mercy. Thank you, Heavenly Father, for giving me the vision, confidence, discipline and means to pursue my dreams.

This book would not be in your hands without the generosity and enthusiasm of the gracious Gems featured on these pages. Thank you to the 44 STEM Gems who share my passion for closing the gender gap and encouraging girls and young women to pursue STEM fields. With crazy busy schedules, these phenomenal leaders made the time to communicate with me over and over again to make this book a reality. In the beginning, most of them were strangers. But now, they are my friends, role models, peers, colleagues, champions and heroes.

I have been blessed with the guidance and companionship of so many who have assisted me in the preparation of this book. I start with the person who was on board from day one and just as eager to get to work as I was: my cousin Ayana Wilson. A STEM Gem herself, Ayana was one of the first people I called with the idea to write this book. She got my vision immediately, and was instrumental in bringing this book to life. Ayana helped me with the initial research, putting in countless hours of internet searches to determine which STEM fields to feature. Then, many more hours to identify and locate women in these fields. Our next step was to contact the women and schedule an interview. Ayana took the lead with conducting interviews, helped source photographers for photo shoots of the women and later helped with the first round of editing. I am blessed and thankful for her commitment, passion and dedication. Ayana, you are a Gem.

Second, I must thank three hugely talented women who all helped to make sure the stories and chapters were written with girls and young women in mind. With a pre-teen daughter herself, Laura Mitchell understood firsthand the target audience. She made sure the language we used in the stories appealed to girls and even tested the wording with her daughter and her daughter's friends. I appreciate Laura most for her professionalism, passion and dedication from start to finish. Then, came Francie Latour. A veteran journalist and storyteller, Francie dove in to the book, editing for content, style and overall structure. She made sure that each line would draw readers in, each sentence was clear and easy to understand and each paragraph and chapter flowed cohesively from one to the next. Hands down, Francie's talent as an editor made this book pop, exceeding my expectations time and time again. Lastly, Rakia Clark came onboard as proofreader of the final copy, checking for consistency in grammar and overall flow. Thank you Laura, Francie and Rakia for the unique gifts you each brought 100% of the time to make this book a success. You are Gems.

Next, I'd like to thank my book designer, Elaine Callahan. Elaine has been a part of every aspect of this two-year journey with me, from initial concepts to final design and layout. We have had hundreds of conversations along the way, and each time she helps me put my vision on paper. In one particular conversation, Elaine asked me to name three words to describe how I want the book to feel. I came up with four: approachable, inspirational, powerful and feminine. Elaine took these words and created the beautiful design you see on these pages. I couldn't have told her exactly to do what she did; it was her own creativity and passion for this project that led her to create a stunning cover and design of the entire book based on my four adjectives. In her own right, Elaine is a Gem.

I'd like to thank my friends and colleagues who helped me along this journey; there are too many to name, but you know who you are. A special thanks to Randy and Jeanette Latimer for brainstorming titles for this book and helping me to come up with the title *STEM Gems*. I want to thank The Gwinnett School of Mathematics, Science & Technology in Lawrenceville, Georgia, and the six young ladies who read sections of *STEM Gems* and gave their testimonials on camera: Apurva, Lucy, Nosayaba, Rachel, Sabrina and Tiffany. I'd like to thank those who beta-read sections of *STEM Gems*: Alba, Amber, April, Deanna, Eboney, Carolanda, Ellen, Jennifer, LaShanda, Leslie, Matthew, Nicole, Nina, Shana, Shayna, Tamaria and Valerie. Thank you for your valuable input and editorial comments.

Finally, I would like to acknowledge and thank from the deepest parts of my heart the people who have not only supported my lifelong journey but are currently walking with me: my family. Dad, Mom, Jennifer, Cecil, Matthew, Leslie and my daughter Zoë. You have supported me in ways only family can. I am grateful for your unconditional love and support. ●

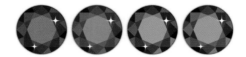

Introduction

This book that you hold in your hands might change your life. At least, that's my goal.

I've been you. I've sat in middle and high school classrooms, listening to career day presentations and pondering my future. I've filled out questionnaires about my interests and wondered how high scores in cognitive reasoning or an unquenchable love of the outdoors or an affinity for colorful metaphors could ever translate into a future that seemed real. Imagining ourselves ten or fifteen years in the future is tough. The present always seems to capture our attention with more passion, more intensity.

I'll let you in on a secret: You don't have to figure it all out now. You don't even have to figure it all out this week or this year. The 44 inspiring women in this book — STEM Gems who *shine* in their respective fields of **S**cience, **T**echnology, **E**ngineering and **M**athematics — collectively changed career courses over a hundred times. They might change careers a hundred more. So what sets them apart from others who pursue dreams and miss the mark?

My best answer is in this book.

Back in high school, I loved chemistry and all things math. I appreciated amazing teachers who challenged me to dig deeply into the material and to ask questions. In chemistry, the hands-on experiments were memorable and exciting. Testing changes in pH and discovering interactions between molecules? Awesome! And in math, I grew to appreciate the beauty in patterns, in logic and in real-world applications. Math builds on itself, and my teachers taught me the necessary pieces to get to each next level. I found that instant gratification when you "get it" exhilarating.

Beyond school, my family gatherings could just as easily have been STEM conventions. My father was an electrical engineer with degrees from the Georgia Institute of Technology (Georgia Tech) and Stanford University. Many uncles, aunts and cousins became mathematicians, scientists and engineers. (You'll find one in this book.) Eventually, my brother Matthew majored in applied math and economics at Harvard University, and my older sister Jennifer rocked electrical engineering at Georgia Tech. My most influential role model was my mother. She was a shining example of what women can accomplish in STEM. An environmental engineer with a math degree from the University of California, Los Angeles and an engineering degree from Georgia Tech, my mother made sure that I was always engaged in challenging activities and programs to strengthen my STEM foundation.

You might conclude that being in STEM is in my DNA — that somehow I had a genetic predisposition to STEM. Despite being born into the same family, my younger sister Leslie pursued a passion that wasn't STEM-related. And like Leslie with her chosen career, many of the women in this book were the first in their families to enter into a STEM career. I'll tell you and they will too: STEM isn't a special brain. STEM doesn't come from a life of privilege. STEM is simply an exposure to what is possible and an internal belief that anyone can be a STEM Gem.

Truly, *anyone* — including you!

I'll let you in on another secret: In high school, despite the rather prevalent career choice of my parents and relatives, I had no concrete idea what engineers did. What did my parents *do* each day? Did they work with other people or with machines? What about engineering ignited a passion within them? I began asking questions, attending summer engineering camps at various colleges and looking ahead to my future. I eventually decided to pursue a career in chemical engineering because, though I was unaware at the time of the many opportunities I would have with a degree in engineering, I held true to my belief that Math + Chemistry = Chemical Engineering. I attended the Massachusetts Institute of Technology (MIT) and the University of California, Berkeley (UC Berkeley), earning bachelor's and master's degrees in chemical engineering.

While at MIT and especially while in graduate school at UC Berkeley, I learned I was an anomaly, someone unique and rare simply because of my gender. I attended classes dominated by men. Fortunately I had women in my life in STEM fields, but I sometimes wondered about my peers who didn't have family gatherings of engineers and scientists to inspire them. To whom did they look when they graduated and went out into the world to make it a better place? Would women continue to be viewed in their field as a rare novelty? Would women be treated as talented professionals for the skills they bring to the field first and gender second, or even twenty-second on their list of qualities admired in a co-worker or boss?

During two of my summers in college, I interned at a chemical plant that manufactured polymers, or plastics used in a wide range of applications from everyday products including bags and bottle caps to performance-critical products used to help make airplanes safer and improve the fuel efficiency of automotives. At this plant, one other woman and I comprised the only female engineers in the entire operation. I longed to stand out for my thirst for knowledge, my ambition in my field, my talents and my skills. Largely, however, I stood out simply because I was a woman in a sea of men.

The gender gap is real. But it doesn't have to be. Not anymore.

Knowledge is power. And power is knowing what interests you and going after it.

Something had to be done to inspire girls and young women — you! — to pursue your STEM interests. This book began as a crusade: assemble some of the brightest women in diverse STEM areas to inspire the next generation through their struggles and triumphs, in their words and the words of those who witnessed their achievements. I wanted to provide you with first-hand accounts of what these women do, how they began their journey, who impacted them, how they are changing the world and what advice they have for young women today. I wanted to highlight wildly unique careers so that bubble of what is possible expands your imagination. I wanted to do my part to close the gender gap in STEM.

So, how should you approach this book that has the potential to be a life-altering experience?

The 44 unique stories contained in this book are possible destinations on your map, but they are certainly not the only ones. Think of them as way-stations to even more possibilities beyond. You will frown at the challenges and injustices these women faced and smile at what the human spirit can overcome. You will journey to outer space, dig deep into ancient Peruvian soil and root for those women on the front-lines, fighting the most critical and impactful diseases on the planet. You will witness the cool-factor you only thought possible in a Hollywood movie. And in the end you will have 44 women in your army of inspirational role models whose stories will endure in your mind and heart for the exciting ride ahead.

This book began as a crusade, but it became so much more. When I assembled the biographies, the story had yet to be finished. There were commonalities, threads, beautiful patterns that illuminate when brought to the surface. That's when I realized all these amazing STEM Gems needed to share this book, these answers, with the most important person of all: you.

I call this section *Crystals* because all gemstones take the form of crystals in the formative stages of growth. The *Crystals* portion is about *you* — about dreaming when STEM isn't already in your blood, about celebrating your gender in the face of adversity, about sketching that route between this moment and your dreams. You will learn what you can do this school year, this summer, next week, tomorrow and even today to start on your dream path to be a STEM Gem. The action checklist at the conclusion of each chapter will guide you beyond a mere reading experience. This critical portion gives you immediate, actionable steps to tackle your STEM dreams.

The advice I give you in his book is exactly what I did myself. No one's STEM road is ever easy, and I am no exception. I worked hard. I took advantage of opportunities that came my way, and I never lost a sense of curiosity about the world. Inspiration was all around me; and with this book, inspiration surrounds you, too.

Someday, you will pick up a magazine in a doctor's office or catch a story on the evening news or see an internet headline about one of our 44 STEM Gems, continuing to inspire. It has happened to me more than once in the creation of this book, and I know it will happen for you, too. These hard-working, gifted women are just beginning to come into their full potential, and the world will never be the same. They are 44 in number, but they represent so many more. They represent countless women in STEM every day, all over the world. They represent my mother, me and, yes, even you.

If you found this book in a public library, share it with everyone you know — even the guys. If someone you love gave it to you, mark it up, highlight it in your favorite color, dog-ear the pages, spill soup on its edges and trade it with a friend. (Just be sure to get it back!) Talk about these women at the dinner table so your little sister and cousins and neighbors will know that they, too, can be STEM Gems. Dream. Stay open-minded. Listen — *really* listen to the women in this book who have come before you. Revisit these pages often. Turn to them when a test score comes back lower than you had hoped. Take comfort in our 44 STEM Gems who were once you.

You can pursue the intellectual curiosities that fuel you and do amazing things.

Lastly, I want to hear from you. Follow me on social media. Post your thoughts, ideas, and questions on the many posts and images that you see. Share a photo of you pursuing your STEM dreams. Start a STEM Gems Club in your school — visit the STEM Gems website to get started. Share pics of you and your STEM Gems Club members engaging in fun activities. Connect with me; I want to see you shine. I want the world to see you shine.

I wish I had this book when I was a teenager. But what are wishes without action? This book is my action. What will be yours? ●

Stephanie Espy

Web: www.STEMGemsBook.com
LinkedIn: @Stephanie Espy
Facebook, Twitter and Instagram: @STEMGemsBook
#GiveGirlsRoleModels

STEM GEMS Science

STEM GEMS Technology

Archaeologist

Atmospheric Scientist

Biologist and Geneticist

Animation Technologist

Bio-technologist

Computer Coding Creator

Entomologist

Forensic Scientist

Global Health Scientist

Holography and Virtual Reality Technologist

Hysteroscopy Technologist

Internet Gaming Technologist

Immunologist

Microbiologist

Network Scientist

Internet Identity Advocate

Online Security Expert

Solar Energy Technologist

Oceanographer and Geophysicist

Physicist

Planetary Scientist

Startup Champion and Entrepreneur

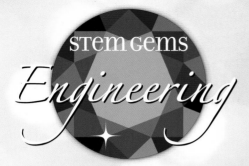

STEM GEMS
Engineering

STEM GEMS
Mathematics

Chemical
Engineer

Computer Scientist
and Engineer

Electrical
Engineer

Actuary

Architect

Biostatistician

Environmental
Engineer

Materials
Engineer

Mechanical and
Fire Engineer

Cancer Modeling
Mathematician

Data Scientist

Dynamical Systems
Mathematician

Nuclear Engineer

Product Designer and
Mechanical Engineer

Robotics
Engineer

Economist

Geophysicist

Graph Theory
Mathematician

Web Application
Engineer

Network Systems
Mathematician

Number Theory
Mathematician

Urban Planner
and Designer

STEM GEMS
Science

STEM GEMS
Technology

STEM GEMS
Engineering

STEM GEMS
Mathematics

Introducing Our STEM Gems

What does it take to get some of the most influential and innovative women of the STEM world to take time out to participate in one very special book? As it turns out, the mere mention of you, the reader.

Amazing, right?

See, these women are seeking out cancer cures, turning the sun's rays into viable energy and advancing crime-fighting technology. They are testifying before Congress, building skyscrapers and inventing robots that will someday touch distant planets. But these 44 leaders, each inspiring in their own right, have more in common than a passion for science, technology, engineering and math. They are just as passionate about inspiring the next generation of young women to embrace STEM.

In selecting these STEM Gems, I focused on women who are thought leaders in their fields. I paid attention to the newsmakers and the ones who should be newsmakers. I combed STEM organization and higher education websites for innovators and risk-takers, women making a difference, women challenging the status quo with new ideas. Each one reflects a unique career path, opening new doors to the incredible diversity of opportunities that await you! Each woman also has a personal story to tell, dating all the way back to childhood. That's when STEM starts. That's when STEM has the greatest impact on our collective futures.

Diving into their lives, accomplishments and careers, I came to know them as girls and young women, unearthing that pivotal moment or influence or experience that shaped their remarkable futures. I wanted them to speak in their own voices to you, the reader. Who better to figure out how to close the gender gap in STEM than the women who have triumphed over gender adversity?

Read about all your STEM Gems in one sitting, or read one Gem each day so that their stories come alive in your imagination. Share them with an important girl or woman in your life. Dive into their worlds. Doodle inspiration beside them. Dream.

These women invited me into their worlds, sharing private thoughts and emotional truths. For that, I am grateful and humbled. Consider their stories a special invitation, a confidence shared among sisters with a mutual love for science, technology, engineering and math. Simply by reading their stories, you are now a part of the STEM Gems sisterhood. ●

stem gems
Science

JENNIFER CHAYES, *Network Scientist*

INEZ FUNG, *Atmospheric Scientist*

HELENE GAYLE, *Global Health Scientist*

LAURIE GLIMCHER, *Immunologist*

CHRISTINE GOFORTH, *Entomologist*

JANET JANSSON, *Microbiologist*

MICHELE KOONS, *Archaeologist*

MARCIA KEMPER McNUTT, *Oceanographer and Geophysicist*

KAREN OLSON, *Forensic Scientist*

CAROLYN PORCO, *Planetary Scientist*

LISA RANDALL, *Theoretical Physicist*

PARDIS SABETI, *Computational Biologist and Geneticist*

STEM GEMS
Science Intro

More than any other discipline in the STEM acronym, science defies any one definition. Science is both a field of study and the process by which we satisfy our curiosity about the world around us. Science is the gravity tugging at our bellies on a roller coaster ride, the lantern in the abdomen of a firefly and a common language that crosses political and cultural boundaries. Where technology is modeling, science is knowing. Where mathematics is rules, science is hypothesis. Where engineering is design, science is discovery. And while science cannot move forward without technology, engineering and mathematics, science, at its core, is simply the quest for understanding.

Science is traditionally divided into two categories: the social sciences, which relate to human behavior, and the natural sciences, which seek to understand the natural world. Though educators debate whether or not to include the social sciences under the STEM umbrella, they generally consider only the natural sciences when referring to STEM. Natural science includes disciplines ranging from physics and chemistry to geology, meteorology, botany and biology. Other scientific disciplines include formal sciences like statistics and applied sciences like computer science. From particle science, which examines the parts of an atom, to astronomy, which takes on the observable and vast universe, if any human has ever been curious about an aspect of his or her environment, there is a scientific field dedicated to its pursuit.

According to internationally renowned marine microbiologist Nicole Dubilier, "being a scientist isn't simply a career choice; it's a way of thinking, a way of life." In the lives of the women scientists you will soon meet — an immunologist and a geneticist, a climatologist and a microbiologist, a physicist and a planetary scientist — you'll discover that a curiosity about our world was present from an early age. Karen Olson was a schoolgirl capturing fingerprint patterns with packing tape and dust before she became a leading innovator in forensic science. Archaeologist Michele Koons excavated a New Jersey beach long before she implemented new, high-tech methods for excavating ancient ruins in South America. And before Marcia Kemper McNutt became a world-renowned expert on mapping oceanic floors, she was a little girl visiting San Diego's Scripps Institution of Oceanography and dreaming about the world's sea animals.

Today's society is poised at the edge of a vast frontier of knowledge, one in which science intersects powerfully with technology, breakthroughs are shared instantly via the internet instead of in academic journals and the sheer volume of data researchers have at their fingertips calls for a new word — zillionics. Science will likely advance more in the next 50 years than it has in the past 400 years. From perfecting the scientific method to disproving the theory that Earth is the center of the universe, past science has moved at a glacial pace compared to what the future will bring. The road ahead will see tremendous advances in biology and medicine, two areas of study that boast significant representation by women.

The cause of the gender gap in science is puzzling. According to a 2012 Gender Equity Report by the U.S. Department of Education, high school boys outnumbered girls in physics classes, but girls were evenly represented in biology studies and surpassed the number of boys in chemistry studies. This trend continues into post-secondary education, where the physical and life sciences account for 57 percent of female STEM degrees, compared to 31 percent of male STEM degrees. So why are women attracted to some areas of science more than others? Theories abound. As part of a larger study called Perceptions of Women in Academic Science, some 2,500 male and female biologists and physicists from leading universities in the U.S. were surveyed and interviewed. Almost half of all participants believed that women might be discriminated against in physics. Additionally, some theorized that women gravitate toward more "emotional labor," dedicating themselves to scientific advancements that will help others. Still others attributed the gap to cultural stereotypes that keep women from pursuing male-dominated science fields.

The scientists assembled here defy gender-based theories. Lisa Randall rose to the top of the physics world because she wanted to pursue the big picture of why we are all here. Christine Goforth, known as the Dragonfly Woman, developed an intense passion for insects. Jennifer Chayes's lifelong pursuit has focused on mathematical algorithms. Physician and global health leader Helene Gayle followed the path of medicine because other women in her life told her "this is something you can do." She believes confidence is the key to strengthening the number of women in science. "It takes people believing that it's possible. The idea of do-ability is so important."

On the following pages, you'll see glimmers of what is possible. These scientists stand at the edge of that vast frontier, one hand reaching toward progress, the other extended to the new generation of young, curious women.

One final aspect of science deserves mention. Science marches on. Always. Science will never be complete. There will always be new questions, new insights, new scientists to take the baton in our never-ending quest to reveal the truths about our world. Scientific advancements rely on generations to come. Scientific advancements rely on you.

Are you ready to take the baton? ●

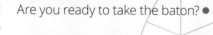

jennifer chayes
Network Scientist

Behind Dr. Jennifer Chayes' path to leadership in science lies a surprising secret.

Dr. Chayes works as a managing director of Microsoft Research New England in Cambridge, Massachusetts and Microsoft Research New York City. With a PhD in mathematical physics from Princeton University, she is a pioneer in the emerging field of network science and in phase transitions — the change from one state of matter into another.

But as a teenager, Dr. Chayes was a high school dropout.

"I didn't like school. I was kind of bored," she says. "I went back to a school for dropouts. I dropped out a few times and went back a few times and finally they let me finish. When I did my last stint at the school, I ended up teaching math to the other dropouts." Dr. Chayes scored very well on her College Board exams, which allowed her to attend Wesleyan University. When she reflects on her high school years, she embraces her unconventional route. "Challenging authority enabled me to pursue science differently. If you're going to be a scientist, you have to challenge the norm."

In hindsight, it's not surprising that Dr. Chayes was destined for much more than her GED. She still recalls being an impressionable four- or five-year-old and hanging out with a group of neighbors who had a blast solving math puzzles. She got an early spark in math when a fantastic seventh grade geometry teacher introduced her to mathematical proofs. And most important, she had a strong work ethic that belied her high school performance. More than anything, Dr. Chayes says, young women who have had a tough start in school need to know that "they have the right to challenge authority. They just have to get the working hard part down."

At Wesleyan, Dr. Chayes took a physics class that kicked boredom to the curb. Physics, along with math, ignited her imagination and transformed her into a student who hungered for an ever-evolving learning challenge. The daughter of Iranian immigrant parents, she had always been taught that excellence meant becoming a doctor or lawyer. But a freshman year math professor recognized her gift for math and opened her up to a different definition of excellence: academics and research. Dr. Chayes went on to receive her bachelor's degree in biology and physics, graduating first in her class. After earning her PhD at Princeton, she completed her post-doctorate work in the mathematics and physics

Photo Credit: Microsoft Research

departments at Harvard University and Cornell University. She became a professor of mathematics at the University of California, Los Angeles and was poised for a long career in academia when industry knocked on her door.

The echoing of patterns across different realms, and the potential to connect and solve problems in these realms through research, lie at the heart of Dr. Chayes's scientific passion. "I come up with an algorithm for computer science

"If you're going to be a scientist, you have to challenge the norm."

Dr. Chayes was recruited to join Microsoft Research in 1996. She loved that in addition to the company's cutting-edge product development, Microsoft also wanted to pursue the theoretical science shaping the technology of the future. Together with her mathematical physicist husband, Dr. Chayes co-founded the Theory Group at Microsoft's research lab in Redmond, Washington, where she created methods to analyze the design, structures and behaviors of various growing networks such as the internet. "My research has spanned a lot of different things: math, physics, biology, computer science, machine learning, social sciences, economics. I tend to see patterns emerge in different places. So in tech, you see social networks. In biology, many of the processes that take place inside our cells are biological networks. I see these same patterns in different places. It's a lot like artists seeing the same motifs in different domains. People should emphasize the kind of high level creativity and analogy that drives STEM research."

research that can tell me something about possible drug treatments for cancer. That's very magical to me — that the same kinds of math and motifs will stretch across different domains." She is equally passionate about her legacy as a teacher: many of the graduate and post-doctoral students who spend time in her Microsoft lab have gone on to successful careers.

As a mentor, she advises her students to be confident, remain optimistic and to persevere. "Not giving up is very important — just saying to yourself, 'if I'm insecure, it might not correspond to reality. It may just be that society has put into my head false ideas about what I can do and I just need to ignore them.'" She wants young women to know that STEM research satisfies creativity and that *anything* is possible. Dr. Chayes's surprising route to exceptionality proves it. ●

Inez Fung
Atmospheric Scientist

Professor Inez Fung grew up on the beaches of Hong Kong's southern shore. For her, the beach represented freedom. She floated in the water, watched the clouds and felt the waves ripple beneath her. In the spring of 1967, political unrest between Hong Kong and China led to riots, prompting Professor Fung to seek higher education outside her homeland. She initially attended Utica College in New York but later transferred to the Massachusetts Institute of Technology (MIT). She received a bachelor's degree at MIT in applied math and became the second woman in MIT's history to earn a PhD in meteorology. She is now a professor of atmospheric science at the University of California, Berkeley and a world-renowned leader in climate research.

Professor Fung has a "tremendous love and respect for the planet — how the whole system comes together." Starting in the early 1980s, she worked with chemists, geographers and other scientists to develop mathematical models that track variations in carbon dioxide levels in the atmosphere, both over time and across continents. She was also at the forefront of solving the mystery around carbon sinks — regions of ocean and forest that play a crucial role in absorbing the earth's carbon emissions. Professor Fung's research identified land in the northern hemisphere as a major "missing" sink soaking up carbon dioxide.

Professor Fung always had a talent for math. "I was interested in everything and mathematics came easier to me than literature. I like numbers. There is elegance in numbers." When Professor Fung applied to graduate school, she did not have straight A's. She attributes her academic struggles to one thing: boredom. Her studies had yet to ignite her passion. But an undergraduate applied mathematics course introduced her to earth science and changed all that. The course nudged her away from a career in theoretical calculations. Once she found a connection to something concrete, she knew she would use mathematics to impact her world.

In graduate school, Professor Fung studied with meteorologist Dr. Jule Gregory Charney, an advisor and mentor who had a profound impact on the path of Professor Fung's research. Although she initially focused on hurricane studies, Dr. Charney encouraged her to learn chemistry and biology so that they could start a new project to understand the variations of CO_2 in the atmosphere. Sadly, her mentor passed away before their collaboration could be realized, but Professor

Fung would grow that seed of an idea into a major field of study through her groundbreaking research on our planet's carbon cycle.

Her current research focuses on the cycle of carbon dioxide in our atmosphere and how this and other greenhouse gasses will shape the earth's climate in the future. A greenhouse gas is any gas that absorbs the sun's heat and stores it in the earth's atmosphere. Because she can't recreate the earth's climate in a laboratory, Professor Fung constructs large-scale 3D mathematical models to measure greenhouse gas emissions. As a leading expert in her field, she led a team of U.S. and U.K. scientists in issuing a major 2014 report on climate change for policymakers and the public. Their conclusions were grave: carbon dioxide levels in the atmosphere have risen to higher levels than at any other time in the past 800,000 years, contributing to the planet's overall warming. Although there is always some degree of uncertainty regarding the minute details of prediction, Professor Fung is quick to point out that scientific "uncertainty does not challenge my certainty about the fact the planet will warm. Climate change is happening. We see it in temperature, we see it in the melting ice and we see it in sea-level rise."

Professor Fung's contributions to her field extend far beyond carbon cycle research. She also studies the earth's dust cycle, the process by which dust particles that absorb and reflect radiation in the atmosphere fall into the oceans, boosting iron levels in the sea and fueling the productivity of the marine ecosystems. Professor Fung is the founding director of the Berkeley Atmospheric Sciences Center, which brings chemists, biologists, ecologists and mathematicians together to address critical problems in climate science. She also founded the Berkeley Institute of the Environment,

an initiative focused on research and training the next generation of environmental leaders. In addition to leading the HydroWatch project, a multidisciplinary study in one of the University of California's Natural Reserves that uses innovative technology to track the life cycle of water, Professor Fung is also on the science team of the Orbiting Carbon Observatory, a new satellite that will measure the abundance of carbon dioxide over the earth. She was named one of *Scientific American's* 50 leading researchers of 2005 and earned the World Technology Network's 2006 Award for the Environment.

"Science is fun and exciting," says Professor Fung. "My reward isn't money. You can't compensate for that magic moment when you say 'Aha' and you find the answer."

Almost 50 years later, Professor Fung's deep contributions to climate science have brought her full-circle to that girl who floated and dreamed on the waves all those years ago. She is modeling the ocean, the atmosphere, the trees and soils, using supercomputers not just to predict the planet's future, but to protect it. ●

"My reward isn't money. You can't compensate for that magic moment when you say 'Aha' and you find the answer."

11

HELENE GAYLE
Global Health Scientist

Dr. Helene Gayle hopes to put herself out of a job one day.

Dr. Gayle's passion is global social change. Her appointment as CEO of the McKinsey Social Initiative (MSI), as well as her previous roles, have positioned Dr. Gayle to make positive impacts on complex, global problems.

MSI was launched by the global consulting firm McKinsey and Company to develop innovative solutions to major global challenges. MSI's first program, entitled *Generations*, tackles global youth unemployment. This role allows Dr. Gayle to utilize her varied experiences in both the public and private sectors to make the greatest impact.

Prior to joining MSI, Dr. Gayle was president and CEO of CARE USA, the U.S. branch and founding member of one of the largest international humanitarian organizations in the world. Her leadership advanced the organization's primary goals: to end the cycle of extreme poverty and aid by fostering healthy, balanced societies where all members are free to realize their potential. As the leading decision-maker for an organization that reaches more than 83 million people through 997 projects in 84 countries, Dr. Gayle was a crusader for bettering the human condition on a global scale. Forbes magazine named her the 78th most powerful woman in the

world for her international reach and impact, and over the years she has garnered praise from world leaders including President Barack Obama and the late South African President Nelson Mandela, yet on a day-to-day basis Dr. Gayle concerned herself with the survival needs of the world's most destitute populations. "We believe that it's possible to eliminate extreme poverty over the next couple of decades. We know what needs to be done and we have the tools, but do we have the will as a world community to do it?"

Born into a generation that witnessed and brought about massive social and political change in the 1960s, Dr. Gayle has a sense of sheer will that runs deep. She grew up in Buffalo, New York, where her social worker mother inspired her to believe she could be the change she hoped to see in the world. "My mother really gave that sense of giving back to the community. She'd say, 'you've got a good brain and a big mouth — use it.'" Her mother also exposed her to students from other parts of the world, and Dr. Gayle began to take an interest in anti-apartheid and liberation struggles. "I had a real interest in global issues. I was also very interested in what could be done to improve the plight of African Americans." She believed that by studying psychology, she

Photo Credit: © Allen Clinton/CARE

"Read books about everyday people who decided they wanted to be part of something larger than themselves."

could better understand the issues that African-American communities faced. Medicine became her career of choice; pediatric and public health became her passion.

After earning a bachelor's degree at Barnard College, a master's degree in Public Health at Johns Hopkins University and an M.D. at the University of Pennsylvania, Dr. Gayle completed her residency in pediatric medicine at the Children's National Medical Center in Washington, D.C. She then entered the Epidemic Intelligence Service program at the Centers for Disease Control (CDC), the nation's leading public health institute, which also plays a major role in international health issues. In 20 years of service at the CDC and then at the Bill and Melinda Gates Foundation, Dr. Gayle has made significant contributions to the advancement of HIV/AIDS research, education and prevention. "Just a few years ago, less than one percent of people who needed HIV treatment had access to it, and now it's up to 55 percent and growing. We are now on track to absolutely eliminate pediatric HIV infection globally." The unique HIV prevention project she spearheaded in India for the Gates Foundation had impact in halting the spread of HIV there.

Dr. Gayle's move to CARE in 2006 made her the first woman and the first African-American leader of the organization, and gave her the chance to broaden her work and help an even greater number of people. "I was drawn to CARE because it offered me the chance to address some of the underlying social and economic factors that fuel health inequalities and keep people trapped in poverty." Her vision for CARE included shifting the sole focus away from aid and relief and really seeking to understand the dynamics that created the state of dire need in the first place. A huge part of that understanding came with the realization that "if you can change the life of a girl or woman, you didn't just have an impact on that individual. That really created a catalytic change for families, for communities and ultimately for societies. Because when you bring girls and women into the equation, you bring a different kind of balance. You bring a different voice."

For young women interested in a career in global health, Dr. Gayle advises "reading people's stories. It makes you realize what is possible. Read books about everyday people who decided they wanted to be part of something larger than themselves — Ms. Rosa Parks, Ms. Maya Angelou, Ms. Charlayne Hunter-Gault just to name a few." She also recommends getting experience in the field by working in a lab during summer or traveling to places where students can be exposed to people who help others. Most important? "Follow your passion. Do something that inspires you, that makes you excited. If you are doing something you enjoy, that's the first step toward achieving your goals."

With that kind of passion, who needs to hope? Dr. Gayle is determined to fight global issues one community and one day at a time. ●

Laurie Glimcher

Immunologist

On the first day of medical school, Dr. Laurie Glimcher called her mom in a panic. All the other students seemed so perfect — perfect grades, so put together, so completely intimidating. Dr. Glimcher worried she wouldn't succeed. Her mother treated her to a nice dinner out, dropped her back at her dorm and told her that she would do just fine. Dr. Glimcher believed her.

Another day, early in her research career at the Dana-Farber Cancer Institute in Boston, Dr. Glimcher became discouraged that her experiments were not going as planned and left her lab early. On the way home she ran into her father, Dr. Melvin Glimcher, an accomplished orthopedic surgeon and biophysicist who made tremendous advances in prosthetics during his career. When Dr. Glimcher expressed her frustrations with her research, her father's response surprised her. "Oh, no. That is the wrong approach. It's when the experiments are not going well that you dig in and you don't give in and you work and you work."

In addition to her own hard work, Dr. Glimcher credits her family as a driving force in her career as a scientist. Her mother armed her with self-confidence, her father nurtured her interest in science and her grandmother, who once led political campaigns during the Great Depression, left her with the lasting impression that women can do and be anything. She also believes her three children have kept her grounded and connected to the important things in life throughout her career. "They reminded me that in the long run, if I didn't make a certain discovery, someone else would — I was far from irreplaceable as a researcher, [but irreplaceable as a mother]."

Many of her peers would disagree.

As an immunologist — a doctor who focuses on the body's ability to fight off disease and infection — Dr. Glimcher has made breakthrough discoveries in T-lymphocyte cells, also known as T-helper cells. These cells regulate the activities of other immune cells and tell them how to respond to invasions that are foreign to the body. Her lab studies how T-helper cells develop and activate other molecules and cells. She hopes to learn why the body's immune system sometimes turns on itself and attacks its own tissues, in order to better understand and develop treatments for diseases like cancer, osteoporosis, rheumatoid arthritis and allergies.

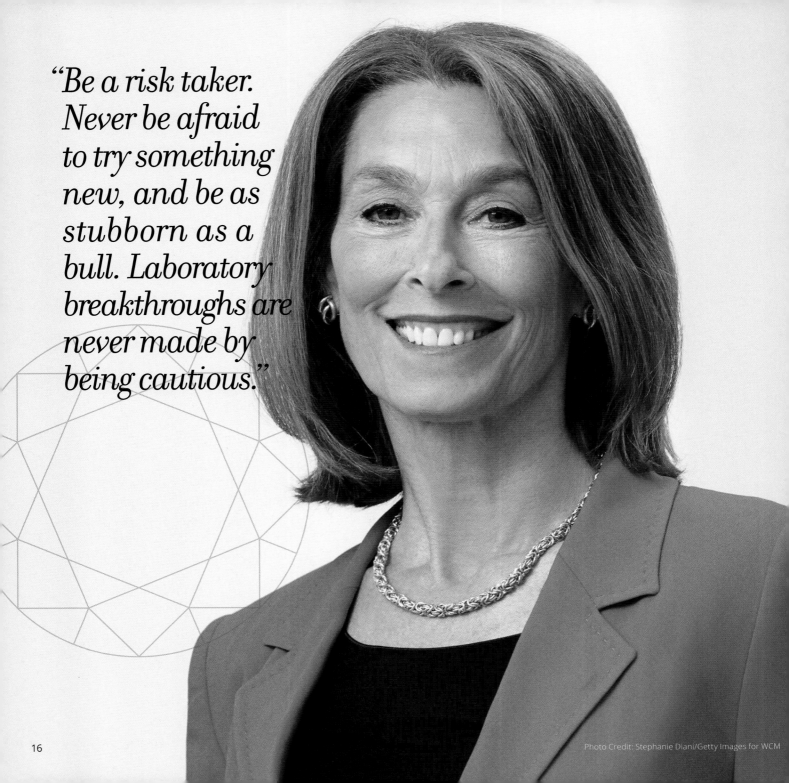

"Be a risk taker. Never be afraid to try something new, and be as stubborn as a bull. Laboratory breakthroughs are never made by being cautious."

16

Dr. Glimcher has contributed more than 350 articles to medical literature, presided over the American Association of Immunologists (AAI), was elected into the prominent National Academy of Sciences and is the recipient of numerous awards, including the Feinstein Institute's Advancing Women in Science and Medicine Award in 2013 and the L'Oréal-UNESCO for Women in Science Award in 2014 for her pioneering research and leadership as a role model for women in science and medicine. She considers her AAI Excellence in Mentoring Award one of the most meaningful honors of her life, because she believes that part of her responsibility as a scientist is to help train the next generation.

Her pursuit of science began as a teenager in her father's lab at Massachusetts General Hospital. She remembers being captivated by rat and chicken bones swirling around in beakers and printers churning out colorful graphs. Growing up, her summers were spent between her father's lab and a vacation home on Martha's Vineyard, Massachusetts, where she would dissect frogs and try to revive dying flowers with potions she invented. Though biology and English literature captured her attention early on, she felt the pull of medicine, switched gears and earned her M.D. from Harvard University in 1976. She became a senior physician at the Brigham and Woman's Hospital and a professor of medicine at Harvard, where she headed one of the top immunology labs in the world.

Her advice to women considering a science-based career comes straight from her father: "Be a risk taker. Never be afraid to try something new, and be as stubborn as a bull. Laboratory breakthroughs are never made by being cautious.

There are so many talented and smart young women, but sometimes they lack the same self-confidence that a lot of men have. Women tend to underestimate their abilities, while men often overestimate theirs. Don't be afraid to stand up for yourself. Ask for what you need and just go for what you want." She also believes that scientists must pursue their research and experiments with passion to be successful.

Dr. Glimcher has always been a vocal advocate of building support networks for women scientists while they raise families. As the leader of a large laboratory at Harvard Medical School, she provided laboratory technicians as extra hands for female post-docs and graduate students who were the primary caregivers for their children. "The women for whom I provided that went on to do very well. They ended up as tenured professors at academic institutions. Some of them went into the private sector and did very well there. Having that boost really made a difference. I did not find resentment from their male colleagues. They understood." She was then able to convince the leadership at the National Institutes of Health to establish a similar program for their grantees.

As the first female dean of any medical college in New York State, Weill Cornell Medicine in Manhattan, Dr. Glimcher continues to build networks for female scientists who don't have the support she had while raising her three children. She plans to raise money for an endowment that will continue to offer this critical support. Dr. Glimcher never wants young women to have to choose between a career and raising a family. She is proof that with the right support, both are possible. ●

CHRISTINE GOFORTH
Entomologist

One warm July day in 2009, Mrs. Christine Goforth and a friend visited a lake near their homes in Tucson, Arizona, to collect water samples to study. Although it was typical to see a few dragonflies stirring near the grass surrounding the lake, nothing prepared Mrs. Goforth for the sight of several *hundred* dragonflies darting, whirring and swarming the lakeside. Captivated, she and her friend took notes and even returned several more times to appreciate a rare, special occurrence in nature.

The dragonflies moved on, but Mrs. Goforth's desire to understand the mystery of dragonfly swarms remained. Known as "The Dragonfly Woman," a nickname given to her by colleagues to capture her never-ending fascination with the creatures, Mrs. Goforth has made it her mission to fill a gaping hole in scientific knowledge about why and how dragonfly swarms form. Because these swarms can be elusive, she has harnessed the power of social media and the internet to follow swarm sightings. With thousands of members, the Dragonfly Swarm Project has evolved into a thriving investigation of citizen scientists, with participants submitting online observations and reports of dragonfly swarm behavior.

In addition to her dragonfly obsession, Mrs. Goforth studies the respiration and behavior of giant water bugs, or belostomatids, in Arizona's Sonoran Desert. "Giant water bugs are crazy cool animals, and my work has helped determine how their eggs benefit from the care they receive from their fathers. That's right — *Dad* takes care of the babies, a very unusual behavior in insects." Although scientists have known for 100 years that these giant water bug fathers care for their offspring, Mrs. Goforth was among the first to seek out the reason for this evolutionary behavior. She found that these super-fathers provide a delicate balance of oxygen and moisture to the eggs.

Mrs. Goforth knows a little something about super fathers.

Her father was a computer engineer and amateur geologist who loved sharing his hobby of mineral collecting with his two daughters. When Mrs. Goforth wasn't digging in the dirt with him, her outdoor-loving family was camping or fishing or bird watching. Whether it was observing a desert tortoise in the yard or a sun spider in the laundry room, she recalls spending many hours captivated by the animals and insects in her environment. At one time, her family even had 24 pets. "I think all of these experiences got me really interested in animals and animal behavior."

Photo Credit: C.L. Goforth

"A lot of the very best scientists and other STEM leaders are people who have turned something they're obsessed with into a career."

Mrs. Goforth didn't always embrace insects. She recalls being three or four years old and experiencing a three-inch-long palo verde beetle drop out of a tree onto her shoulder. Much flailing of the arms and chaos ensued. "Those beetles are scary — they bite and they're terrible fliers — so it was a horrible experience." After another encounter in Arizona's Chiricahua Mountains — a huge field brimming with ladybugs — the young, impressionable Mrs. Goforth developed a healthy respect for insects. By the time she needed a 4-H project in 9th grade, she and one of her neighbors had already started an insect museum in a tiny room under the stairs at her neighbor's house. It was during this project that Mrs. Goforth realized that being an entomologist was a real job. "I worked toward that goal from that moment on," she recalls. "When I got to college, I met an awesome professor, Dr. Alex Vargo, who had earned an entomology PhD in the 1970s when there weren't nearly as many female entomologists, so I thought she was inspiring."

Mrs. Goforth attended Colorado College, then went on to graduate school at the University of Arizona before starting her career as a teacher. From then on, she knew she wanted teaching to be her primary focus. She received a National Science Foundation GK-12 award that allowed her to spend a year teaching kids about nature in an outdoor education center. She is currently working to complete her PhD while serving as the senior manager of citizen science at the North Carolina Museum of Natural Sciences. A champion of the museum's educational programs and laboratory projects, she brings researchers and curious non-scientists together to answer scientific questions of all kinds.

Mrs. Goforth encourages young women interested in STEM careers to follow their interests. "I loved my dad to pieces, but he once gave me a very bad piece of advice that I'm glad I ignored. He told me that my job and my hobby shouldn't be the same thing. Well, I can say that you *will* be a better STEM professional if you love what you're doing so much that you would be doing it even if it wasn't your job! A lot of the very best scientists and other STEM leaders are people who have turned something they're obsessed with into a career." She advises women to "be prepared to work harder than the men you'll go to school with. There is *still* this completely incorrect assumption by some that women aren't as capable as men in STEM careers. That's absolutely not true — we are every bit as good as the guys, and in many cases we're better because we work harder to earn our place in STEM fields. Don't listen to anyone who tells you that you can't do something. You can be anything you want to be if you put your mind to it." •

Janet Jansson
Microbiologist

Around the year 1500, Leonardo da Vinci predicted man would learn far more about the movement of celestial bodies than about the soil under our feet. More than 500 years later, his hunch turned out to be true. While space missions have observed our solar system billions of kilometers from Earth, more than 90 percent of microorganisms have never been isolated in a lab and studied for their properties. Why are these little buggers so important? Nature's microorganisms carry out critical, life-sustaining functions such as cycling carbon and other nutrients, promoting the growth of plants and preventing disease. Space has its own dark matter, but microbiologist Dr. Janet Jansson prefers the largely untapped world of Earth's dark matter: microbes.

Microbes are microscopic living organisms found in air, soil, water — even on and inside our bodies. Bacteria, viruses, fungi, algae and protozoa are all examples of microbes, the oldest form of life on Earth.

For more than 30 years, Dr. Jansson's passion has been microbial ecology — the study of microbes in the environment and their interactions. Her expertise lies in using a new, big-data approach to scientific analysis called "omics" to better understand the key functions of microorganisms that live in complex microbial communities like soil, sediment and even the human gut. From the impact of global warming on Alaska's permafrost to the progression of illnesses like Crohn's disease, Dr. Jansson's advancements have had a major impact on our understanding of these tiny, complex microbial communities.

Dr. Jansson spent her formative years in Albuquerque, New Mexico. Daughter to an elementary school teacher and an electrical engineer, she received nurturing guidance and support from her parents, who positioned her for a successful science career. In addition to being a voracious reader, Dr. Jansson embraced nature from a young age. Camping, visiting national parks and hiking all had an impact on the eco-minded scientist she would become. Dr. Jansson recalls that she has "always loved animals and nature and had a lot of empathy for the environment."

Although her father encouraged her to pursue a degree in chemical engineering because of the opportunities the field provided to women, Dr. Jansson's true passion came to life in one particular "aha" moment in a lecture at New Mexico State University. "Professor Bill Lindeman said that research

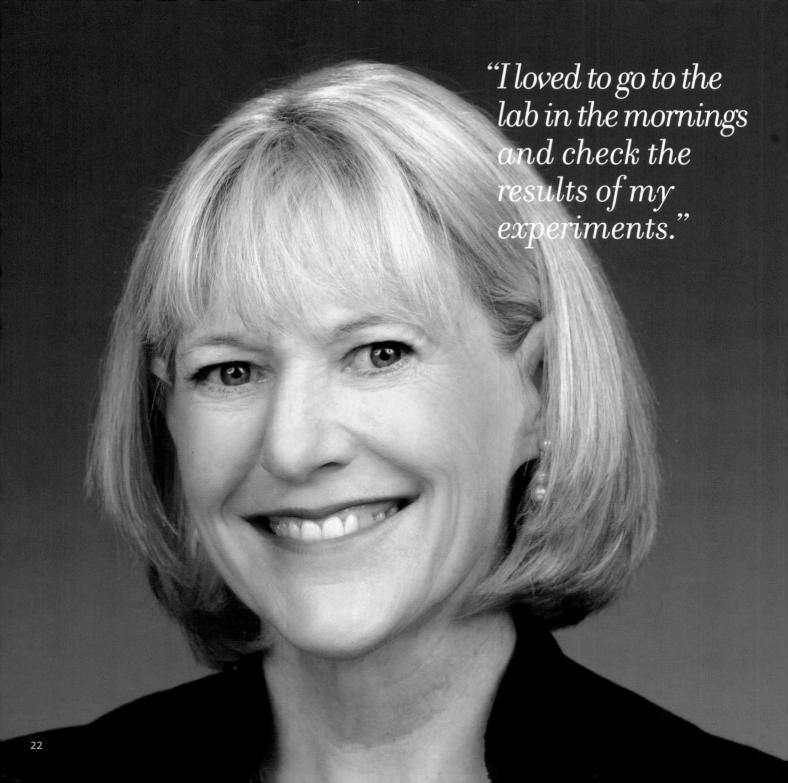

"I loved to go to the lab in the mornings and check the results of my experiments."

in soil microbiology was a growing area with a lot of opportunities for scientists interested in environmental research. I approached him after class and asked if he had any work for me in his laboratory. I ended up working in his lab that last couple years of my undergraduate work, first as a dishwasher, then preparing media and finally doing some experiments with the graduate students. This was the opportunity that helped me to realize my future career. I loved to go to the lab in the mornings and check the results of my experiments."

Dr. Jansson never intended to acquire master's and doctoral degrees (at Colorado State University and Michigan State University, respectively), but after her bachelor's degree, "there were no jobs that really interested me. I continued to study because I loved research." After earning her PhD, she went to Sweden and established a successful research career for the next 20 years, eventually becoming a vice dean and professor of environmental microbiology at the Swedish University of Agricultural Sciences. In 2007, she was recruited back to the U.S. as a senior staff scientist at Lawrence Berkeley National Laboratory, where she led the Ecosystems Biology program. In 2014, Dr. Jansson became the director of the biological sciences division at Pacific Northwest National Laboratory in Richland, Washington, run by the U.S. Department of Energy. Dr. Jansson believes the most exciting aspect of her research is "the opportunity to do high-impact science that addresses important areas, such as climate change. I really like the way that scientific experts at the Pacific Northwest National Laboratory work together as a team to tackle science problems that are not possible to study at single universities."

In their investigation of microorganisms extracted and thawed from blocks of thousand-year-old permafrost ice, Dr. Jansson and her team found that the samples rapidly awakened and released methane and carbon dioxide. The findings have huge implications for understanding the environmental impact of global warming in the Arctic region.

After the April 2010 Deepwater Horizon oil spill in the Gulf of Mexico, Dr. Jansson used her multi-omics approach to determine the impact of the environmental disaster on the water, the beach and the sediment communities. By using omics, she and her team can jump straight to sequencing DNA or studying proteins or metabolites that microorganisms produce, instead of waiting to cultivate microbes from the environment.

Dr. Jansson is proudest of her achievement to become full professor at a Swedish university at a time when only four percent of the professors in the country were women. Although microbiology shows less of a gender gap than other scientific fields, Dr. Jansson still has concerns that women need a support system as they climb the academic ladder during their child-rearing years. "It can be very detrimental to be away from one's scientific discipline for too long a period of time, due to the fast pace of science and the need to stay competitive. In this respect, I was fortunate to have raised my children in Sweden where we have generous parental leave for both parents."

When not in the lab, Dr. Jansson enjoys hiking, gardening and exploring nature. She knows that every cup of soil contains 100 billion microorganisms — 10 times the number of stars in our galaxy — just waiting to be discovered. ●

MICHELE KOONS
Archaeologist

Picture yourself on Peru's arid north coast. It is one of the driest places on Earth, receiving only two-tenths of an inch of rain per year — 15 times *less* rainfall than the driest desert in the United States. Dirt and sweat add a second and third layer to your skin. On this unyielding terrain, you enter one of the richest ancient burial sites in the world, filled with the artifacts of a complex society you hope to unearth. In honor of the ancestors who once called this sacred land home, a local shaman cleanses your archaeological dig site by spitting rosewater on your back and head.

First, you and your team unearth two huge llamas laid out as sacrifices. Then, past adobe brick walls that line a tomb, you discover a coffin inlaid with copper designs fashioned into a mask. You have found the tomb of an ancient Moche priestess.

This is no Hollywood movie. It's more like a page straight out of Dr. Michele Koons's field journal.

Dr. Koons is an Indiana Jones-style explorer, a museum curator and an expert on Andean and environmental archaeology. Archaeology has long focused on artifacts to study and document historic and prehistoric cultures. But Dr. Koons represents a new generation of STEM-oriented archaeologists who are merging traditional methods with cutting-edge technology. In her work, she uses high-tech inventions like drones and ground-penetrating radar to make 3D maps of sites, along with traditional techniques, to uncover secrets of past civilizations. Her passion lies in discovering problems in ancient cultures that mirror problems in modern society, particularly in the areas of farming and irrigation. "Dealing with environmental change and natural disasters is not new, and we can learn a lot about strategies and repercussions by examining the response of the people and societies of the past."

As a child, Dr. Koons often dug for treasure every summer at her family's beach house on the New Jersey shore. Encouraged by her uncle, who often spun tales of ancient Roman coins and chariots in his own backyard, she reconnected with her love of other cultures and her appetite for exotic travel in college, when a University of Pittsburgh-sponsored *Alternative Spring Break* trip took her to Bolivia. "My mind was blown away by the people and the culture and the history." She immediately changed her major from physical therapy to anthropology and Latin American Studies.

Since archaeology is a sub program of anthropology, it was only a matter of time before Dr. Koons's passion for

25

discovery landed her in the specialized field. A study abroad program in Chile cemented her career choice when she had the opportunity to photograph some of the world's oldest mummies. For a time after college, Dr. Koons worked as a contract archaeologist, an expert who is called in prior to building projects on public land to ensure there is no disruption to burial or other historically significant sites. "Towards the end of my college career, I became more serious about archaeology and the scientific techniques that are needed for research. I pursued archaeology and the science side in graduate school." Dr. Koons received her master's degree from the University of Denver. A mentor at the university encouraged her to get her PhD. She attended Harvard University and earned her doctorate in 2012 studying the Moche culture, a complex and fascinating society that lived pre-Inca (300-900 AD) on the Peruvian coast. "I'm motivated to do work that's relevant to people's lives today. The Moche did a lot of irrigation for agriculture. With no water, you need great engineers and great politics and great planning. So my more recent research has focused a lot on water management and politics and how those played out in the past and how we can learn from that."

Since earning her doctorate, Dr. Koons has been curating artifacts for the Denver Museum of Nature & Science, a job she calls "fantastic" for many reasons, including its family-friendly environment. Her museum responsibilities include keeping meticulous records of the institute's collections, developing innovative exhibits and programs for the public and continuing research into ancient Latin American and southwestern U.S. cultures.

As a young blond female, Dr. Koons has faced an interesting set of challenges working as an archaeologist in Latin America "When I am working in rural Peru I dissociate from gender

"It's not an easy thing to have it all. But you have to follow your gut. If you want it, you can do it."

because if I am identified using traditional gender roles, then I am not taken seriously. I almost see myself as a third gender when I'm there as I don't fit the stereotypical expectations of females or males within the field setting. It's a coping mechanism to get the job done." Dr. Koons recognizes both the rewards and the challenges of her time as a graduate student. "My program at Harvard mainly consisted of female students, but there is a pervasive feeling that you can't have it all — meaning a family and a career — if you're a woman in academia. I didn't feel as if I was treated differently, but I saw that no females were being hired in the all-male department."

She encourages young women interested in the highly competitive field of archaeology to follow their passion. "You really have to work hard to make a career out of archaeology. Don't let details get in the way of that passion. And that's really hard. It's not an easy thing to have it all. But you have to follow your gut. If you want it, you can do it."

Dr. Koons is proof that STEM boundaries are dynamic and ever-evolving, thanks in part to advances in science and technology. She is an inspiration to young women everywhere who wish to roll up their sleeves, get their boots muddy and take on the world, STEM-style. ●

marcia kemper mcnutt
Oceanographer and Geophysicist

The summer after her first year in graduate school, Dr. Marcia Kemper McNutt learned how to blow things up. Not with any old land explosives, but underwater explosives used in mapping the deep structure beneath the ocean floor. Alongside Navy Seal teams, she graduated at the top of her training course before returning to graduate school, where she enjoyed the admiration of her all-male peers. "As one of the few women in graduate school at the time, it helped to have an opportunity like that to show that I was as tough as any of my classmates. No one messed with me." Her enthusiasm for driving motorcycles no doubt helped that image, but what most impressed — and continues to impress — Dr. McNutt's colleagues is her passion for uncovering the great mysteries of the world's oceans.

She is a pioneering geophysicist and a world expert on the ocean floor in the southern hemisphere. Dr. McNutt is also an impassioned communicator and ambassador for science; she is the first female editor-in-chief of *Science* magazine since the publication's founding in 1880.

A key figure in oceanographic research for close to 40 years, Dr. McNutt has inspired countless students and career scientists with her dedication. In addition to public service, she participated in 15 major oceanographic expeditions, more than half of those as chief scientist. Her contributions include advancing knowledge about ocean island volcanism in French Polynesia, the uplift of the vast Tibetan Plateau in Central Asia and the use of highly sensitive radar altimeters in Earth's orbit to map the sea floor's terrain. In 2003, Dr. McNutt was named Scientist of the Year by the Achievement Rewards for College Scientists Foundation, and she also earned the James B. Macelwane Medal (1988) and the Maurice Ewing Medal (2007) for her significant research accomplishments.

Dr. McNutt grew up far away from Earth's oceans in Minneapolis, Minnesota, but a summer visit to San Diego's Scripps Institution of Oceanography when she was just six years old marked the beginning of a lifelong quest to understand and protect this global resource. After earning a perfect score on her SAT and graduating at the top of her high school class, Dr. McNutt majored in physics at Colorado College and pursued graduate studies at Scripps, where she earned a PhD in earth sciences. She credits her supportive family as being the most important factor in her success.

"My mother and father allowed me to pursue every dream, unfettered, regardless of whether they understood anything I was doing."

The excellence Dr. McNutt displayed as a student continued into her career. After conducting a three-year study in earthquake prediction with the U.S. Geological Survey (USGS), she became the E.A. Griswold Professor of Geophysics at the Massachusetts Institute of Technology. She later went on to direct the Monterey Bay Aquarium Research Institute and join the faculties of both the University of California, Santa Cruz and Stanford University. In 2009, President Barack Obama chose Dr. McNutt to be the first woman in history to lead the 135-year old USGS. The very next year, the U.S. Secretary of the Interior hand-selected Dr. McNutt to chair a working group of scientists to measure the oil spilling into the Gulf of Mexico following the explosion and sinking of the Deepwater Horizon oil rig. She continued her appointment until 2013, when she became editor-in-chief of the 126-year-old academic journal *Science*, which boasts the largest paid circulation of any peer-reviewed, general science journal in the world.

The challenge of ensuring that future generations of STEM leaders represent America's diversity remains a concern for Dr. McNutt. She believes that higher education, government and private industry are doing their part to stimulate STEM interests through special incentives and scholarships, but major challenges for women in science remain. "Potential STEM students need to be identified in junior high, or earlier, and involved in hands-on activities and mentorship programs. The sooner you start learning anything, the easier it is."

For now, Dr. McNutt's challenges as chief editor of *Science* involve issues around the communication of ideas, rather than the exploration of them. In this domain, too, it is clear the scientific community believes in her leadership. Dr. Robert Gagosian, CEO of the Consortium for Ocean Leadership in Washington D.C., sees Dr. McNutt as an intellectual force with the influence to bring bold new ideas. "She has that kind of tenacity to really push hard on what she believes in." Her dedication to the advancement of science, both in the field and in the sharing of ideas, is sure to lead the next generation of scientists into the unchartered waters of discovery. ●

"My mother and father allowed me to pursue every dream, unfettered, regardless of whether they understood anything I was doing."

karen OLSON
Forensic Scientist

There are more than 200 different cell types in the human body. Within the nucleus of each of these cells is DNA, a string of atoms that encode the cell with a specific biological function. DNA is found in human blood, hair strands, skin and even in the saliva passed to a cup while drinking. Everyone's DNA is slightly different from everyone else's, which makes it a valuable tool in solving crimes.

The advent of forensic DNA analysis has transformed the nature of criminal investigations. With its unique identifying signature, DNA can breathe new life into unsolved cases, link multiple crimes to a single perpetrator and exonerate the innocent. But with this powerful new technology, sometimes applied to evidence samples that are microscopic in size, comes the very real problem of mixed DNA profiles: collected samples that contain the DNA of two or more individuals.

In her work as a forensic research scientist at the Defense Forensic Science Center (DFSC), a military facility based in Georgia, Dr. Karen Olson hopes to help investigators to connect and solve crimes committed by the same offender — even when individual DNA profiles in a sample cannot be fully distinguished. A specialist in testing and evaluating forensic technology, Dr. Olson provides critical feedback to manufacturers about their devices, allowing them to refine the technology into something that is useful for forensic and military uses.

In the field of forensics, time is often the most critical factor in identifying suspects. For Dr. Olson and others who work on perfecting forensic technology, the goal is to shrink the DNA analysis testing process from days or weeks to a mere 90 minutes, encompassing DNA extraction, purification, amplification, separation and detection. Dr. Olson considers influencing the development of new crime-fighting technology the most thrilling part of her work. "It's very rewarding to see the suggestions I have made for improvement worked into the final products and to see my research transformed into products and methods that enhance the ability to solve crimes."

Dr. Olson grew up in Eagan, Minnesota, at a time when public school budgets for science experiments were meager. She credits two resourceful grade-school teachers, both women, for crafting exciting scientific labs on a tight budget. A study on fingerprints, and another that featured dental floss pressed into a gel capsule to represent DNA, sparked her interest in

"Overcome your fears by gaining experience and practice."

forensics. "Looking back, perhaps the fact that two of the most engaging science teachers in my early school career were women removed the stigma from my mind that science was somehow a career that suited men more than women."

When she enrolled at the University of Wisconsin-La Crosse, Dr. Olson was primed for a forensics career, but one of her freshman lab professors advised her to reconsider that path because of its limited career opportunities. He recognized her gift for chemistry and actively encouraged her to pursue the field. Encouraged further by an organic chemistry professor, Dr. Olson went on to obtain a master's degree in 2008 and a PhD from the University of California, San Diego in 2012. Although she was still set on a career in forensics, she is glad she followed her professors' advice. Had she not found her way to forensics through chemistry, "I don't think I would have had as challenging and rewarding of a journey, nor would I be as good of a scientist."

Dr. Olson now applies her scientific expertise at the DFSC, serving the U.S. Army and other Department of Defense (DOD) organizations worldwide in DNA analysis, digital evidence, drug chemistry, firearms and tool marks, forensic documents, latent fingerprints and trace evidence. She is committed to making current investigative technology faster, lighter and more reliable. Dr. Olson also mentors interns and DOD's Science, Mathematics And Research for Transformation (SMART) scholars. She encourages young women interested in forensic science careers to read all they can about the field, shadow scientists and pursue internships at local crime labs. "Overcome your fears by gaining experience and practice. I really hated giving presentations in graduate school. It made me nervous, and I was always worried that someone in the audience would ask a question I couldn't answer. My advisor understood the fear but wouldn't let me get out of the presentations. Instead, he helped me make great presentation slides and gave me strategies for creating a smooth talk. As a result of a lot of practice, I won the 'best talk' award the first time I had to present my research in front of my peers."

Dr. Olson views workshops, classes and conferences geared toward young women as critical components to closing the gender gap in STEM. Parents and teachers also play a key role, she says: From a young age, girls need to both hear from the adults around them that all careers are possible and be shown that this is true through interaction with role models. As one of those role models herself, Dr. Olson has certainly left her fingerprint on future generations of women in forensic science. ●

carolyn porco
Planetary Scientist

"I feel like I have lived my life at Saturn. It's been such an enormous thrill and a privilege to have been part of it and to know that when I'm old and looking back on my life I will feel that I did the coolest thing anyone could ever possibly do with their life."

No one but Dr. Carolyn Porco, herself, can capture the wonder and awe of the STEM career she has lived. The term "planetary scientist" doesn't seem to do justice to her contributions in space exploration. In the past 40 years, Dr. Porco has participated in many historic missions as an imaging specialist with the National Aeronautics and Space Administration (NASA), such as the Voyager in the 1980s, Cassini's present orbit around Saturn, the New Horizons spacecraft mission to Pluto and the Kuiper Belt in 2006. Tasked with capturing and studying remarkable images from robotic spacecrafts, image specialists like Dr. Porco do more than just take breathtaking photographs of our cosmos. Their work, as she describes it, is to "understand the processes that are at work in the natural world, in particular those that have been responsible for the birth, development and evolution of the bodies in our solar system." Images of the cosmos obtained by teams of planetary scientists become scientific evidence of new phenomena. Dr. Porco has made a few discoveries from these images herself, some of which include: one of Neptune's ring arcs, the finding that "spokes" on Saturn's rings change according to the planet's magnetic field, the manner in which satellites create features in planetary rings, the finding that sound waves within Saturn produce wave features in its rings and the discovery of 101 geysers erupting from beneath the south polar terrain of Saturn's icy moon, Enceladus. All of these significant discoveries, and many more, are Dr. Porco's legacy to astronomy — a legacy that started from humble beginnings and a memorable cosmic connection when she was a teenager.

The daughter of Italian immigrants, Dr. Porco grew up in the Bronx, New York in the 1960s, a decade that brought the world's first images of Mars and Venus, the *Star Trek* television series and the historic first moon landing of Apollo 11. "The whole decade was space-obsessed," explains Dr. Porco. "My interest in science was inborn. I just gravitated to it immediately. I loved the absolutism of it — the fact that what is true is not merely decided by some authority figure but can be discovered. And I loved learning how things really worked. It seemed so mystical to me."

She tells of a pivotal moment during her childhood when a friend acquired a telescope and invited Dr. Porco to her rooftop to explore the limitless sky. Finding Saturn through that lens gave Dr. Porco her first taste of connecting with

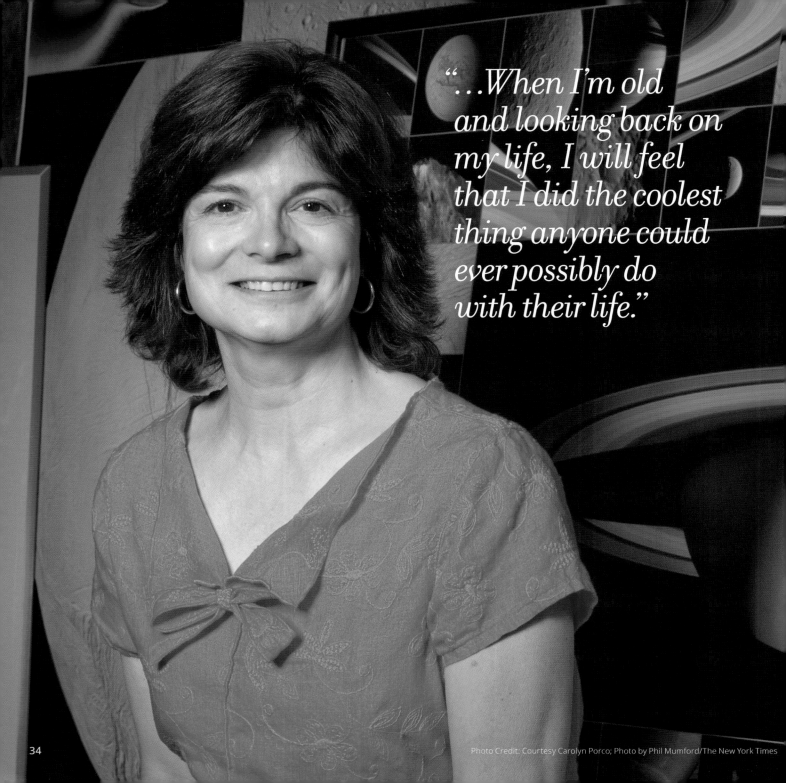

"…When I'm old and looking back on my life, I will feel that I did the coolest thing anyone could ever possibly do with their life."

34

the cosmos. "You feel like you've discovered it yourself. And in some ways you have. You've discovered it *for* yourself." This experience, along with her natural philosophical curiosity about the nature and meaning of human existence, led her to astronomy. "The major religions and philosophies of the world — Catholicism, the religion of my birth, Hinduism, Buddhism, existentialism — failed to answer my questions about the meaning of life and my own existence. Somewhere along the line, asking the question 'So what I am doing here?' became 'So where *is* here?' "

Dr. Porco earned a bachelor's degree from State University of New York, Stony Brook in 1974 and a PhD from the California Institute of Technology in 1983. Shortly after, she joined the faculty at the University of Arizona's Department of Planetary Sciences and became a member of the NASA Voyager's Imaging Team. Then, in 1990, Dr. Porco set her sights on the Cassini mission to explore Saturn. "Thank my lucky stars, I was very audacious. I thought I'm not just going to be on the imaging team, I'm going to *lead* the imaging team. I had some stiff competition. But I won."

Her contributions to astronomy are not limited to missions. Inspired and mentored by one of the most revered astronomers and cosmologists of our time, Dr. Carl Sagan, Dr. Porco plays a special role in bringing space exploration to the wider public. Through social media and the internet, she educates audiences of all kinds about planetary exploration. She lectures frequently, publishes both scientific papers and popular science articles in leading publications like *Science, The New York Times* and *Scientific American* and has appeared on numerous television programs and news networks as a consultant and expert. When Dr. Sagan began work on the blockbuster motion picture sequel to his novel *Contact*, he wanted Dr. Porco to be a character consultant on the movie's heroine, Ellie Arroway. Dr. Porco recalls him telling her, "'Of all

the female scientists I know, you come closest to being like the character we wish to portray on the screen.' I assumed he was referring to my driven, passionate, perhaps overzealous nature, which he had ample opportunity to observe since we both had been members of the Voyager imaging team. I was enormously flattered and jumped at the chance." Dr. Porco also was singularly responsible for conceiving the idea of sending to the Moon the ashes of another mentor, geologist Dr. Eugene Shoemaker, who taught the Apollo astronauts to recognize lunar rocks of unusual scientific importance. Dr. Shoemaker's ashes were carried to the Moon aboard the Lunar Prospector mission and buried there in July 1999.

In addition to traveling and speaking about Cassini's exploration of Saturn, Dr. Porco also directs the imaging lab at the Space Science Institute in Boulder, Colorado and conducts ongoing research as a leading scholar at the University of California, Berkeley. Her current research involves Enceladus, a small Saturnian moon whose icy geysers and salty, organic-rich sea source make it the most accessible body for the search of life in the solar system beyond Earth.

Dr. Porco believes that success in the sciences, when "given an adequate to above-average measure of analytical ability, comes down almost entirely to personality. Traits like drive, persistence, focus, confidence, insightfulness, emotional intelligence, ability to rebound from setbacks, ability to accept criticism, enjoyment of solitude and an abiding, intense desire to *know* separates out those who succeed from those who don't." Her advice to young women considering a career in planetary science is heartening. "Doing planetary science is probably a lot easier than trying to be a successful concert pianist. And it's enormously gratifying." She is passionate about ensuring that *all* women — not just American women — have access to education. "That is *the* only hope for our world." ●

LISA RANDALL
Theoretical Physicist

Piano movers experience gravity as an overwhelming pull. Because of it, the act of lifting a piano up a flight of stairs can take back-breaking energy. But physicists understand that in the grand scheme of things, the force of gravity is fairly puny. It may hold down a piano, but against the force of a tiny magnet, it can't even hold down a paper clip. The mysteries of gravity have long fascinated scientists: Why is it so weak? How does it relate to the other known forces operating in our universe — the electromagnetism that pulls the magnet and the strong and weak nuclear forces? Is there any answer to the problem that would achieve what physicists see as the ultimate prize: a single, unified theory of the universe?

These and other questions form the basis of Professor Lisa Randall's research as a theoretical physicist. Professor Randall's work centers on developing models that explain fundamental forces, elementary particles, the existence of extra dimensions and the possibility of parallel universes. With nearly 40 groundbreaking scientific papers, she has emerged as a global leader in particle physics.

Professor Randall began exploring the physics of space and time more than a decade ago. String theorists propose the existence of 10 dimensions (including time). But for Professor Randall's research, she needed to consider only one additional dimension which focused on a theory with four dimensions (three spatial dimensions plus time) and an extra fifth dimension that might explain phenomena in our universe. Her findings, published in 1999, offered a compelling explanation of the weak gravitational force that an individual particle would experience. Her research also advanced a model of the universe we observe as existing within a four-

dimensional "pocket" inside higher dimensions. It was a pioneering and mathematically rigorous model, and the world of physics took notice, honoring her with awards such as the National Award of Nuclear Science and History and the 2012 American Institute of Physics' Andrew Gemant Award, which recognizes individuals who have made "significant contributions to the cultural, artistic or humanistic dimension of physics."

Professor Randall points out that a lot exists beyond what we see. "In the history of physics, every time we've looked beyond the scales and energies we were familiar with, we've found things that we wouldn't have thought were there. You look inside the atom and eventually you discover quarks. Who would have thought that? It's hubris to think that the way we see things is everything there is."

Largely influenced by New York's "intense community where there are lots of bright people around," Professor Randall

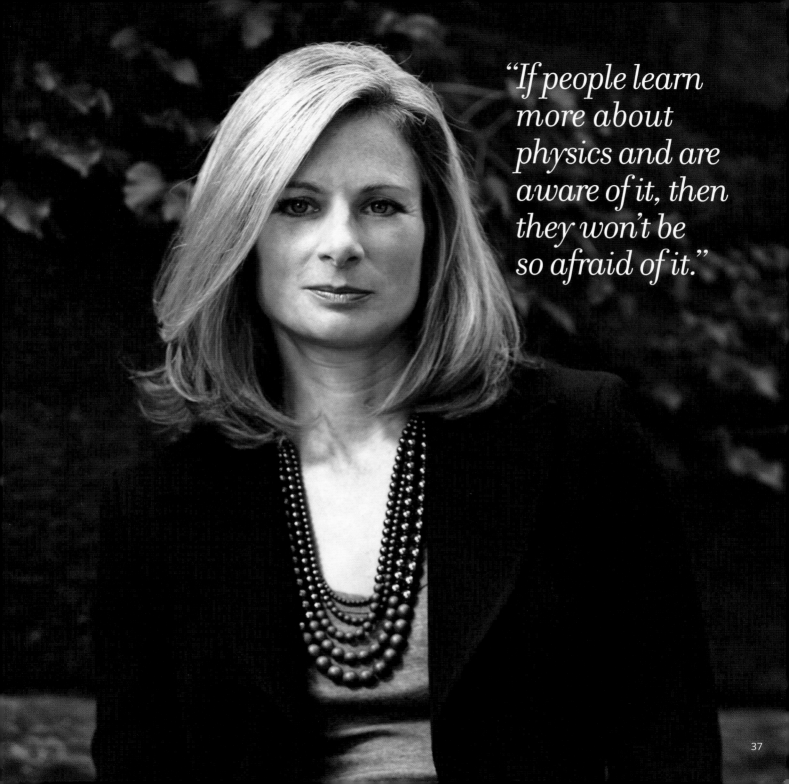

"If people learn more about physics and are aware of it, then they won't be so afraid of it."

37

loved reading and math as a child. In her teens, she rode the subway each morning from her home in Queens to Manhattan's Stuyvesant High School, where she won a Westinghouse Science Talent Search for a number theory project on complex numbers. Although physics initially drew her attention because of its concrete solutions to problems, Professor Randall soon realized that pursuing the unanswered questions about our universe was far more exciting.

Professor Randall completed a bachelor's degree in physics from Harvard University in three years, added a PhD and went on to professorships at the Massachusetts Institute of Technology (MIT) and Princeton University before returning to Harvard, where she became the first woman to earn tenure as a theoretical physicist.

She is most excited about our current era because new technology makes previously impossible experiments possible. Although optimistic that the Large Hadron Collider (LHC) — the largest and most powerful particle accelerator in the world, located in Switzerland — could be the key to radical new insights into the nature of our universe, Professor Randall believes that some discoveries will take time. Though physics may not have the daily impact of the computer or medical sciences, the discovery of new forces, new elements of nature and new theories places us all at the "edge of human knowledge."

After Harvard's former president, Dr. Lawrence Summers, famously suggested that fewer women were scientists because of a fundamental difference between males and females, Professor Randall joined a committee at Harvard to address the lack of women in science and engineering and to combat outdated ideas that men are innately better at math than women. She and the committee argued that giving undergraduate women more opportunities and tools for research may be the key to increasing the representation of women in STEM careers.

Though her science is traditionally high on intimidating jargon — multiverses and branes and supersymmetry — Professor Randall has dedicated herself to keeping theoretical physics down to earth, making her work relatable to lay audiences. Her wildly popular books, including *Knocking on Heaven's Door: How Physics and Scientific Thinking Illuminate the Universe and the Modern World* and *Warped Passages: Unraveling the Mysteries of the Universe's Hidden Dimensions*, take readers on a thrilling ride through the latest scientific insights at the frontiers of string theory.

Not surprisingly, her honors extend far beyond the world of science into mainstream popular culture, with publications like *Time*, *Newsweek* and *Esquire* hailing her as one of the most important scientists of her generation. She has graced the glossy pages of Vogue and appeared on über-hip television shows like *The Daily Show with Jon Stewart*, among others. Professor Randall hopes that "if people learn more about physics and are aware of it, then they won't be so afraid of it."

In 2006, Professor Randall found a fresh way to popularize science like never before. Along with Spanish composer Mr. Hèctor Parra, she developed the multimedia opera *Hypermusic Prologue*. The high-concept story tells the tale of a composer/physicist who abandons the man she loves to explore the fourth dimension of space, while he remains trapped in the three spatial dimensions we all experience. *Hypermusic Prologue* gave Professor Randall a creative outlet to communicate her passion for exploration and discovery.

At the edge of human understanding are the theories and experiments — and sometimes even art — that express our thirst for big-picture answers. Professor Randall is poised on that edge, inspiring a new generation of STEM students to reach for higher dimensions. ●

PARDIS SABETI
Computational Biologist and Geneticist

Ask Iranian-born computational biologist and medical geneticist Professor Pardis Sabeti her dreams and she'll tell you her ultimate goal is to "help train students to be good people as well as good scientists." That, and to have fun. As the lead singer and bassist for the indie rock band Thousand Days, she already has fun covered. And fronting a band is a pretty extraordinary accomplishment given Professor Sabeti's current day job, or actually jobs. She is an associate professor of biology at Harvard University. In 2015, she lead a team of scientists who took on a daunting task: working around the clock to decode the genome of the deadly Ebola virus, whose genetic code was rapidly mutating as it ravaged the African countries of Guinea, Sierra Leone and Liberia. Her work has earned her national headlines in publications from the *New Yorker* to *The New York Times* to *Popular Science*, using words like "trailblazing" and "genius" to describe her accomplishments.

As a young girl, Professor Sabeti and her family fled from Iran on the eve of a political revolution. Her father, who had been a high-ranking official in the Iranian government, inspired her with his courage, beliefs and determination to make a difference. She developed a love of math when her sister, who was two years older, set up a pretend school for her each summer that intensely focused on everything the older sibling had learned that year. By the time Professor Sabeti reached the same subjects in school, she could focus on excellence instead of simply gaining knowledge.

Though her high school days and university studies at the Massachusetts Institute of Technology and England's Oxford University were filled with achievements such as National Merit Scholar and Rhodes Scholar honors, her journey to understand human genetics and how it relates to malaria — a serious, mosquito-borne disease caused by parasites in red blood cells — was not an easy road. Instead of using existing tools to analyze new data, Professor Sabeti focused on developing new tools to analyze existing data. "Many people thought that what I was trying to find in my research was a distraction," she recalls. "It seemed as if I was just going to go nowhere." Keeping her head down and tuning out the naysayers was, perhaps, one of the most trying things she has ever done. "When I was doing my PhD at Oxford, my research was going in a new direction, and I had a lot of failures that made it seem like I was flailing.

"Find a voice, which requires buckling down and really getting to know yourself, and trust yourself."

Though I was pursuing something I believed in, I understood that society will judge you until you're proven. And perhaps if you're a woman, the judgment is ever more severe."

One fateful morning around 3 a.m., Professor Sabeti added data to a formula she had developed and "everything came together." By focusing her technology on sets of genes called haplotypes, she proved that it was possible to identify recent changes to the human genome, a landmark discovery in fighting disease. As a result of her intense drive to succeed and her untiring belief in herself, her breakthrough changed the world of computational biology forever.

Her own determination to make a difference led her from the lab to the rapidly developing nation of Nigeria. This time, she focused on the Lassa virus, a recently discovered and deadly virus similar to Ebola that world nations consider a serious risk to national security. Her fearless confrontation of a disease that impacts hundreds of thousands of people throughout Nigeria is a reflection of the same courage she witnessed in her principled father.

The partnerships she developed with clinicians in Africa around the Lassa virus would become critical in 2014, when she took on Ebola. Leading a team of viral geneticists at the Broad Institute of MIT and Harvard, Professor Sabeti was able to track the virus's mutations as it moved through affected populations. The groundbreaking paper she published in *Science* magazine included five authors who had died from Ebola.

Although Professor Sabeti has achieved more successes than anyone can count, she is quick to relate a recent triumph when asked which of her achievements she cares about most. "One accomplishment that comes to mind occurred a week ago — I just got my reviews back from teaching. I had 400 comments from my students, some of which made me cry. The comments were basically just saying, 'she got me excited about statistics, I would take any class from her.' They just so moved me. Being a great teacher — inspiring my students and empowering them — this is most important to me."

Her advice to young women reflects the trials she has experienced during her career. "Young women need to build their own confidence and move forward. Find a voice, which requires buckling down and really getting to know yourself, and trust yourself."

Professor Sabeti's quest to understand how diseases affect our genes, the cellular building blocks of our bodies, may someday lead to new treatments and perhaps even vaccines. And while she attacks the world's most critical diseases at a mathematical level, she cuts memorable vocal tracks on her band's albums and shreds a mean guitar onstage.

Who says STEM doesn't rock? ●

41

stem gems

Technology

MIREILLE AKILIAN, *Hysteroscopy Technologist*

ERIKA EBBEL ANGLE, *Bio-technologist*

SHAHEROSE CHARANIA, *Startup Champion and Entrepreneur*

LORRIE FAITH CRANOR, *Online Security Expert*

MARY LOU JEPSEN, *Holography and Virtual Reality Technologist*

HOLLY LIU, *Internet Gaming Technologist*

ANDREA LUECKE, *Solar Energy Technologist*

PILAR MOLINA LOPEZ, *Animation Technologist*

HEATHER PAYNE, *Computer Coding Creator*

KALIYA YOUNG, *Internet Identity Advocate*

STEM GEMS
Technology INTRO

In popular culture, the world of technology has become synonymous with the world of computers. Processors, silicon chips and data memory devices have invaded everything from internet-wired dishwashers to gym clothes that analyze muscle mass during workouts. But we do a disservice to the term "technology" by limiting it to Google glasses and self-driving cars. Technology can encompass humble inventions like duct tape — originally called "duck tape" for its cotton duck cloth material — which has been used for everything from reinforcing steel cables on the Brooklyn Bridge to repairing carbon dioxide filters on the National Aeronautics and Space Administration's (NASA) lunar module. Technology can also include cutting-edge solutions to global problems, like drinking straws that filter water for people in developing nations who have little access to clean water. Amy Smith, an inventor and professor at the Massachusetts Institute of Technology, devised a simple mill that uses airflow to separate grain particles into flour for rural areas in developing countries, where motorized parts are scarce. Even scissors fall under the umbrella of technology. Technology includes *all* kinds of devices, tools and instruments that enrich both science and engineering as well as our everyday lives.

Ancient Greeks and Romans used the term *techne* to refer to both skills and art. Logos is Greek for "word" or "expression," so the term "technology" centers around the written instructions or codes needed to carry out a craft or skill. At first glance, technology and engineering seem too similar to be distinct STEM disciplines. Like engineering, technology harnesses science and math to innovate and push the boundaries of what we think is possible. To better understand the distinction, let's use a simple fire analogy from our ancient ancestors. Because fire can be used to cook food, it is a form of technology. It is a tool, clear and simple. Engineering allows us to perfect the tool — making fire inside a brick chimney, for example, to eliminate smoke and move cooking indoors.

Fast forward 125,000+ years: Human technology has come a long way, and the women you'll meet in this section are among those leading progress. Take Mireille Akilian. Her high-precision, technological advances have revolutionized everything from NASA x-ray image technology to a common surgical procedure that impacts millions of women each year. You'll discover her remarkable contributions, along with those of an internet security warrior, a computer-literacy champion dedicated to putting computers into the hands of all children regardless of economic status and a woman on a mission to level the STEM playing field by bringing coding skills to women and girls. You'll read about techies who harness the sun, create story magic on animated feature films and protect your privacy rights online.

At the center of this surge in tech entrepreneurs is the startup culture of Silicon Valley, California. Although New York is fast becoming a major hub in the startup market, attracting twice as many female startup founders as Silicon Valley, research by The Startup Genome shows that Silicon Valley remains the undisputed tech metropolis. Shaherose Charania, an open innovation expert and leader of the organization Women 2.0, offers an insider's look into this powerhouse region of technology. Her passion and advocacy for women in tech draw thousands of like-minded innovators to her conferences and business opportunities each year. Other leaders you'll meet, like solar energy champion Andrea Luecke and bio-technologist Erika Ebbel Angle, are taking the tech revolution to cities all across the U.S.

In a world that craves better, faster gadgets and apps to organize and share every aspect of our lives, technology has seen explosive growth within STEM, and it has never been easier to enter the playing field. Yet according to the Bureau of Labor Statistics, only 19 percent of software developers are women. Less than 20 percent of bachelor's degrees in computer science go to women, and women hold only 27 percent of computer science jobs in the workforce. Trends suggest these numbers will hold steady or decrease in the coming years. Women engage with technology just as much as men, so why aren't they innovating at the same rates?

Sheryl Sandberg, Facebook's Chief Operating Officer, became the first woman to serve on the social media giant's board of directors in 2012 and has been an outspoken advocate for increasing the number of women in leadership positions. In 2015, sixty-four percent of Facebook users were women, but the percentage of female employees on the tech side of Facebook stood at 15 percent. Studies showed that women are four times more likely to use Pinterest than men, but only 21 percent of Pinterest techies are female. What does this mean for the age of "new media?" It means that content, creativity and innovation are largely dictated by one group: men.

The pitfalls of a male-dominated technology culture are perfectly highlighted by the work of Holly Liu, Co-founder and Chief of Staff of the gaming site Kabam. When she and her team first considered gaming opportunities, they found that existing Facebook games lacked a deep, engaging experience. A huge fan of traditionally male-dominated strategy games, Liu had a vision to bring these more immersive games to Facebook's female-heavy users. Her vision turned into a successful reality. Kabam is now the leader in free-to-play core games, expanding past early titles such as *Kings of Camelot* and *Dragons of Atlantis* to focus on high-quality, high-budget mobile games.

Despite the gender gap, hope is on the horizon. Liu, for one, isn't discouraged. She quotes baseball icon Babe Ruth — "It's hard to beat a person who never gives up" — when speaking to young women. "Male-dominated fields can only get better with more women, and that cannot happen unless you are, and continue to be, there." Jocelyn Goldfein, Director of Engineering at Facebook, famously told the Associated Press, "The reason there aren't more women computer scientists is because there aren't more women computer scientists." And Sandberg recently said that she believes future generations can close this gap. "A world where half of our countries and half of our companies are run by women would be a better world." With role models like Liu, Sandberg and Goldfein in high-profile spaces, young women are awakening to the opportunities in tech.

The 10 STEM Gems highlighted here represent a small fraction of the vanguard of women emerging as leaders in technology. Working in different domains, they have all rallied around a model of innovation that is inclusive, and they have helped to crack the code on inspiring young women to pursue all things tech.

A girl code 125,000+ years in the making. ●

MIREILLE AKILIAN
Hysteroscopy Technologist

Dr. Mireille Akilian became a mechanical engineer because she wanted to design and fix cars. Specifically high-performance cars, like Porsches or BMWs. "I always knew I wanted to have a PhD in engineering," Dr. Akilian says — though it turned out her advanced degree would have its biggest impact not on the speedway, but in the hospital room.

Far from making her mark in the outward symbols of material wealth, Dr. Akilian has made a difference in an extremely intimate, unseen space, one that has huge implications for women's health. Her innovative breakthroughs have revolutionized the technology countless surgeons use to diagnose and treat health concerns specific to women's bodies. Dr. Akilian oversees a team of engineers at Smith & Nephew, a global medical technology company, working to advance the technology used in hysteroscopes, the minimally invasive, small-diameter tubes with cameras that surgeons use to examine the uterus. These new, high-precision devices offer them a way to examine, and in some cases remove, diseased tissue without subjecting a patient to major surgery — a direct "see and treat" approach that represents a dramatic improvement over previous procedures in which surgeons took blind samples. Through her work, Dr. Akilian is providing women everywhere with a better quality of life. But her achievements aren't limited to health care, or even just to Earth.

At the Massachusetts Institute of Technology (MIT) Space Nanotechnology Laboratory, Dr. Akilian helped to shape and assemble extremely precise, thin optic glass sheets that act as mirrors to reflect x-ray images taken from space-launched telescopes. The technology she developed reduced the surface warping of these fragile sheets, a major contribution that enabled scientists at the National Aeronautics and Space Administration to better capture x-rays from distant galaxies and learn about the evolution of the universe.

So how does a young woman who dreamed of cars end up creating technology for surgery and space imaging? Growing up, Dr. Akilian loved the outdoors, biking and going on long walks with her best friend. At night, she would read whatever books she could find on her mother's shelf. A physics teacher in seventh grade provided a fun and memorable learning environment. "I remember being fascinated by the laws that governed everything around us. This was when I started analyzing my daily surroundings in a scientific way." Though

no one person inspired her to pursue STEM, Dr. Akilian's love of physics and math proved a natural fit for engineering.

Dr. Akilian attended the American University of Beirut in Lebanon, where she received a bachelor's degree in mechanical engineering. Her quest for a PhD brought her to MIT and its Space Nanotechnology Lab. After a brief time as

trust "by meeting my deliverables consistently, demonstrating knowledge in the field and helping them whenever needed." She advises young women who may be intimidated by entering into a STEM field that "fear of something is not knowing it. If you have an interest in a specific area, just research it or practice it. The fear will go away because you will have the right tools and experience to handle it."

"Fear of something is not knowing it. If you have an interest in a specific area, just research or practice it. The fear will go away[.]"

an engineering consultant, Dr. Akilian sought a greater sense of fulfillment in her work. She found it as a research and development manager at Smith & Nephew, whose mission is to use medical technology to improve lives. The most exciting part of her research is "having fun while continuously looking for better ways to serve women. There is always new technology to come up with and assess. The feeling of delivering a device using this technology to the hands of surgeons and seeing it perform as expected is indescribable."

At times, working in a male-dominated field has proved challenging, but Dr. Akilian learned early on that to be successful meant earning her male colleagues' respect and

Dr. Akilian believes the secret to attracting more women to STEM careers is to dispel the notion that STEM is difficult or boring. "Ensure that women receive proper education and training so they have the right level of confidence and skills to prove themselves in the field and the rest will follow."

Reflecting on her own career path in hysteroscopy, Dr. Akilian smiles thinking about the kind of breakthrough technology she envisioned creating as a girl and how radically dreams and paths can change. These days, her main hobby on wheels involves bike riding, not high-end roadsters. "Porsches didn't quite work out for me," she says with a note of humor, "but the PhD definitely paid off." ●

erika ebbel angle
Bio-technologist

Dr. Erika Ebbel Angle visited a crocodile farm in Cancun, Mexico when she was 11 years old. She learned that fatally wounded crocs end their own lives by flipping over and slipping into a coma. When it was time to return to school and select a science fair project, Dr. Erika couldn't stop thinking about this crocodile fact. She wondered if cells in the human body commit suicide when infected by a virus, similar to the croc's biological drive to bring on its own death. Dr. Erika's quest to test her hypothesis sparked an interest in microbiology and chemistry that has remained with her to this day. The support she has received along the way has had a tremendous impact on her own path in biochemistry and her ability to nurture future generations of scientists.

Dr. Erika's quest began with supportive parents and a mentor at the local public health laboratory named Mr. Michael Nachtigall, who guided her through her first six formative years as a young scientist. She tested the effectiveness of two herbs that prevented the herpes virus (the safest virus Mr. Nachtigall had in his lab) from infecting cells, hoping to isolate the active anti-viral compound in these herbs. Mr. Nachtigall challenged her to begin to think like a scientist. "Even if he knew that I was going to fail or that the experiment wouldn't work, he let me find that out for myself because he knew that the process was just as important as the end result. I learned that failure was a normal part of the research process. Additionally, through trial and error, I learned the value of perseverance."

As her experiments became increasingly more complex, she sought help from biotech researchers and laboratories. Participating in high-level science fairs exposed Dr. Erika to older student role models, many of whom had plans to study at the Massachusetts Institute of Technology (MIT). Before long, Dr. Erika also began to set her sights on MIT. Once enrolled, she majored in chemistry because it gave her the flexibility to pursue a career in medicine or biology.

Around this time, Dr. Erika entered the Miss America contest on a dare. After two thwarted attempts to win the crown, she became Miss Massachusetts and garnered much attention for being a super-wiz scientist *and* a pageant winner. Her participation in the pageant became less about rising to a challenge and more about the powerful message she brought to young women: Defy stereotypes.

Encouraged by area students who became interested in science careers after hearing about her unusual path, Dr. Erika founded Science from Scientists, a non-profit organization in Massachusetts that unites STEM professionals with students in fourth through eighth grades twice per month. Her local celebrity status increased the popularity of the program, which gives more than 5,000 students from 43 schools access to leading scientists who teach hands-on labs. Science from Scientists has enjoyed such phenomenal success in Massachusetts that in August 2014, Dr. Erika established the program in San Francisco. Her beauty-pageant fame eventually led to a connection with another mentor, Dr. Wayne Matson. He convinced her to work with him on her biochemistry PhD at Boston University. Together, their mission is to solve real-world medical issues and transform health care.

In addition to launching "The Dr. Erika Show," an educational TV show in which kids struggling with science projects get advice from Dr. Erika (in her tiara and lab coat) and other scientists, Dr. Erika is Co-founder and CEO of Ixcela, Inc., a biotech company that develops pin-prick blood tests to assess and provide actionable solutions to improving gut microbiome health. Poor gut microbiome health has been shown to increase one's risk of getting diseases such as ALS, Parkinson's, Alzheimer's, diabetes, heart disease, IBS and certain auto-immune conditions. The mission of Ixcela is to help individuals to improve their gut microbiome health and thus minimize their chances of developing these diseases. The most thrilling aspect of her latest work is "that we are able to help people minimize their risk of disease. The goal is to help people understand what their risks are to reduce their likelihood of disease. It gives the patient control to be able to do something long in advance."

Dr. Erika continues to advocate for girls in STEM. "There are so many moments when students, girls especially, can fall off the path because someone tells them they can't be a scientist because it's hard, boring or because girls just don't do that sort of thing. We need young women to know that they can pursue STEM fields and still be feminine." Dr. Erika also wants education to be as valued in popular culture as fashion and celebrity to encourage girls to pursue higher education. "Why aren't female STEM leaders on the covers of *Vogue* and *Time* magazines? Society needs to change."

Her advice to young women considering a STEM path of study is to "find mentors who can support you. It is much more difficult to do it alone. It means being proactive. You're not expected to know how to do it all yourself. None of us were born with all this knowledge." She adds, "As a woman in STEM, you will face stereotypes, and you just have to help them go away. The most effective way to do that isn't by becoming huffy and storming off. If they think you're unintelligent, make them realize that their assumptions are wrong."

Much like the assumption that a woman can't be a super-wiz scientist and a pageant winner? Well played, Dr. Erika. ●

"Find mentors who can support you… It means being proactive. You're not expected to know how to do it all yourself. None of us were born with all this knowledge."

51

"Try, try, try, and if you fail, try again. And if you fail, try again."

SHaHerose CHarania

Startup Champion and Entrepreneur

Ms. Shaherose Charania has always been a tech junkie. From the moment she unwrapped her first America Online (AOL) startup disc and discovered the internet as a girl, she was hooked. By the time she entered her final two years in college at the University of Western Ontario in Canada, she was primed to become a major contributor to the ever-changing landscape of technology. Imagine her surprise, then, when her computer science classes gave her a bleak introduction to daily life in a tech career: "You spend 30 percent of your time in the lab. And the lab was dark and hot and it smelled like feet because it was filled with dudes who hung out there all day long. And I thought, 'Forget it. I'm not going to hang out in this stinky room.'" Ms. Charania completed her studies as a business major with a minor in management information systems, packed two backpacks and headed to Silicon Valley, the epicenter of technology.

She wanted to start a company. But she had just moved to California's Bay Area from Canada and knew she would need a support network to make her entrepreneurial dreams come true. As she immersed herself in the high-tech community, she realized that being an entrepreneur wasn't just a career choice, but part of her basic identity. "I didn't know that that was the full expression of myself because entrepreneurship wasn't brought up in school as an option at all. The only entrepreneurs I followed were Steve Jobs and Bill Gates, and, come on, I can't really relate at all to anyone like that. My dad was a small business entrepreneur, but that archetype also didn't resonate with me. I wanted to have an impact with my work." She also realized that in the world of high-tech startups, "innovation was moving forward and moving fast and if women weren't involved, what was that going to mean

for the types of products that were going to be released or the types of problems that were going to be solved through technology? Women have to be part of the discussion."

These two realizations set Ms. Charania on a path to becoming one of the leading champions of women in technology and entrepreneurial startups. Working as a product manager in startup companies like Jajah, Talenthouse and Ribbit, she found that the small, informal meetings she and her female tech friends held in their apartments began to snowball in popularity. Women wanted opportunities to network and build the same framework of support Ms. Charania had sought when she first moved to the Bay Area. Larger gatherings and conferences soon followed. What began as a social experiment in 2006 evolved into Women 2.0, an inclusive, diverse, community-driven media brand that "creates content, community and events for aspiring and current innovators in technology." Women 2.0 has provided assistance to thousands of early-stage technology startups and offered educational and networking workshops for tens of thousands of women from California to New York to Spain.

Ms. Charania is passionate about bringing women to technology-driven fields and believes the recent surge of women in entrepreneurial startups will yield "better products, products that speak more directly to the other 50 percent of the world, products that are designed differently and address problems that a guy would not have thought of. It just means better business, better ideas." Her philosophy on tech is simple: "Serve the underserved, connect the unconnected and impact people in positive ways."

In 2010, Ms. Charania became an advisor to startup companies through her idea lab, Founder Labs. She considers Founder Labs a place where "smart, driven people build new web and mobile startups." The same year, *Fast Company* recognized Ms. Charania as one of the "Most Influential Women in Technology." She is widely featured in high-profile publications such as *The Wall Street Journal, Business Week, USA Today* and *The Huffington Post*.

Her advice to those interested in starting a business is to "try, try, try, and if you fail, try again. And if you fail, try again." She suggests young women seek out mentors who can offer real advice and "keep a close group of people that are in your peer group, people that you really trust, that you can go to and ask the difficult questions without any fear. Your idea, your company is only as strong as the people you surround yourself with and as good as the people you choose to start the idea with. Choose wisely."

Thanks to advocates like Ms. Charania, tech meccas like Silicon Valley and beyond are starting to better reflect the diverse population of tech consumers. ●

Lorrie Faith Cranor
Online Security Expert

In 2009, hackers stole 32 million passwords from the social games website RockYou and posted them to the internet. The infamous case, which prompted a class-action lawsuit, left users who had the same usernames and passwords for sensitive accounts vulnerable to identity theft. For internet security experts, the incident became a cautionary tale about the extremely lax, unoriginal password habits of online users — like *iloveyou*, or *123456789*, or just *password*.

For computer scientist and online security expert Professor Lorrie Faith Cranor, the RockYou hack also inspired something entirely different: a dress. In a humorous take on the security breach, Professor Cranor designed a word cloud motif with many of the predictable (and some less predictable) password phrases stretched in neon colors across a dark purple fabric. The larger the password appears on the dress, the more often it was used. The password 123456 was so commonly used that it spans the entire length of the dress. The fashion statement was the follow-up to *Security Blanket*, an artistic quilt that landed Professor Cranor a spot on the pages of *Science* magazine.

When she is not engineering tongue-in-cheek designs, Professor Cranor is blazing new trails as a technologist in digital privacy. In 2003, *Technology Review* magazine named her a top 100 young innovator for her substantial contributions to online security. She holds four degrees from Washington University in St. Louis, ranging from engineering to computer science to technology and human affairs, and is now a professor of computer science and of engineering and public policy at Carnegie Mellon University. She also worked for seven years as an AT&T-Labs researcher, co-authored *Security and Usability* — an influential and widely referenced book on usable privacy and security — and co-founded Wombat Security Technologies, where she served as chief scientist for several years.

Passionate about the need for simple but effective security software, Professor Cranor has emerged as an advocate for the protection of personal privacy, adding her voice to the fight to end the U.S. government's mass surveillance program. She compares online privacy to the privacy we seek in our everyday lives. "As we walk about in the physical world, we raise and lower our voices and we raise and lower our window shades and we turn our faces, and we are all constantly adjusting to regulate our exposure and our privacy. And it comes naturally; we don't spend a lot of time

"I've always thought of myself as an interdisciplinary person. It's a great career path for people who have many interests."

thinking about it. But when we go online, it's no longer natural because we don't have these readily apparent, physical things where you can just easily close that shade, and it's obvious what you're doing. So we have to rely on software tools to help us with this privacy regulation process."

For most internet users, the complexities and cost of such software tools make secure communication prohibitive. "If you want to send me an email," Professor Cranor explains, "and you're concerned about someone intercepting it and reading it — if you wanted to encrypt that email, you'd have to get an email encryption program, and I'd have to get the same one in order for you to send me a secure email. Wouldn't it be nice for email to be encrypted automatically?"

While her parents — a college math professor and a biomedical engineer — played the biggest role in her decision to pursue a STEM field, Professor Cranor's love of engineering kicked into high gear in middle school during a summer internship at a government research lab. "They were working on acoustics for the Navy, on submarines, and they needed to understand the acoustical properties of propellers. So they had me lower microphones into a pool where they tested hulls and propellers to gather data. That was really cool."

In her first engineering courses in college, Professor Cranor learned that she thrived at the meeting point where different disciplines intersect. She shifted her engineering focus to incorporate public policy. "I've always thought of myself as an interdisciplinary person. I remember thinking in middle school that I wanted to be an architect because it combined math and art." For Professor Cranor, the combination of engineering and public policy holds tremendous potential for social impact that is both broad and deep. "Political leaders need to understand the science before they make decisions," she says, and she has helped elected leaders do just that, testifying before Congress and the Federal Trade Commission.

Although Professor Cranor has not suffered from overt discrimination as a woman in a male-dominated field, she has had her share of challenges. "Sometimes you're at meetings and the men are all talking and sometimes I think I have to speak up extra loud to be heard. As a mother of three children, another issue for me has been to push for more family-friendly policies at my university, and I think that's something that men benefit from as much as women do." Her advice to young women interested in pursuing technology is to go for it. "It's a great career path for people who have many interests. There are a lot of exciting opportunities in this space."

And if your internet password is *iloveyou* or *123456789*, change it to something more unique but still memorable. You wouldn't want your password to end up on Professor Cranor's next creative endeavor, would you? ●

mary lou jepsen
Holography and
Virtual Reality Technologist

Imagine a day when we'll be able to transmit our ideas directly to computers — when technology will be able to decode our brainwaves enough to interpret human thought. Imagine a movie director visualizing a scene and then instantly downloading that creative vision from her mind to a laptop, to share with her cast and crew. Imagine an artist's vision projected onto a digital canvas or a composer's ideal symphony downloaded into a sound system in real time.

Sound far-fetched?

Not for Dr. Mary Lou Jepsen, a computer scientist and electrical engineer at the forefront of some of the most cutting-edge optical and display inventions of our generation. Research on the brain has already shown a powerful correlation between human thought and real images; for example, imagining an object, like a jelly donut, creates the *exact* same result on a brain scan as observing a real jelly donut. The technique used to produce these brain scans, known as MRIs, use strong magnetic fields to create images of the body. So what kind of technology could bridge the gap between current MRI capabilities and the 1000-fold resolution increase needed to decipher human thought? Dr. Jepsen, already a tech superstar when it comes to enhancing the resolution on brain scan systems, believes the answer lies in better magnets, not bigger ones.

While decoding brain waves is still many years away, the technology holds immense promise for patients who suffer traumatic brain injuries or who can no longer speak or remember due to illness, as well as for those who simply want to bridge cross-cultural language barriers. As she continues to push the boundaries of her field to design the inventions that will seamlessly connect computers with human thought, Dr. Jepsen also has her eyes set on a parallel prize: championing the education of young women around the world by making basic computing technology accessible to all.

Dr. Jepsen grew up in Windsor, Connecticut on a Christmas-tree and strawberry farm. No one in her family had a background in technology, but they instilled in her a belief in the power of education to change things. Her interest in optics, the science that studies light and the way light impacts

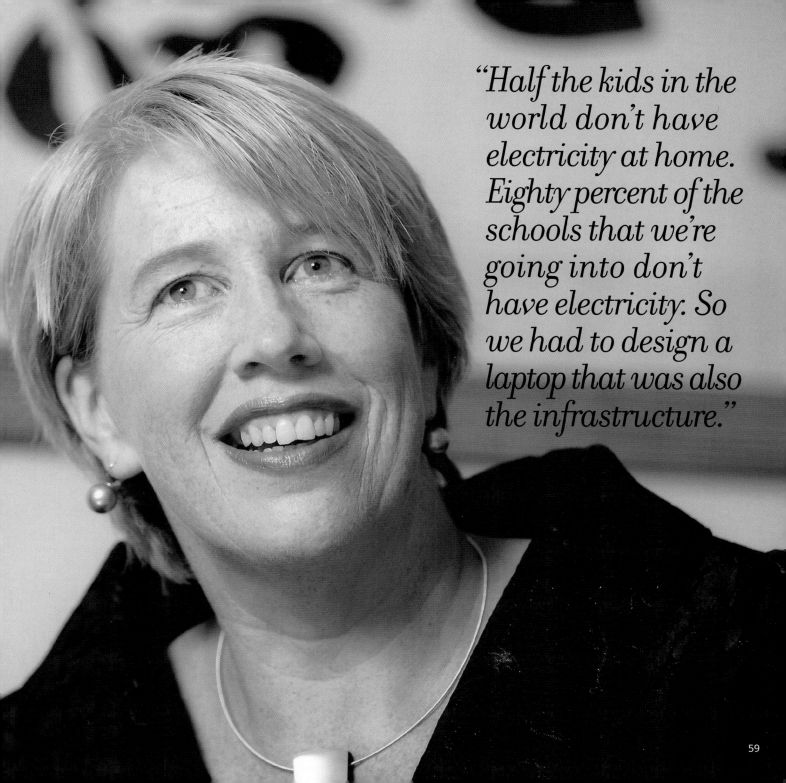

"*Half the kids in the world don't have electricity at home. Eighty percent of the schools that we're going into don't have electricity. So we had to design a laptop that was also the infrastructure.*"

59

objects, developed from a fundamental interest in both technology and art. Her studio art and electrical engineering degrees from Brown University in 1987 led her to a master's degree in holography from the Massachusetts Institute of Technology in 1989. Dr. Jepsen's advancements in holography, the study of lasers to create three-dimensional images, allowed her to construct a holographic replica of Cologne, Germany's historic district. She also proved it was possible to project video onto the moon's surface "for all humanity to see."

Dr. Jepsen's vision to impact the world through her research led her to develop cutting-edge, high-performance screens for cell phones and computers featuring low-power screens with a more readable black-and-white display in direct sunlight. Soon after, she founded Pixel Qi, a company that specializes in creating low-power LCD displays. And when she imagined "millions of girls all over the world who will never stand on a stage, who will never win an award of any kind," as she had, she co-founded One Laptop Per Child, an organization that develops and distributes low-cost ($75), solar-powered laptops to millions of poor children around the globe — giving them access to information, education and power.

Every major computer company laughed at her idea and told her it couldn't be done.

Dr. Jepsen did it.

"Half the kids in the world don't have electricity at home," Dr. Jepsen explains. "*Half* the kids. Eighty percent of the schools that we're going into don't have electricity. So we had to design a laptop that was also the infrastructure. It has mesh networking, which is the last mile, 10-mile, 100-mile internet solution. The solar repeaters and active antennas that we've added into the mix cost about $10 apiece and help to relay the internet. If one laptop in a village is connected to the internet, they all are."

Her passion for images became deeply personal after she was diagnosed with a brain tumor in 1996. Having a portion of her brain removed and relying on a combination of medicines for her recovery made brain science personally relevant for Dr. Jepsen, who describes the past 18 years as "trying to get my intelligence back after surgery."

Dr. Jepsen's vision isn't limited to medical advances. For three years, she led the display division of Google X, a top-secret part of Google dedicated to revolutionary tech ideas. Most recently, she joined Oculus, a Facebook-owned startup company dedicated to taking virtual reality to the next level. As head of the Oculus team, Dr. Jepsen will invent screens, optics, electronics and hardware with the lofty goal of exposing a billion people to virtual reality. Her future predictions, which include wearables such as sunglasses that instantly identify people around you, might seem more science fiction than fact, but Dr. Jepsen is already busy creating those predictions of the future.

The world has taken notice of Dr. Jepsen's gifts. She is consistently ranked in the top 50 computer scientists of all time and was named one of *Time* magazine's 100 Most Influential People of All Time.

Dr. Jepsen considers herself an experimentalist at heart. The world considers Dr. Jepsen an experimentalist with heart. Whether it's neuroscience or rumored elevators to the moon (shh!), you can bet Dr. Jepsen will be at the forefront of the next mind-blowing technological reality. ●

HOLLY LIU
Internet Gaming Technologist

Ms. Holly Liu, Co-founder and Chief of Staff of Kabam, a leading internet free-to-play gaming company, is the heroine in her own Camelot. She has battled the knights of self-doubt, joined forces with mighty teams of programmers and entrepreneurs and created an online gaming empire that employs nearly 1,000 people from San Francisco to Beijing, China and other parts of the world. In 2013, *Forbes* magazine named Ms. Liu a *Top 10 Women Entrepreneurs to Watch* and *Fortune* magazine named her one of the *10 Most Powerful Women in Gaming*. Her motto — "Think big" — informs every decision she makes. Large dreams lead to large rewards.

The daughter of Chinese immigrants, Ms. Liu gravitated toward teachers and mentors who challenged her non-native English skills and struck a good balance between strictness and sensitivity. During summers off of school, she enjoyed spending time with her parents, who were teachers, learning about her native culture and attending extra academic classes. As she grew older, she tried her hand at painting and a very short stint in carpentry, building stools with neighborhood friends. She also traveled abroad to Europe and Asia.

Ms. Liu took undergraduate classes in programming at the University of California, Los Angeles. Though she lacked confidence with the more abstract concepts in programming, she pressed on in graduate school at the University of California, Berkeley to learn Java, often pairing up with other students she felt she could learn from and work with well. Before long, her tenacity would pay off.

With a bachelor's degree in mass communications and a master's degree in information management systems, Ms. Liu entered the job force at America Online (AOL) as a senior user interface designer and leader of community web products. During her three years at AOL, she launched several creative side projects, one of which eventually evolved into Kabam. She had initially envisioned a social network geared toward uniting and empowering employees within companies. Then she hit a stumbling block, after figuring out that company employees preferred connecting through a company-sponsored interface much more than through a third-party network. But Ms. Liu wasn't deterred for long; she

"Think big."

Photo Credit: Kabam

and her team ultimately regrouped and created Kabam as a social gaming site that would unite their greatest passions: people and technology.

The failure of Ms. Liu's original idea provided her and her team with an opportunity to learn valuable lessons, refine their business model and aim bigger. "Admitting you have a problem is hard because it means you failed. You left your company [AOL] and everything you had to go work on something which you felt would change the world. The failure is painful and palatable." Ms. Liu and her team had made a promise to their investors and couldn't quit. Despite a series of obstacles and false starts, Kabam grew to become the leading entertainment community on Facebook. When the U.S. economy began struggling in 2008, the downturn dramatically impacted their business, as they had adopted an ad-based business model. Ms. Liu and her team responded to the new challenges by making critical changes to their business model, ending their practice of contracting out to other companies to create content and focusing on goal-oriented games that tend to build a stronger online community. Those key changes helped to transform Kabam into the $1 billion company it is today.

Ms. Liu led product design for Kabam's flagship game, *Kingdoms of Camelot*, and had a hand in the initial design for the mobile extension of the franchise, *Kingdoms of Camelot: Battle for the North*, which became the top-grossing app in 2012 for the mobile Apple operating system. More recently, she has shifted her role from creating products to creating great employee experiences. As Kabam's chief of staff, her goal is to ensure that all employees work as a collective, supportive team to ensure the company's future success.

Though she sometimes misses the design and engineering aspects of her early career days, she now has a much wider and deeper impact on the company and its culture. She inspires the people who inspire the games.

For Ms. Liu, the first step to closing the gender gap in STEM is to acknowledge that challenges exist. "Some women will say, you know what, I don't see the gender challenges. I think that's detrimental. I think we must acknowledge the challenges because they are there." She believes that more women in high management positions will create an environment where it is no longer unusual to work for a female boss. She also suggests that reframing STEM courses to emphasize strengths that society encourages women to cultivate — project management and communications instead of theoretical thinking — will entice more women to try, stay and excel in STEM careers.

What can young women do on a more personal scale to rise above those gender gap challenges? Ms. Liu believes the largest difficulty facing women are the expectations imposed upon them. The "battle to know what's me and what's imposed on me," is a challenge Ms. Liu still faces, but it's a battle in which every young woman should engage. "Never, ever make your gender an excuse, but be aware. That awareness can help you move along." She also advises young women to "not hold back, to dream as big as possible, attack goals with full force and not stop until it's over. Not trying in the first place in anticipation of rejection limits a dream, and that in turn holds one back from performing optimally."

Who needs Merlin as a guide with rock-solid advice like that? ●

andrea luecke
Solar Energy Technologist

If we could harness all the sun's energy reaching Earth for one hour, how much power would it represent? Could it power a city? A country?

Think bigger. Much bigger.

That one hour of solar energy would contain enough energy to meet the demands of every individual on Earth for one *year*. Yet, as of 2016, 99.99% of solar radiation goes to waste. Capturing solar energy remains low on the priority lists of lawmakers, businesses and homeowners. Ms. Andrea Luecke, Executive Director and President of The Solar Foundation, believes it is time for "solar energy to be a greater part of the climate discussion. Solar is universal and benefits all walks of life." She is using her gift of communication to inspire people to embrace the clean energy that comes to us free each sunny day.

Ms. Luecke is the mastermind behind the National Solar Jobs Census report series, the first rock-solid method for tracking solar jobs in the U.S. each year. Starting with a baseline statistics report in 2010, the study has been updated each year to document changes and analyze trends in the solar energy jobs market. Ms. Luecke's methodology is so widely respected that President Barack Obama, the Department of Energy and others use the report to inform their decisions regarding investments in solar, a key part of our country's energy future. For example, the 2013 National Solar Jobs Census report indicated that the rate of new solar industry jobs grew 10 times more than the national job rate for the previous year, creating more than 24,000 new jobs. As a result, Ms. Luecke says, the Obama administration "partnered with industry, universities, local communities and the Energy Department's national laboratories to aggressively drive down the cost of solar-powered electricity generation and to develop and deploy cutting-edge technologies that will create new businesses and jobs." Her work and passion for solar energy proves that broad real-world impact in tech extends far beyond the computing and gaming industries.

Ms. Luecke's biggest role model as a child was her grandmother. "She got me hooked on STEM. She was a self-taught homeopathic doctor. She read every single book on healing serious illnesses through food. She was very informed and very much an activist against pesticides because they pollute water and cause cancer in people and degrade our ecosystem. She taught me about the importance of air and water quality. Because of her, I wanted to be a marine biologist."

As a college student, her childhood passion for the environment began to focus around a burning question: How have human societies become such a major source of environmental degradation? In study-abroad programs at the University of Minnesota, which took her to far-flung regions from Mexico to Ecuador to Spain, she started to make a critical connection

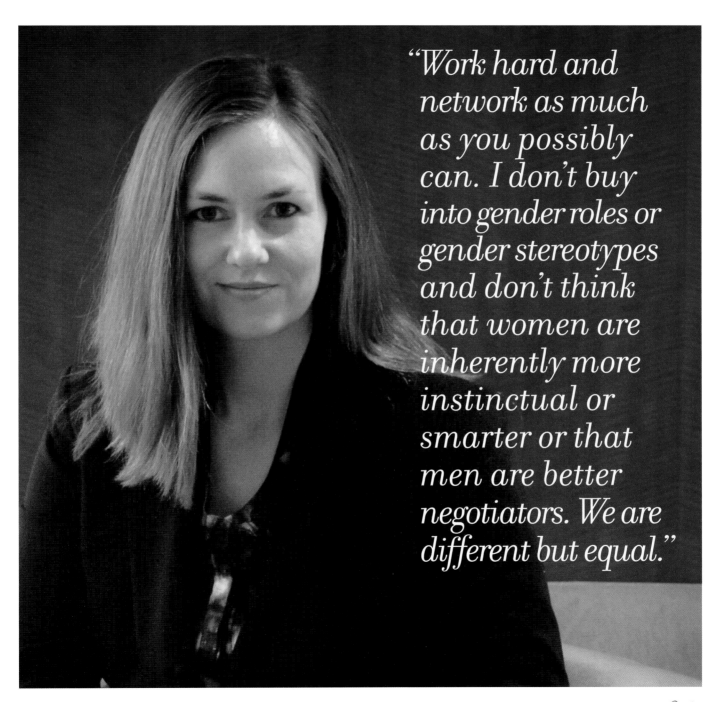

"*Work hard and network as much as you possibly can. I don't buy into gender roles or gender stereotypes and don't think that women are inherently more instinctual or smarter or that men are better negotiators. We are different but equal.*"

between the environment and poverty. "I witnessed poor people from beautiful cultures, living in pristine parts of the world, like the rainforests of Belize or Ecuador, feel trapped into selling their land to oil companies and ranchers in order to feed their families. This is how I became interested in sustainable international development — helping people make a livelihood that allows them to prosper so they don't get caught up in a vicious cycle that negatively impacts their natural environment and perpetuates their poverty." While in Ecuador, Ms. Luecke worked with farmers to use natural resources and preserve river cleanliness. While in the Peace Corps, she also helped a rural women's cooperative market their argan oil in Morocco while safeguarding the future of the native, endangered argan trees. Ms. Luecke calls her Peace Corps service invaluable — not just as a much-needed pause before the academic rigors of graduate school, but also as a time to read, study independently and reflect.

As part of the Peace Corps Fellowship graduate program, Ms. Luecke ran Milwaukee Shines, a solar project funded by the Department of Energy's Solar America Cities program. She also created one of the first Property Assessed Clean Energy (PACE), a program in the Midwest that helps local businesses finance energy efficiency and renewable energy updates, and launched one of the first business councils for manufacturers who choose solar power. In 2010, Ms. Luecke moved to Washington, D.C. to run The Solar Foundation, a non-profit group whose mission is to increase understanding of solar energy through strategic research that educates the public and transforms markets.

Though Ms. Luecke did not enter the solar industry as an engineer, her diverse business and cultural studies background adds an important aspect to solar discussions. "I am a subject matter expert on a lot of different aspects of solar, from jobs and economic impact to getting the grid to become more resilient through renewable energy. The truth is that most people don't understand what solar is and how it works. Because I don't have a technical background, I can translate the industry benefits to people in ways that many engineers can't."

Ms. Luecke also spearheads the National Solar Schools Consortium, an outreach program that not only motivates schools to switch to solar energy to save costs, but also gives students opportunities to learn about solar in a hands-on environment. The Consortium aims to build more solar-powered schools in the U.S., impacting millions of students. Ms. Luecke is hopeful some of those inspired students will be young women who grow up to consider solar industry careers.

Only one out of every five workers in the growing solar industry is female; within that small minority, there is a deepening disparity in the percentages of African-American, Latina and Asian women pursuing the field. "Solar is very — no, extremely — male-dominated. Our research shows that 18.7 percent of the solar work force is female and other research shows only 4 percent female at the board level." For Ms. Luecke, that's not just bad news for women, but for the industry, as companies with diverse employees and leaders tend to perform more competitively in the business market.

Ms. Luecke's advice for young women interested in the solar industry is the same advice she gives to everyone: "Work hard and network as much as you possibly can. I don't buy into gender roles or gender stereotypes and don't think that women are inherently more instinctual or smarter or that men are better negotiators. We are different but equal." She is proud to be a STEM leader who seeks out opportunities to increase diversity in the solar field. "I'm one of very few women in an executive position. I'm in active pursuit of women to join our team and our board. My board is fortunately sold on the idea that diversity makes business sense. It's not just the right thing to do — it makes business sense."

With Ms. Luecke at the helm of the solar movement, our country's energy future has never been brighter. ●

PILAR MOLINA LOPEZ
Animation Technologist

In the 1920s, an animation artist's canvas consisted of transparent paper attached to pegs in their desks. Animation cartoonists drew one frame at a time, often using colored pencils after the initial pencil sketches. Pieces of glass were then placed over the final drawings and photographed. The photos would then be strung together and run through clunky cameras that weighed close to 2,000 pounds.

Fast-forward to today, and computer animation has radically transformed the practice of animation, inspiring a new generation of creators and building new bridges between art and technology. Instead of using colored pencils to capture a character's changing hair color as it darkens with the sunset, computer engineers utilize a software program called a shader. Typically programmed in the C++ language, which enables easy communication between artist and computer, shader software allows animation artists to subtly tweak color levels within an image. The result is graphics that bring stories to life with visually stunning effects.

Ms. Pilar Molina Lopez is a face of modern animation: computer scientist, engineer and currently an assistant technical director at Walt Disney Animation Studios. She joined the studio as a trainee through Disney's Talent Development Program. Today, she works hand in hand with artists to perfect films through innovative technology — including the brilliant 2016 film *Zootopia* which includes themes surrounding diversity, tolerance and the importance of being who you want no matter what others tell you. Ms. Molina Lopez's previous projects include work as a technical director for Kandor Graphics on the 2013 feature film *Justin and the Knights of Valor* where she programmed and maintained various shaders and as a research and development intern for Blue Sky Studios on the wildly popular 2014 film *Rio 2*.

Ms. Molina Lopez grew up in Spain, where she attended the same co-ed school from the age of four through high school graduation. "That school was a huge part of my life. I loved it there. Unfortunately, the curriculum did not include a computer course until high school, and even then it did not include programming." That basic course introduced her to the world of computers. She remembers always being attracted to the newest technology — from gadgets to video games — and when she got her first introduction to the internet, "it blew my mind. I realized computer science could be exactly what I was looking for. It would allow me to use math and engineering to build the things I loved as a user. Luckily, I was right."

Math was always Ms. Molina Lopez's most-loved subject, and she credits her parents and brother for her interest in engineering. "When I was a child and they wanted to give me a toy, sometimes they used to buy me construction toys. I also got dolls and things like that, but they were not worried that construction toys are normally considered 'boy' toys. I loved those toys. My brother loved them, too, and that way we could play together. I like to believe that this could be one of the facts that contributed to my interest in engineering."

Ms. Molina Lopez considers her mother her biggest inspiration in her decision to pursue a STEM career. "She also developed her career in a field where men largely outnumbered women. I grew up seeing her succeeding, and that made me believe there was nothing I couldn't pursue. She used to tell me that, if I worked hard for it, there was nothing I couldn't do." Ms. Molina Lopez graduated from Spain's Universidad de Granada with a bachelor's degree in computer science. She began working for a telecommunications company and realized that she was not inspired by the more conventional areas of computer science and engineering. She wanted to use her skills to tell stories. She had always loved computer graphics, so after some self-tutoring on programs used by local animation studios, Ms. Molina Lopez landed a job at a small animation studio in Spain. Shortly after her stint at the studio where she developed her first shaders, she earned her master's at Columbia University in New York, where she was a research assistant for Columbia's Computer Graphics Group. She still considers her education a work in progress, as she strives to "keep learning every day."

Ms. Molina Lopez is proud to pass along the best advice she was ever given as a student considering a STEM career: Never give up. "Find out what you want, work hard for it and be

> *"Find out what you want, work hard for it and be patient. Hard work is essential. You will find mentors… Ask them for help and advice. Surround yourself with people who are better than you are."*

patient. Hard work is essential. But you won't be alone. You will find mentors — professors, co-workers, partners — along the way like I did. Ask them for help and advice. Surround yourself with people who are better than you are." She also encourages young women to find positive in the negatives they might encounter. "You may find people who won't believe in you. Listen to them as well. These people will make you fight harder and will also make you stronger."

Who knows? Her never-give-up attitude might be just the inspiration Disney animators need for their next heroine. ●

HEATHER PAYNE
Computer Coding Creator

In her late 20's, Ms. Heather Payne wears many hats: an entrepreneur, an angel investor who financially backs small startups, a champion of women's tech skills. Over the years, her ambition has taken her from manager of her local McDonald's as a teenager near Toronto, Canada, to Hong Kong and China, where she discovered her passion for coding. Perhaps the hat she most enjoys wearing is that of a creator.

"Imagine back when humans invented the printing press," says Ms. Payne. "At that time, there was a select group of people that could read, write and distribute their ideas using the printing press, and, for a time, this small, elite group took advantage of that technology to shape history. That's what's happening now: There's a relatively small group of people that know how to code, and they're the ones creating the technologies that the rest of us use. If you don't become a part of this group, you will forgo the opportunity to shape the future of our country, society and the technology we use every day. People should learn to create — not just consume — things on the web."

Ms. Payne wants to ensure that women are increasingly represented "behind the screens" in that creation process. Together with a team of women, she created the nonprofit organizations Ladies Learning Code, a labor of love that unites women in 24 cities across Canada with a common mission: to put women front and center in shaping technology's future. The organization's counterpart for youth, Kids Learning Code, hosts digital literacy workshops designed to take tech-hungry learners from newbie coders to fluent mobile and web

programmers. In 2012, Ms. Payne started another business, called HackerYou. HackerYou's courses — developed in response to high demand for a deeper level of skills beyond Ladies Learning Code — are taught by working programmers and designers, not academics, and focus on skill-building, not theory. There is no certificate upon completion. "If you care about a certificate, HackerYou is not for you," explains Ms. Payne. "People come because they value this style of learning, the type of experience where it is about building a portfolio, not about putting in the hours."

In childhood and adolescence, Ms. Payne squeezed the most out of every opportunity to learn from the people around her. "Whether it was someone a few years older than me at school or someone I met through family or friends, there was always someone around to serve as a role model to become just a little bit better, or happier, or more well-rounded." As soon as Ms. Payne was able to work, she took a job at McDonald's. Fast promotions soon followed. "I was the youngest member of the management team for a long time. I learned a lot about processes, managing people and creativity during those years." When it came time for Ms.

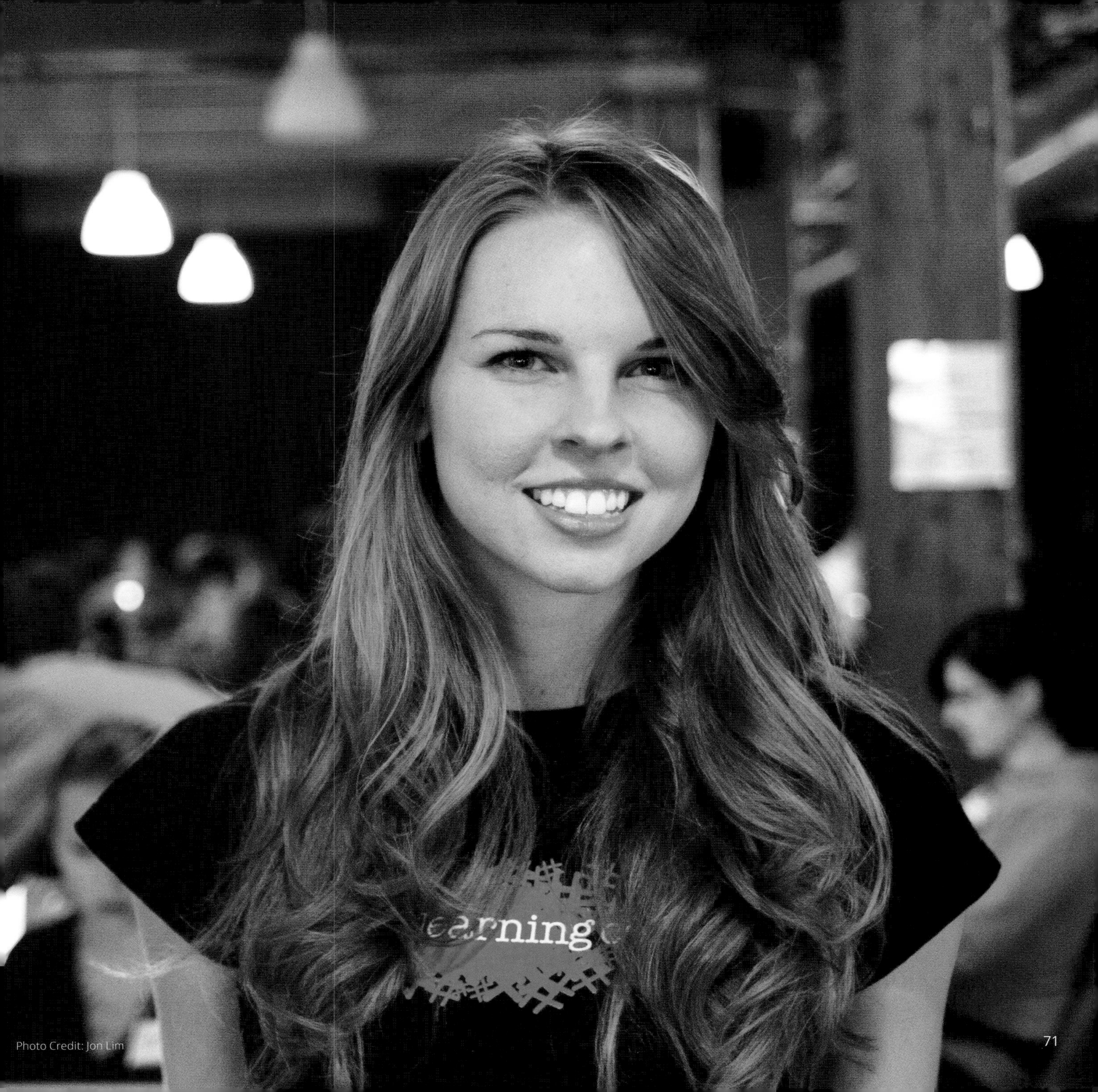

Photo Credit: Jon Lim

> *"Be extremely ambitious. People should learn to create — not just consume — things on the web. Even if you never actually launch a website, knowing that you can is empowering."*

Payne to reflect on what she wanted to study at university, she remembered how much she enjoyed her management job at McDonald's. Studying business seemed a natural fit.

As part of a five-month student exchange program while at Western University in Canada, Ms. Payne studied in Hong Kong. Upon graduation, she moved to mainland China to work towards a master's degree in international relations. To prepare for her return to Toronto, she decided to learn to code to help enhance her resume with marketable skills. "Within a few months, I launched my own website, and I was hooked on the process."

She returned home to Canada and secured a job with a sizeable company; it was on a business trip to Los Angeles for that company that she had her revelation. She learned of a workshop organized by PyLadies, a group of coders who taught the Python computer language to women, and saw the need for something similar in her own Toronto community. She sent out a Tweet, hoping to gather a few women who might be interested to meet informally at a coffee shop. The response was staggering: Via Twitter, people in the community volunteered their resources — meeting space, programmers, equipment — and Ladies Learning Code began. Since launching in 2011, Ladies Learning Code has instructed and mentored more than 16,000 adult participants (including men).

Ms. Payne is especially proud of the Girls Learning Code program. "I know that for the girls who come consistently to our workshops, coding is going to change their lives. Those girls who are coming once or twice a month to learn Ruby and Python are not only gaining skills that will help them down the road, they're seeing how cool it is to become involved with technology. I wouldn't be surprised if, 10 years from now, we have women working in the technology industry that can say they got their start at Girls Learning Code."

Ms. Payne believes that if technology conversations included names such as *Stephanie* Jobs and *Martha* Zuckerberg, women wouldn't feel so out of place in the industry. While nurturing the next generation of women tech leaders is her passion, it is also a growing challenge, as she seeks to expand her workshop series to include more women while also maintaining a personal bond with each participant. Ultimately, Ms. Payne is an entrepreneur at heart, so whatever direction she takes her ambition, she is certain to remain her own boss.

Although Ms. Payne considers coding a hobby (she's learning the Rails computer language from one of her own HackerYou courses), she understands the need for balance. "I'm learning to snowboard, which is a slow and painful process. Oddly enough, I'm also learning how to type properly. I am a terrible typist. I don't know how I do what I do with three fingers."

Her best advice for girls considering a career in entrepreneurship and technology? "Be extremely ambitious." She advises girls to arm themselves with the tools to be a creator of the web, not just a consumer. "Even if you never actually launch a website, knowing that you can is empowering." ●

Kaliya Young
Internet Identity Advocate

In the summer of 2011, Ms. Kaliya Young launched a David-and-Goliath battle against global internet giant Google with nothing more than a punctuation mark.

A die-hard advocate for online privacy and the use of pseudonyms to remain anonymous on the web, Ms. Young did not wish to use her real last name when she joined the popular social media service Google+. So she entered her last name as "." — the period at the end of a sentence. Google was not amused. The company, whose Google+ service requires users to register with real names only, suspended Ms. Young's profile for many months. Finding herself up against a multi-billion dollar corporation, she did not back down. Instead, she became a leading influence in the so-called *nymwars*, the exploding debate between online services, government and internet users over public and private identity in our digital lives.

"If we don't get this right, we will be living in a world of un-free people who are not able to voice their opinions freely and to democratically discern how we want to be governed," says Ms. Young, who famously goes by the pseudonym *Identity Woman*. "The systems of control and oppression will be embedded into all our devices."

Some social media platforms have policies that prevent users from having complete control over their identity. Under terms of service, an individual can have one account using a real name. But Ms. Young argues that people have compelling reasons for wanting to keep their lives separate and should have the freedom to do that. A school teacher might want to keep her identity as an educator separate from her active religious life. The life or safety of a political dissident in a totalitarian country could depend on communicating under a pseudonym.

In 2005, Ms. Young co-founded the Internet Identity Workshop along with other like-minded idealists to create a space dedicated to "finding, probing and solving identity issues." During the first year of her career, she often found herself the only woman at meetings. She needed a name for her blog and decided to call it *Identity Woman*. The nickname stuck, and she now continues her advocacy by blogging and tweeting under that digital cover name. Ultimately, Ms. Young says, she envisions an era of online privacy protected through identity lockers, controlled by individuals — not corporations — as a kind of storehouse for pseudonyms and different online personas. Users would then choose where and when to use these multiple identities.

Ms. Young showed early promise in STEM when she was selected in seventh grade to attend a national science fair

Photo Credit: Doc Searls

> *"I hit a wall in high school. Math was taught in a way that was hard for me to learn it — very linearly, and I learn holistically."*

based on an experiment she designed that tested the strength of cotton against different substances at different temperatures. But her road to a career in technology wasn't always obvious. "I hit a wall in high school," she recalls. "Math was taught in a way that was hard for me to learn it — very linearly, and I learn holistically."

With a growing passion for public policy and social justice movements, Ms. Young attended the University of California, Berkeley, where she designed her own self-directed major, political economy and human rights. In 2000, she attended a conference hosted by Planetwork, a leading organization that uses information technology to address the environmental crisis and social and economic justice. Inspired, Ms. Young immersed herself in technology and outlined a plan to build a distributed social network amongst change makers. This lead directly to collaborating with tech advocates who shared her vision for user-centric digital identities.

Ms. Young's focus on inclusiveness in a more democratic digital world led her to launch Unconference.net, an events design firm that uses Open Space Technology to organize non-traditional, highly collaborative conferences and meetings. She also founded She's Geeky, a national series of conferences aimed at helping women in tech make connections, share skills and explore new ideas. She views She's Geeky as a safe place to "explore topics and questions they would never raise or discuss in mixed company."

Her passion for an ethical digital world also inspired her to launch Digital Death Day, an event that brought 35 professionals from around the world to discuss what should happen to online users' digital footprint after they die. In this domain and others, Ms. Young's pioneering work has elevated her to global recognition. *Fast Company* magazine named Ms. Young one of the most influential women in tech in 2009, and in 2012, the World Economic Forum honored her as a Young Global Leader, an award given to "bold, brave, action-oriented, entrepreneurial individuals who commit both their time and talent to make the world a better place."

Her best advice to young women thinking about a career in technology is to attend a conference in any area that might be of interest. "It might seem like a lot of money to go to a conference, but think of it — you will learn so much and save yourself years of pursuing a field or a potential career and many tens of thousands of dollars on education." She encourages all young women to seek out potential student discounts on conferences, check out She's Geeky and network early on with women across the world of tech.

The fight to protect online identity will be a long and controversial one, especially as concerns about global security rise. But Ms. Young has an early victory to build on. In 2014, after three years of protest by her and others, Google finally reversed itself and stopped requiring Google+ users to use legal names — proving that with nothing more than a period, it is possible to be a leading voice in global change. ●

STEM GEMS
Engineering

CYNTHIA BREAZEAL, *Social Robotics Engineer*

CAROL ESPY-WILSON, *Electrical Engineer*

PAULA HAMMOND, *Chemical Engineer*

SARAH KOVALESKI, *Nuclear Engineer*

SYLVIA LEE, *Environmental Engineer*

BARBARA LISKOV, *Computer Scientist and Engineer*

KIMBER LOCKHART, *Web Application Engineer*

SARA McALLISTER, *Mechanical and Fire Engineer*

AINISSA RAMIREZ, *Materials Engineer*

DEBBIE STERLING, *Product Designer and Mechanical Engineer*

STEM GEMS
Engineering INTRO

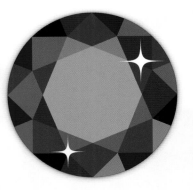

From the building of primitive shelters in ancient times to the crafting of today's nanotechnology, engineering has always been about designing simple, elegant solutions to difficult problems. Starting with the early Neolithic settlers in 4000 BC, the earliest civil engineers improved on the log roller method of transportation to construct the wheel, an engineering masterpiece that shifted human evolution from nomadic tribes to settlements. In 475 BC, when China needed to protect its borders from the invading Huns, engineers built the massive, 5,500-mile-long fortification known as the Great Wall of China. And in the early 20th century, engineers carved out the Panama Canal to give merchant ships a more efficient route between the Atlantic and Pacific oceans.

The word "engineer" is derived from the Latin word *ingeniare*, which means to construct or craft, but don't think engineering is limited to designing dams or determining the structural soundness of a building. Although early civil and mechanical engineering leaned heavily on principles of physics — consider the Great Pyramid of Giza, which stood as the tallest man-made structure for 3,800 years — modern engineering increasingly relies on mathematics, technology and other aspects of science, including chemistry, genetics, electricity, biology, computers, materials and the environment. Engineers become astronauts and surgeons, architects and lawyers. They invent faster and lighter computers, create high-performance athletic gear, design the synthetic colors and textures in our cosmetics and develop satellites to withstand the harsh conditions of orbiting in space. Outside of nature, virtually everything we come into contact with had its origins in the mind and hands of an engineer.

Engineers are the doers of the STEM acronym. They translate a great idea at point A into a real-world product at point Z. For every invention and innovation, an engineer holds the "toolbox" that gets it done. Many of the engineers you'll meet in this section recall childhoods defined by a hunger to understand the mechanics of the objects that surrounded them. They were tinkerers, meddlers, young women who weren't satisfied until they figured out *how* things work. As a middle schooler, mechanical and fire engineer Sara McAllister spent hours in the garage with her father, handing him tools and learning to build and repair cars and just about anything else she could put her hands on. Chemical engineer Paula

Hammond recalls being fascinated when she was young by the inner dynamics of her ant farm. Multiple STEM Gems, including nuclear engineer Sarah Kovaleski, cite a childhood love of Legos for giving them tactile experiences that fostered their inquisitive minds.

In addition to being relentlessly curious, these young women were also relentlessly determined. "My closest friends and family will tell you how easy it is to get me to react by saying 'I don't think you can...[do something].' I can't help it — I have such a visceral reaction to expectations that limit my potential, I react by proving that *I can*," says web application engineer Kimber Lockhart, whose tenacity propelled her through a computer science degree at Stanford University and into her first startup, which she founded *before* graduating from college. Electrical engineer Carol Espy-Wilson grew up in a household influenced by three brothers, all of whom pursued engineering. Though disadvantaged, she eagerly pursued and won scholarships to attend engineering programs at schools like the University of Wisconsin-Madison and the Georgia Institute of Technology. And when it came time for social robotics engineer Cynthia Breazeal to select a major in college, she found that her fascination with robots was stronger than any other inclination.

According to the 2011 Women in STEM study conducted by the U.S. Department of Commerce, "engineers are the second largest STEM occupational group, but only one out of every seven engineers is female." Of the men who choose to major in STEM in college, 48 percent choose engineering — two and a half times the rate at which women make the same choice. During the past decade, efforts to change those statistics have begun at the top levels of American government to ensure that our future includes innovations from *all* members of society. National mentoring programs such as those initiated by the Department of Energy and Department of Transportation as well as the National Aeronautics and Space Administration are working to connect women engineers to young women and girls from the elementary-school to the college level. Setting a high bar for gender equality in STEM, President Barack Obama appointed engineer Sally Jewel to a cabinet position as leader of the Department of the Interior, which manages and sustains all of America's land, water, wildlife and energy resources. With leaders like Jewel and the engineers assembled in these pages, the future of engineering promises to be groundbreaking *and* balanced.

Predictions about what engineers will be doing in the future abound. Most experts agree that faster technology will push engineers to design and develop at an increased pace. As the demands grow more complex — who doesn't want faster, better, healthier? — the engineers of the future are likely to draw on expertise from several areas. Engineers will make technology smarter and alternative energy more economical. Advancements in virtual reality will make almost anything seem real. Medical engineering will help doctors more effectively treat and overcome illness and disease. According to Joseph E. Coates, author and president of a Washington D.C. policy research firm, "women will become increasingly central to the profession and will bring with them new issues, concerns and design strategies."

Can you imagine all the opportunities engineers have to change the world? ●

CYNTHIA BREAZEAL
Social Robotics Engineer

Imagine a world where robots aren't engineered merely to perform fixed tasks, like wash dishes or sweep minefields. Imagine a world where robots develop social intelligence by interacting with humans and evolve into thinking, feeling companions, much as the beloved R2-D2 and C3-PO robot characters of *Star Wars* fame.

That's exactly the kind of robotic world Professor Cynthia Breazeal envisions.

Professor Breazeal is well on her way to making that vision a reality. At the Massachusetts Institute of Technology (MIT) Media Laboratory, she built Kismet, an emotionally expressive robot that has captured the imagination of all who have come into contact with it. Professor Breazeal created Kismet by studying the developmental psychology of human infants, then using that model to design a synthetic nervous system for the robot — from an artificial brain and sensors to mechanical body parts. Kismet and its next-generation successors are precisely the kinds of hands-on, real-world inventions that drive her passion for social robotics engineering. "I would much rather build something and interact with it than philosophize about it. Or philosophize about someone else doing it."

In many ways, Professor Breazeal's upbringing shaped her destiny. She was born to a mathematician father, who worked at the Sandia National Laboratory, and a computer scientist mother, who worked at the Lawrence Livermore National Laboratory. Both facilities, co-located near what is known today as Silicon Valley, California, specialize in the advancement of science and technology research in areas critical to U.S. national security. It isn't hard to imagine that Professor Breazeal became captivated by science and engineering at a young age. Although she seriously considered a career as a medical doctor or an astronaut, her initial love of robots never left her. She credits the iconic, fictional droids from *Star Wars* with sparking her fascination. "I was old enough to know they didn't really exist, and I was old enough to know that they may never exist as long as I was alive," says Professor Breazeal, who was 10 when she first saw the movie. "But that was the moment I became aware of the notion of this special kind of robot. These robots were full-fledged characters that had rich personalities, that had friendships with people."

Eventually, she earned a bachelor's degree in electrical and computer engineering from the University of California,

81

Santa Barbara. When she started thinking about doctoral work, she still had plans to become an astronaut, specializing in the robotic technology that missions depend on to carry out scientific work in space. She began her PhD research with Dr. Rodney Brooks — considered the world's leading authority on autonomous robots — and his group at the MIT Artificial Intelligence Lab. In 1993, her mentor turned his attention to creating humanoids. To execute the monumental task of creating a highly social and emotional robot, Professor Breazeal pioneered a unique integration of engineering and

judge in the FIRST Robotics Competition, a national team-based engineering contest for students, and has been an integral part of exhibits at the Boston Museum of Science that promote science and technology. Professor Breazeal considers herself fortunate to have had a primary role model in her scientist mother. She now aspires to fill that role for young women. She wants young women to know that the hard sciences and engineering are rich with opportunities to be creative, but to get to that place of creative empowerment, students must commit to learning the fundamentals. "If you

"I would much rather build something and interact with it than philosophize about it."

social psychology in her research. She wrote about her experiences in the book *Designing Sociable Robots*, published by MIT Press, and also worked as a consultant on Steven Spielberg's movie *A.I.: Artificial Intelligence*. In addition to earning numerous academic and popular honors, such as *Time* magazine's Best Inventions of 2008 for a robot named Nexi, she serves on the advisory board for the Science Channel. Today, Professor Breazeal is recognized as the pioneer of social robotics.

Near and dear to her heart is the desire to turn K-12 girls on to careers in engineering and science. She has served as a

want to do robots there's going to be traditional math and science involved. So you can't shy away from that stuff... When you're in high school or grade school you're learning these very basic things that — at least when I was growing up! — tend to be kind of dry. Appreciate that those skills are so powerful. They allow you to create and think about things with tremendous creative empowerment."

Professor Breazeal recently founded a new high-tech company, Jibo, Inc. to bring social robots to the world. This just might make her vision of helpful social robot companions for all a reality. ●

carol espy-wilson
Electrical Engineer

Our ability to talk to computers the way we talk in everyday speech has come a long way. Early voice recognition required slow, careful pronunciation of every sound to get computers to correctly recognize spoken words. Now, we can talk to Siri, the iPhone's built-in personal assistant, as if we are talking to a friend. Even with advancements in understanding how the human tongue, lips, jaw and other articulators come together to form speech, we don't yet have software that can adequately cope with speech variables such as accents, dialects or unusual speech patterns. Factor in variables such as the type of phone a person is using or ambient noise and the science behind accurately recognizing conversational speech becomes an imposing challenge.

Thankfully, Professor Carol Espy-Wilson is up to that challenge.

Professor Espy-Wilson and her team of engineers at the University of Maryland are crafting 3D geometric models of the human vocal tract to better understand the relationship between the characteristics of physical speech signals and the corresponding position of speech articulators. They are also developing a system that maps those physical signals to parameters for the relative positions of the lips, teeth, tongue and jaw. With a better understanding of the brain's processing of sound, the articulators that produce it and the human factors that influence it, Professor Espy-Wilson hopes to push the frontier of speech recognition to a level of accuracy such that your car could distinguish your voice from your sister's by a simple vocal command. She also envisions software that could aid those who have difficulty producing speech, either because of disability or because their native language lacks specific sounds. The applications of the technology seem limitless; already it has made national headlines for detecting depression through biological markers such as vocal features and facial expressions. Professor Espy-Wilson is now Founder and CEO of OmniSpeech, a company she began as a direct result of her research.

Professor Espy-Wilson's career path might have been very different had she not had a family that encouraged her to excel. She grew up in Atlanta, Georgia in a lower-income neighborhood and attended low-performing public schools. "While some of my teachers cared about whether students learned the material, I had some who did not. And I had some who had very low expectations of us." She admired her father's exceptional math skills and strong work ethic as a

"Don't let fear keep you from doing anything. Face your fears."

remodeling contractor, her three older brothers' paths into engineering and her mother's unwavering belief in education. This family support, along with a special high school counselor who encouraged her to attend pre-engineering academic programs, boosted Professor Espy-Wilson's confidence and filled in her educational gaps. So did the nearby Georgia Institute of Technology, where she took trigonometry and calculus classes while she was still in high school. Before she graduated, she petitioned her high school to offer trigonometry so others could benefit. As a result of her petition, the school began offering trigonometry to all students.

Professor Espy-Wilson met her undergraduate degree with equal moxie. At the encouragement of one of her brothers, she followed in his engineering footsteps at Stanford University. She found, however, that the most difficult part of being an undergraduate wasn't her studies. "The academics were very isolating. I was in classes where few people had a background like me. Many of my classmates attended private schools or at least well-resourced schools, and I was the only African American my year majoring in electrical engineering." Having felt isolated as an African American during her summer jobs in industry, she decided to pursue an advanced degree after graduating from Stanford in 1979. She considered pursuing her PhD at many universities, with the Massachusetts Institute of Technology (MIT) ranking as the most intimidating of all. "I was afraid. Once I realized that, there was no choice. I had to go to MIT. I promised myself when I was a child that I would never allow fear to guide my decisions." Professor Espy-Wilson became the first black woman to earn a PhD in electrical engineering at MIT.

Her numerous awards testify to the impact her research has made, both in the classroom and in her area of expertise. She has also won numerous grants from the National Science Foundation and National Institutes of Health (NIH), including an NIH Career award. She believes strongly in giving back and helping others, and her commitment to nurturing others was recognized when she was inducted as a Fellow by the Acoustic Society of America. "One of the reasons that was quoted for my induction as a Fellow was my mentorship. That meant a lot to me because I work really hard to train my PhD students in all areas so they can be successful in the academy or in industry."

Professor Espy-Wilson suggests that if young women want to be entrepreneurs, STEM fields are a great place to start. "Having a life where you're being creative and where you are answering questions and developing technology to better society can naturally lead to being entrepreneurial." And as she learned with that crucial MIT decision, "Don't let fear keep you from doing anything. Face your fears."

In a future where computers and humans move toward a seamless interaction, Professor Espy-Wilson's progressive research is fundamental to fostering that effortless connection, distinguishing the endless patterns and traditions of speech that make cultures unique. Thanks to electrical engineers like Professor Espy-Wilson, the human element is alive and well in STEM. ●

PAULA HAMMOND
Chemical Engineer

Chemical engineer Professor Paula Hammond is finding ways to battle cancerous tumors, protect soldiers on the battlefield and harness energy, all in a micro-space that is one one-thousandth the width of a human hair. Her research is invisible to the human eye, but her contributions to her field and to society are as immense as her fascination with science.

Professor Hammond creates polymers, chemical compounds that contain many small molecules strung together. Examples of naturally occurring polymers include proteins and DNA, but Professor Hammond manufactures these clusters artificially, to develop new energy sources and even to revolutionize medicine's approach to cancer. Her energy projects involve building extremely thin films containing nanotubes, nano-sized cylinders of carbon that convert fuel sources like hydrogen into electricity. These tubes generate incredible power in a tiny space, which makes them applicable for everything from micro-batteries to the solar cells of the future.

To help people visualize the sorts of polymers she uses in her biomedical research, Professor Hammond compares them to tiny soap bubbles designed to carry tumor-fighting chemotherapy drugs through the body. She engineers these "stealth" soap bubbles to appear harmless to the human body so that the immune system does not flush them out. When the polymers reach the tumor, they travel through blood vessel "leaks" in the tumor and release cancer-fighting drugs at precisely the site where they are most needed. Professor Hammond has also used her nanoparticle research to develop polymers that can be injected into wounded soldiers on the battlefield to deliver rapid blood-clotting and life-saving antibiotics. Bringing her chemical engineering expertise to cell biologists and other scientists in order to advance real-world applications is what Professor Hammond finds most thrilling about her vocation.

A bookworm and nature-lover from Detroit, Michigan, Professor Hammond says her parents were pivotal in her decision to pursue a STEM path. Her father has a biochemistry degree and her mother holds a master's degree in nursing. Though they never pressured her into a STEM career, they had high expectations that she would go to college. Professor Hammond credits her all-girls Catholic school with providing a disciplined learning environment where there was no fear in asking questions. "There is a dynamic that sets in during the tween years where you don't want to open your mouth and ask questions because there's a sense of evaluation by

your peers. This anxiety can become more marked when you're in a mixed classroom, gender-wise. In an all-girls school, there's no very strong social tension or gender tension. It frees you up to dive in and answer questions and get involved in class. That provides a level of confidence that is unique for women." It was at this school that a chemistry teacher recognized her talent for the subject and encouraged her to pursue a chemical engineering path.

Professor Hammond went on to excel at the Massachusetts Institute of Technology (MIT). Upon receiving her bachelor's degree, she worked as one of the first African-American process engineers for Motorola. She found she missed university life, so she attended graduate school at the Georgia Institute of Technology and later returned to MIT to earn her PhD in 1993. She adores the quirky, accepting learning climate at MIT and is proud to be the university's David H. Koch Professor in Engineering and the head of a research lab named after her.

The impact of her research has led to many industry awards — from the National Science Foundation to the Environmental Protection Agency to chemical company DuPont to the multi-national conglomerate 3M. In 2010 she was named Scientist of the Year by the Harvard Foundation for her work in advancing minorities and women in science, engineering and math. Her research on polymer batteries informed President Barack Obama's October 23, 2009 speech on clean energy, and her medical innovations designed for the battlefield will soon be used by paramedics and hospitals.

Professor Hammond hopes that all women, at some point in their lives, enjoy that same freeing experience she had in her all-girls school. "Regardless of when it's experienced —

> *"Some will be surprised to see you at the table but you can't allow that to intimidate you. Turn it into an opportunity to engage and instruct. Prove them wrong."*

be it high school or college or sometime after — having that experience for a period of time when you're shielded from presumptions and expectations around gender can be very freeing." Her advice to young women thinking about a career in chemical engineering is to remain persistent. "Never accept that something is not conquerable, that you cannot overcome. Difficulty is a fact of life and of work. Accept it." And as she learned walking the production lines at the Motorola plant, where workers were amazed to learn she was an engineer because she did not fit the stereotypical profile, "some will be surprised to see you at the table but you can't allow that to intimidate you. Turn it into an opportunity to engage and instruct. Prove them wrong." ●

sarah kovaleski
Nuclear Engineer

Every workday morning at the crack of dawn, Ms. Sarah Kovaleski squeezes her minivan into a parking lot filled with pickup trucks at the nuclear power plant at Ameren Missouri, a midwestern electric utility company. Ms. Kovaleski is the first woman to manage a team of 40 engineers responsible for maintaining the technical design of this nuclear power plant. Together, they ensure that every aspect of the plant's design and operations conforms perfectly to all federal regulations. "At a nuclear power plant there are things that must be done perfectly. This is serious stuff, and there is no room for error."

As the Director of Design Engineering, Ms. Kovaleski is responsible for ensuring that every design standard and detail — all of the drawings, calculations and engineering evaluations — match what is installed in the plant. She also oversees the implementation of new and improved equipment and ensures that all changes and upgrades follow rules set forth by the government for safe operations. The diligent work of engineers like Ms. Kovaleski has dramatically decreased the health-related risks associated with nuclear energy in 100 facilities across 31 states in the U.S.

Ms. Kovaleski didn't discover her passion for nuclear engineering until she was a senior in her suburban Milwaukee, Wisconsin high school. Prior to that, her passions involved reading, math and science, participating in French immersion programs to de-code her parents' "secret language," and becoming a hardcore Brewer's fan and baseball rulebook expert. "My dad kept trying to get my younger brother to learn some of the stats and how to score the game, but my brother had other interests. I learned first out of rebellion because my dad had not asked me, and then because it was truly fun. I was never dissuaded or discouraged from STEM interests. It simply did not occur to me that some people thought girls don't do the things I do. I played with Legos, enjoyed my baseball statistics and dove into math and physics lessons because they were fun." In high school, she attended an orientation at the University of Wisconsin-Madison College of Engineering and realized the possibilities associated with the field. "It all sounded exciting, but when they described the field of nuclear engineering, my imagination was sparked! I knew at that moment that I was going to be a nuclear engineer. Here was a field that represented a new frontier, spanning everything from the existence of our own sun to the use of atomic energy to generate electricity."

"If there is a subject that sparks your curiosity and your imagination, follow it and see where it takes you. There will always be people who think you can't do something. You don't have to believe them."

In one of Ms. Kovaleski's introductory nuclear engineering courses, she recalls, she sat at a horseshoe-shaped table with her fellow students. "Among the 15, there were two women, including me. I noticed the woman sitting across from me. She was young, inquisitive and her eager, feminine face stood out among all those men. It took me a surprisingly long time to realize that I stood out like that, too." Although it has never fazed Ms. Kovaleski to be a minority in a STEM field where men outnumber women nine to one, she recalls persisting through "many crises of confidence as a student before realizing that my male peers had these same crises of confidence, too; they just faked confidence while I was agonizing over whether I could cut it as a nuclear engineer."

Ms. Kovaleski went on to graduate school at the University of Michigan, earning a master's degree in radiological health engineering. Her plan was to become a researcher at a national laboratory or university, but when she gave a presentation at a meeting of the American Nuclear Society, the president of a local company that provided engineering services to midwestern nuclear utilities asked her to interview with his consulting firm. This invitation steered her career path from research to industry.

She believes young women in STEM need to stay true to themselves and find their passions. "If there is a subject that sparks your curiosity and your imagination, follow it and see where it takes you. There will always be people who think you can't do something. You don't have to believe them." Maintaining a sense of balance in her life by engaging her hobbies, exercising and spending time with her family is important to Ms. Kovaleski.

During her 16 years in the industry, she has met the challenge of raising a family and growing a career. Early on, she knew she was working just as hard as her male peers but chose not to draw attention to her duties as a new mom out of fear that she might be seen as distracted or less committed to her job. As her career evolved and she stepped into leadership roles, she realized that her bosses and co-workers had been supportive all along and, male or female, they all faced challenges inherent with building careers and meeting family obligations.

Whether leading her team of engineers at a high-stakes power plant or shuttling her kids to soccer practice, Ms. Kovaleski is "changing the face of nuclear power, one minivan at a time." •

SYLVIA LEE
Environmental Engineer

Current water resource forecasters predict that within 40 years, the global demand for fresh water could exceed the world's supply. According to the 2030 Water Resources Group, an international public-private consortium tasked with helping countries achieve water security, "the world will face a 40 percent global shortfall between forecast demand and the available supply by 2030." Countries that share waterways, such as Ethiopia and Egypt, India and Pakistan, and China and its Mekong neighbors, have been locked in ongoing conflict over fresh water resources that flow through their boundaries. Increasing political tensions, particularly in locations already experiencing a water shortage, are placing an enormous strain on the world's fresh water supply. U.S. Secretary of State John Kerry recently remarked, "We've already seen in various parts of the world — in Africa, for instance — people fighting each other over water, and we've seen more conflicts shaping up now over the limits of water."

Environmental engineer Ms. Sylvia Lee has made it her life's work to address the complex issues surrounding the availability and utilization of water around the globe. For seven years after graduating from the Massachusetts Institute of Technology (MIT), she immersed herself in building and designing urban water systems for MWH, a global leader in water and wastewater treatment based in Boston, Massachusetts, because she wanted to make useful structures that contributed to society's need to manage water and wastewater. This career path spoke to her interests in math, science and engineering, but another component was missing: her desire to be on the front lines of shaping public policy. "By the time a water project brings in engineers, most of the major decisions have been made. I became more interested in public policy and raising awareness, a bit more upstream than just the building of things."

So Ms. Lee moved to the World Economic Forum, an international non-profit organization best known for its annual meeting based in Davos, Switzerland, which is "committed to improving the state of the world." In this role, she engaged international corporations such as Coca-Cola and PepsiCo in discussions about the global water crisis in order to raise awareness and inspire change. "As our world becomes more stressed, companies have a major role to play. Having the technical knowledge as an engineer was really helpful." But bringing world leaders to a discussion is no guarantee that action and results will follow. So Ms. Lee moved to Kathmandu, Nepal, where she worked on trans-boundary water issues and helped communities become more adaptable to a changing climate. Her next career move to Skoll Global Threats Fund marked a transition to a

Photo Credit: James Maxwell Hawes IV

private foundation that funds engineering innovations that benefit communities around the globe facing water insecurity and other global threats.

Ms. Lee credits a high school physics teacher, who encouraged her to try a daylong "girls in engineering" program at her local university, for opening her eyes to a career in engineering. "I thought engineers made trains. So I realized 'Oh my gosh, this is what I want to do.' That single day made me want to go into engineering. Had I not gone to that, I don't think I would

I'm in a position to actually do something about that — to look at the landscape, the entire spectrum, and to think every day about what we can do to fix it." Reflecting on her two decades of dedication to water issues, Ms. Lee is most proud that she has been able to encourage large corporations and the media to pay closer attention to the water crises occurring around the globe. One specific point of pride was the role she played in a collaboration that brought together key representatives from clashing South Asian nations to address water issues that the region faces as a whole.

"That single day made me want to go into engineering. Had I not gone to that, I don't think I would have known what engineering was. This is why I believe so much in the power of exposure."

have known what engineering was. This is why I believe so much in the power of exposure." She went on to earn a bachelor's degree in civil engineering from McGill University in Montreal, Canada and a master's degree in environmental engineering from MIT.

Ms. Lee believes the coolest part of her job — aside from the fact that she's lived on three continents and in six countries and has visited over 50 nations — is that it unites her two greatest passions: engineering and working for the public good. "There are a lot of water problems in the world. And

Her advice to young women considering a career in engineering is to not give up. "Go with what inspires you, and you can always figure out how you can be prepared to do it. So if it's civil or environmental engineering that you're passionate about, don't let whether you're good in math or not get in the way. Focus on what you want to achieve and you can always find a way to achieve it."

With climate change intensifying the global water crisis — now more than ever — we need engineers like Ms. Lee: passionate civil servants dedicated to engineering solutions. ●

Barbara LISKOV
Computer Scientist and Engineer

Back in the 1960s, when computers filled entire rooms and inputted data from hole-punched cards instead of keyboards, Professor Barbara Liskov accidently entered the computer science field. She slipped in through the back door as a mathematician but has been a leading innovator in the applied science of computers ever since.

Professor Liskov earned her bachelor's degree in math from the University of California, Berkeley. Working as a programmer in the early days of the computer revolution, she discovered she had a talent and passion for programming and went on to graduate school at Stanford University to push her level of knowledge further. Her work on artificial intelligence led to a PhD in computer science in 1968. Did Professor Liskov feel intimidated as a woman doing pioneering work in a brand new field? (Professor Liskov is, after all, widely regarded as one of the first women in the U.S. to earn a PhD in computer science). "No, I was absolutely not intimidated. I never thought about it at all. I was interested in doing it, there was an opportunity, so I just did it. I think that when you're doing something that's unusual and that people disapprove of, it's very nice to remain oblivious to what they're thinking. I never did pay too much attention to what people's attitudes were." Professor Liskov cites her ability to tune out "negative signals" as being critical to her success.

Since 1972, Professor Liskov has held a professorship at the Massachusetts Institute of Technology (MIT). According to former MIT president Dr. Susan Hockfield, "Professor Liskov is revered in the MIT community for her role as scholar, mentor and leader. Her pioneering research has made her one of the world's leading authorities on computer language and system design. In addition to her seminal scholarly contributions, Professor Liskov has served MIT with great wisdom and judgment in several administrative roles." In 2008, MIT named Professor Liskov an Institute Professor, the highest honor awarded to a faculty member. That same year, she scooped up the highly acclaimed Turing Award, also known as the Nobel Prize in computing.

Of all the achievements in her distinguished career, Professor Liskov is proudest of developing the idea of data abstraction. Data abstraction is a method of inventing modules, or segmented parts, that are useful in building programs. At the start of her career, Professor Liskov realized that the key to efficient software lay in its ability to break large programs into smaller pieces, each of which can be thought about independently. These concepts of modular programming, data abstraction and polymorphism — a programming

96

language's ability to process information differently based upon the type of data — form much of the foundation for modern computer languages such as Java and C#. Professor Liskov led the design and implementation of an early programming language named CLU, the first to emphasize modular programming based on data abstraction. Directly put, nearly every software advantage we enjoy today is rooted in Professor Liskov's innovations.

Not one to rest on her successes, her current research addresses the phenomena of distributed computing and cloud storage. Distributed computing involves software systems that allow computer servers to form multi-layered networks so they can communicate with each other and accomplish a goal. Think about sites like Google and eBay and Amazon which rely on hundreds of thousands — sometimes millions — of computers to run effectively, and you'll come close to understanding the nature and scale of Professor Liskov's work. She is also tackling cloud storage, a rapidly growing method of data storage for businesses and personal users which stores data in an off-site system hosted by a third party service. Ever heard of Dropbox? That's cloud storage. People no longer have to remember to create backup files or risk losing time and information from computer failure. This "no-hassle" solution to computer storage comes courtesy of researchers like Professor Liskov, who work to ensure the technology's reliability and security for users.

The world of technology and computer science is expanding rapidly, and we need all hands on deck. Professor Liskov believes reaching out to young women, pre-university, is the key to increasing the number of women in computer science. "My gut says that the gender gap in STEM is a very difficult problem that has to do with society as a whole. It's not a college problem. It happens much earlier than that. It has to do with how our culture views what women should do. Think about the programs on TV. How many women scientists do you see? How are they depicted? How are the men in technology depicted? Do you think these depictions of women scientists are something that might make a young woman want to go into STEM? So it's a societal problem. It's about the messages we send young women."

"I was interested in doing it, there was an opportunity, so I just did it."

Professor Liskov credits much of her success to supportive parents who encouraged academic excellence, especially in math and science, and who didn't discourage her when her path deviated from the nursing or education careers more common among women of her generation. Her advice to young women thinking about a career in computer engineering is to "do what you're good at and what you enjoy. It's good not to pay too much attention to the expectations of society. My mantra is: don't be intimidated, just do it!" She also suggests taking every math course offered in high school. As Professor Liskov knows, math is only the beginning. ●

KIMBER LOCKHART
Web Application Engineer

Ms. Kimber Lockhart has taken flight in more ways than one. At San Francisco's Circus Center, she trains recreationally in aerial rope, acrobatics and the flying trapeze. But her most impressive feats have come as a software CEO, engineer and champion of women in tech.

Ms. Lockhart is a self-confessed competitor, which was evident at a young age. "My closest friends and family will tell you how easy it is to get me to react by saying "I don't think you can...[do something]. I can't help it — I have such a visceral reaction to expectations that limit my potential; I react by proving that I *can*." Once, in her small-town Iowa high school, she noticed an opening on the varsity track roster in the 400-meter hurdle, a daunting race few attempted. Instead of being content to run second-string, she trained hard and made the varsity team that year. Today, she gives the same advice to women looking toward leadership roles in the tech industry: "Know what you want and find a way to do it. Be willing to take on responsibility beyond the job you already have."

In college, Ms. Lockhart gravitated toward technology. She enrolled in an introductory computer science class at Stanford University and found she loved the challenge and creativity of programming. But moments of self-doubt crept in, threatening to trample her newfound enthusiasm. Many of her male peers had been coding since their early teens. She had no

experience. "It started as one of those *prove I can* moments. As soon as my mind wondered if I could take Stanford computer science, my heart was already planning how I would ace the class."

In the same year she earned her bachelor's degree in computer science, she also co-founded Increo, a tech company that produced Backboard, an innovative software tool that allows online users to collaborate on websites, presentations and documents. Backboard's document preview technology impressed Box — a rapidly growing cloud storage company — so much so that Box purchased the startup in 2009. For Ms. Lockhart, who had taken the reins running the business side of Increo, transitioning back to software programming and development was "one of the hardest things I have ever done. As I became more comfortable, the same skills that made me successful in the past started to emerge." While at Box, she led the 50-member web application engineering team, responsible for building new features and redesigning the user experience. She is now the Chief Technology Officer at One Medical Group, a company transforming

the way patients and doctors communicate by using patient-centered technology. Innovations such as digital lab results, 24-hour appointment scheduling and personalized health summaries allow One Medical Group to drive down the time and cost of healthcare while increasing the quality of doctor-patient interaction.

"I have such a visceral reaction to expectations that limit my potential; I react by proving that I can."

Ms. Lockhart is on a mission to increase the number of women represented in technology. According to the National Girls Collaborative Project, a STEM advocacy organization, women earned only 18 percent of all computer science degrees in 2010-2011. Reflecting on her Stanford days, she says, "Aside from all the practical reasons to increase diversity in technology, it just didn't feel right that I was one of few women in the class." She participated in *she+++: The Documentary*, a short film that explores the gender gap in STEM and encourages girls to consider a career in technology. Ms. Lockhart also co-founded the Box Engineering Diversity Scholarship, a program aimed at female and minority college students who are applying technology to their fields in innovative ways. Her goal with the program is to help foster a richer, more diverse tech community, ultimately benefitting us all.

Her advice to young women considering a technology or engineering path reflects her tireless *prove-I-can* attitude. "Ultimately, you are an individual, you are unique. You have strengths, you have weaknesses. Who you are, what your gender is, is just another dimension of that. If you believe that you're just as likely to be successful as any other person, I think you're more likely to get there." And for those women who encounter that same crippling moment of self-doubt Ms. Lockhart experienced early at Stanford? "Act as though you aren't intimidated. In the same way that when you're in a bad mood, you shouldn't make decisions about your future — when you're feeling intimidated, separate your desires from that feeling. You'll be able to do so much more than you thought was possible." She adds, "the skills gap closes very quickly once women begin studying computer science. By the time the lifelong coders and the women new to the game are ready to be hired, the difference is almost imperceptible. For those who enter the field, the sky's the limit."

Ms. Lockhart knows that sky. Trapeze or engineering new web technologies, she glides through it every day. ●

sara mcallister
Mechanical and Fire Engineer

Scientists at the Wonderwerk Cave, a major archeological site in South Africa, recently confirmed evidence that humans have been using fire for at least a *million* years. A million years of cooking and heating and powering our world. But just because we *use* fire doesn't mean we *understand* fire.

Mechanical engineer Dr. Sara McAllister hopes to change that.

Dr. McAllister is a researcher at the Missoula Fire Sciences Laboratory in western Montana. Her research explores how biomass — the living and recently-living plant matter in a given area — ignites and fuels forest fires. Her experiments range from determining the mass of these natural fuels before and after catching fire, to understanding which materials are the most flammable, to studying how convection (the collective movement of material to rise as it increases in temperature) affects the spread of wildland fires. She also investigates differences among live, green and dead fuels, whose varying water content greatly impacts the behavior of fire. With every experiment she conducts, Dr. McAllister says, she moves closer to her ultimate goal of reverse-engineering the spread of fires.

Dr. McAllister's future in fire wasn't evident in childhood, but her talent for creating and repairing complex gadgets certainly was, with countless hours spent in the garage with her dad, who was always building and fixing things. Thanks to an early jumpstart in math and reading, courtesy of her mother, and supportive teachers along the way, she excelled in school. At 16, her passions for math and physics were ignited after she inherited the family car, a VW Beetle. "I drove that car every day through high school and college. By the time I graduated college, I was obsessed. I went from being the little girl handing my dad tools while he was under the car to *being* the one under the car. I wanted to know more about combustion because, well, that's what makes cars work." She went on to earn a bachelor's degree from the University of Nevada-Reno and master's and PhD degrees from the University of California, Berkeley, all in mechanical engineering.

While she was working on her doctorate, the National Aeronautics and Space Administration recruited Dr. McAllister and her team at UC Berkeley, led by mentor and research advisor Dr. Carlos Fernandez-Pello, to study flammability risks inside the agency's next-generation space shuttle. The new

Photo Credit: Kristine M. Lee, Florence, MT

> *"I went from being the little girl handing my dad tools while he was under the car to being the one under the car. I wanted to know more about combustion because, well, that's what makes cars work."*

lower-pressure atmosphere inside the shuttle required more oxygen, increasing the potential for disastrous fires. The impact of the team's work was significant: Astronauts on space walks are now safer thanks to their study of fire potential in space vehicles. Dr. McAllister and Dr. Fernandez-Pello appeared on the History Channel series *The Universe* to discuss their findings. She also authored a textbook on the fundamentals of combustion.

Dr. McAllister's post-graduate jump to the Missoula Fire Lab came at the suggestion of a friend who was on her triathlon team at UC Berkeley. Her friend's research in the forestry department sparked her interest in wildland fire research. Dr. McAllister entered the Forest Service in 2009 as part of the National Fire Decision Support Center. She loves the challenge wildfire brings. "I think what makes wildfire so elusive is that it is incredibly complicated and requires knowledge not only from many fields within mechanical

engineering, but also from many other fields like chemistry, biology and forestry. It's also extremely difficult to observe. No one wants to get close enough to actually see how it works!" Dr. McAllister is hopeful her research will lead to more effective firefighter training, more accurate predictions in fire behavior and new fuel treatments to slow or stop the spread of fire in communities.

A five-time triathlon competitor and three-time marathoner, Dr. McAllister finds that challenging herself physically is the perfect way to beat stress and stay level-headed when her experiments don't turn out as she had hoped or when she's stuck on a problem. She challenges young women who might be considering a career in mechanical engineering not to give up or be afraid. "You may be one of the few women in your classes, but once all those guys realize you get it and they don't, they'll be asking you for help with the homework and fighting to be your partner on projects." ●

ainissa ramirez
Materials Engineer

STEM classrooms in the 1890s may have had old-fashioned blackboards and parchment paper diagrams, but students still conducted research on everything from atmospheric pressure to the anatomy of birds, as well as in physics, microbiology and chemistry.

The majority of those students also wore skirts.

That's right: Girls once dominated STEM classrooms. According to Mr. John Latimer, a George Washington University professor and author of the 1958 book *What's Happened To Our High Schools?*, 58 percent of girls took physics classes in 1890. By 1955, that percentage had nosedived to just two percent. According to the American Physical Society, high school physics enrollment statistics show girls rebounding from 39 percent in 1987 to 47 percent today, but the trend does not hold true at the college level. Currently, only 20 percent of bachelor's degrees in physics go to women.

Although educators debate the causes of girls' low rates of participation in STEM, Dr. Ainissa Ramirez believes one factor is largely to blame: American culture. Our culture — from girls' t-shirts proclaiming "Algebra sucks" to the 1992 Teen Talk Barbie, who proclaimed "Math is tough," to the invisibility of female STEM role models in our celebrity-obsessed society — discourages young women from embracing STEM subjects and careers at every turn. Dr. Ramirez has become a passionate science evangelist, determined to revolutionize science education through books, videos, podcasts and media events that attract young women to STEM. She also happens to be quite the role model herself.

Dr. Ramirez grew up in a working class neighborhood in Jersey City, New Jersey. Her mother was a nurse and her father was an engineer. Though they encouraged education, "there was no push to do science or math." As a little girl, she saw a television show called *3-2-1 Contact* that featured an African-American girl doing science activities. "I was hooked. I saw my reflection, and the notion of being black and being a scientist were fused together."

Dr. Ramirez earned her bachelor's in materials science and engineering (MSE) from Brown University and her master's and PhD degrees in MSE from Stanford University. While she was a graduate student, she began writing for *Time* magazine, an experience that awakened her passion for sharing science, especially with children — a calling that would significantly shape her future.

"Using science, tech and math, you have the tools to change the world."

After completing her doctorate, Dr. Ramirez worked at Bell Laboratories as a materials engineer, using chemistry and physics to design new materials. There she invented an advanced mixture of metals that utilize the rare and expensive lanthanide elements (located at the bottom of the Periodic Table) to bond metal to glass and ceramics. This new universal solder makes it possible to join any computer part to another part, regardless of material. Think of it as the superglue of the future. Dr. Ramirez focuses on the structure and behavior of atoms to better understand and utilize these minute particles in ways that have major implications. "For example," she explains, "aluminum is a light metal; steel is a heavy one. If you were making a frame for an airplane, you might choose aluminum over steel."

Dr. Ramirez holds more than six patents — trademarks that grant her full ownership of and rights to her inventions. Making materials stronger is the focus of her patents. She says, "If you add small particles to a material, it gets harder. The technical term is called dispersion hardening. I came up with ways to make soft materials strong by adding stuff to them."

During her 10 years as a professor at Yale University, Dr. Ramirez's research explored shape-memory alloys, such as those found on Mars rover vehicles, which remember their shape due to the behavior of atoms under unique conditions. While at Yale, she also began an award-winning lecture series for children called *Science Saturdays* and hosted two popular science videos called *Material Marvels* and *Science Xplained*, for which she became known as the Bill Nye the Science Guy of Yale. In 2003, the Massachusetts Institute of Technology recognized Dr. Ramirez with the TR100 Award, reserved for the top 100 young innovators in the world.

In scientific communication, she found a new and equally deep passion. "I was at a decision-making point where I could've continued along the same path or I could do something that was really scary but could satisfy me far more than anything else had. As soon as I took the leap, I was asked to give a TED talk." In 2012, Dr. Ramirez gave an inspiring speech at a conference hosted by TED, a non-profit organization dedicated to spreading ideas.

Dr. Ramirez has authored over 50 technical papers and has reached a wide audience with her books *Save Our Science: How to Inspire a New Generation of Scientists* and *Newton's Football: The Science Behind America's Game*. She frequently gives talks to groups of teachers to ignite enthusiasm for the type of revolution in STEM education that she believes will be necessary for success in the 21st century: moving away from memorization and multiple-choice tests to a deeper, more collaborative and more playful exploration of scientific ideas. "STEM is like a training camp for key skills like encouraging curiosity and patience and making friends with failure. In this microwave era, STEM teaches patience. Try to quickly make rock candy from sugary water. You can't! It takes time and requires patience, but it is so worth it!"

This materials engineer and STEM evangelist has plenty of advice for young women considering a STEM path. "You need a support system of friends and role models to give you pep talks and an ability to work hard. Using science, tech and math, you have the tools to change the world." ●

DEBBIE STERLING

Product Designer and Mechanical Engineer

Get. Girls. Building.

That's the goal mechanical engineer Ms. Debbie Sterling has in mind with every decision she makes as Founder and CEO of GoldieBlox. Yes, GoldieBlox: an award-winning line of toys whose name plays on the much-beloved storybook character Goldilocks. The words may rhyme, but that's where the similarities end between the helpless fairy-tale protagonist and Ms. Sterling's modern-day creations. In her construction sets and action figures, Goldie is a girl inventor who uses wheels, washers, axles, blocks, cranks, ribbons and a pegboard to help her figurine friends and pet dog solve one challenge after another in a series of adventures. "It's the toy I wished I'd had growing up," says Ms. Sterling. "Goldie is this regular girl, not a genius, but somebody who is really open to trying new things, messing it up but trying it again, and somebody who is not a total tomboy but not a princess either, someone who was just in the middle with a lot of different interests." She sees Goldie as the best possible ambassador of her real-life message to girls: "Take risks. Don't give up. Failure is okay."

Ms. Sterling has lived that message. She grew up in a small town in Rhode Island where she and her sister were exposed to all the typical girl-oriented toys — toys sold on the "pink aisle" at a toy store. Her grandmother was an accomplished cartoonist for Disney and one of the creators of the famous television cartoon *Mr. Magoo*. Although her grandmother died before she was born, she considers her grandmother a mentor who passed along her creativity and courage. It would take both traits for Ms. Sterling to start to see herself as an engineer.

As a youth, whenever Ms. Sterling heard the term engineer she pictured a train conductor. It wasn't until her senior year when her calculus teacher, another pivotal role model, opened her eyes to the possibilities of the engineering field that she considered pursuing it as a major in college. At Stanford University, Ms. Sterling found that she loved mechanical engineering, but the classes weren't always easy. She often felt like she didn't belong and, as one of only a

"Whether it's in Mechanical Engineering 101 in college or in their third-grade science class, girls should never question their value, ability or contribution."

Photo Credit: Courtesy of GoldieBlox, Inc.

handful of female engineering students, believed her ideas were not always heard. After experiencing some difficulty drawing 3D models for a class, she realized that her spatial awareness skills were not at the same level as many of her male peers – not because they were naturally better, but because they had spent their childhoods developing those skills with typical "boy" toys like Legos and erector sets. This realization inspired GoldieBlox.

Ms. Sterling worked hard in college and persevered. She earned degrees in mechanical engineering and product design from Stanford in 2005. After a few years working as a marketing director and volunteering for an organization in rural India, she circled back to her passion: inspiring future female engineers. Ms. Sterling studied the neuroscience of the female brain, which shows that girls tend to learn best with games and play that is story-driven. With this key insight, she crafted prototypes — her first toy models — out of objects found at the hardware store and around her apartment, then wrote and illustrated an accompanying storybook. She took GoldieBlox to toy fairs and faced the same discouraging feedback again and again: construction sets for girls don't sell.

Determined, Ms. Sterling turned to social media. Her campaign on Kickstarter, an online fundraising platform for creative projects, was wildly successful: her team blew past its goal of $150,000 to raise over $285,000 in 30 days! By the end of the year, the toys were available at a major toy retailer and can now be found at Amazon.com and in retailers across the U.S., Canada, the U.K., and Australia.

Ms. Sterling hopes to grow GoldieBlox into a brand with far-reaching social impact. She wakes up each day "excited to tackle the next challenge, all in the name of inspiring more girls and women to explore engineering. Whether it's in Mechanical Engineering 101 in college or in their third-grade science class, girls should never question their value, ability or contribution. It might sound crazy, but I never gave up because I believe that this is what I was born to do."

And you should never give up too. ●

STEM GEMS
Mathematics

SUSAN ATHEY, *Economist*

MARIA CHUDNOVSKY, *Graph Theory Mathematician*

JEANNE GANG, *Architect*

TRACHETTE JACKSON, *Cancer Modeling Mathematician*

BRYNA KRA, *Dynamical Systems Mathematician*

DEBBIE LAWRENCE, *Geophysicist*

STACY LINDBORG, *Biostatistician*

TONYA MANNING, *Actuary*

ANNA NAGURNEY, *Network Systems Mathematician*

RACHEL SCHUTT, *Data Scientist*

STEFANI WILDHABER, *Urban Planner and Designer*

MELANIE MATCHETT WOOD, *Number Theory Mathematician*

STEM GEMS
Mathematics INTRO

In 1623, the Renaissance-era physician, mathematician and astronomer Galileo wrote, "The universe cannot be read until we have learned the language and become familiar with the characters in which it is written. It is written in mathematical language, and the letters are triangles, circles and other geometric figures, without which means it is humanly impossible to comprehend a single word. Without these, one is wandering about in a dark labyrinth."

Four hundred years later, Galileo would likely still hold tight to his philosophy, though he might phrase it in modern programmer lingo — that numbers and number systems are the universe's code, just waiting to be hacked by humans. Galileo wasn't the only one to have a deep reverence for math. Modern theorists believe mathematics is man's greatest invention, a system of patterns, logic and abstract symbols that describe, predict and bring elegant order to the world around us. Math may come last in the STEM acronym, but it forms the underlying basis of the three other disciplines. If STEM were represented as a pyramid, mathematics would be its foundation.

Some of the women you will meet are theoretical mathematicians who explore the "language of the universe" in order to enrich what we already know. Melanie Matchett Wood studies prime numbers with an eye to the future. "We don't know what we will need to know about primes 50 years down the road. That's why we try to figure out everything we can so we're ready, not for the applications of today, but for the applications 50 years from now." Indeed, prime numbers are already the basis of the internet's emerging currency, the bitcoin. Decades ago, advances in abstract number theory laid the groundwork for the encryption systems used in credit card transactions today.

Other mathematicians you will meet, such as Anna Nagurney, a mathematician specializing in network systems, embrace math on a real-world level. Her mathematical chops allow her to study complex challenges that impact society on a broad scale and work with businesses and organizations to implement solutions. Issues such as traffic flow in a busy city, the location of cell towers or the distribution of flu vaccinations in a given area can all be improved by applying mathematic principles. Math is also at the core of Trachette Jackson's achievements in mathematical oncology. She uses math-based models to understand and combat cancerous tumors.

Applied mathematicians can become CEOs, financiers, software engineers, computer programmers, actuaries, transportation and logistics specialists, consultants, health care analysts and data scientists. Many industries need mathematically skilled individuals who are great at problem solving.

Sadly, adaptive problem solving has become less valued as a skill among our youngest learners. Critics of today's U.S. education system believe our secondary schools focus too much on straight calculation and test scores at the expense of challenging young, hungry minds to ask questions and seek out solutions to real-world problems. If we are to meet the demands of a technology-driven society, we must re-learn how to question everything, see failure as a learning tool and make sure girls know that they are just as naturally inclined to excel at math as boys.

Girls are getting the message, but there is much progress to be made. It's true that more young women are pursuing math as a college major than ever before; between 2000 and 2009, figures from the American Mathematical Society show the number of women declaring math as their major rose from 44,500 to 66,000. But those numbers don't necessarily mean that the gender gap is closing. While the figures show a parallel rise in men declaring math majors (from 49,500 to 66,000), those 66,000 men represent a much larger share of the pool of men choosing majors. By contrast, the 66,000 women declaring math as a major is a much smaller percentage of college women choosing majors. And beyond the undergraduate level, the trend is even more troubling: While the total number of women awarded PhDs in mathematics in the U.S. grew between 2000 and 2009, the overall percentage held steady at 30 percent. Alternate data sets from the National Science Foundation suggest a five percent decline in women who earned bachelor's degrees in math during this same period. According to the late Julia Robinson, a mathematician instrumental in decision problems research, "equality in the field of mathematics will occur when male mathematicians no longer consider female mathematicians to be unusual."

While the 20th century emphasized theories and calculations, the math of the future will focus more on real-world problems and scientific applications. Experimental mathematics, where computers crunch large data sets and highlight patterns, will likely drive the development of new theories. And with the role of mathematics increasing in other fields of study, there may come a day when distinct occupations like "engineer," "mathematician" and "physicist" are replaced by "mathematical scientist."

For the STEM Gems assembled in these pages, math was never simply arithmetic or a box of magic tricks using numbers. Some find their passion in shapes, such as the geometry of a Chicago skyscraper or the hexagonal honeycomb of a bee colony. Some exercise their creativity by delving deep into theory and the interconnectedness of numbers, while others strike out into the world and use math to make life better for us all. They are problem solvers and dreamers, working within the parameters of theorems that are decades old while discovering connections that will someday lay the foundation of future innovations.

They are the light in Galileo's dark labyrinth. Will you be next to take the torch? ●

susan aTHeY
Economist

That laptop you won on Ebay? Auction. Law enforcement agencies who want to sell possessions confiscated from criminals? They use auctions, too. And those strategically placed ads that pop up beside your latest internet search? Believe it or not, those are also the results of auctions, known as position auctions, in which billions of internet searches each day trigger auctions among hundreds of thousands of advertisers who want to appear on the screen next to those search results. It is in this incredibly complex world of position auctions that economics visionary Professor Susan Athey has made her mark.

It's rare when a student's graduate work attracts global attention, but early in Professor Athey's career, her PhD dissertation became the stuff of legend in economics circles. Her pioneering work advanced a new mathematical model for analyzing risk and uncertainty. Written when she was still in her 20s, the dissertation prompted its own bidding war of sorts, with elite universities competing to have her join their faculty. She then went on to challenge the work of Nobel prize-winning economist Dr. William Vickrey, who theorized that auction rules played no role in the auction's ultimate outcome. Professor Athey demonstrated that auction rules can have a substantial impact in real-world applications. Next, Microsoft recruited her to advise them on search engine decisions that impact millions of internet users around the world. She is also the go-to person when international governments and businesses want an expert to establish auction-based marketplaces. With these wide-ranging pursuits, Professor Athey has been dubbed a leader charting a new "economic movement, nearly starting from scratch."

So how did this gifted, ambitious woman begin her journey? Professor Athey's appetite for learning was apparent from a young age. She requested additional math problems from her parents and read textbooks in her spare time. "In high school, I started getting bored and skipping class. Realizing that I needed a change, I convinced my school and parents to let me graduate early and head to college." At age 16, she entered Duke University as a triple major in economics, math and computer science. While at Duke, she got her first taste of math's real-world applications in the halls of Congress. "I got a part time job administering a workstation for an economics professor. This professor introduced me to the world of research. Based on my experience in my summer job, we analyzed policies that would help the government auctions for computer services operate more efficiently. My professor testified about our work in front of the U.S. Senate, an experience that inspired me to pursue a career in economics research, a field where mathematical models and statistical analysis can change the way a country works." From Duke,

"There has never been a better time for young women to enter the field of economics. Google, Facebook, eBay, Pandora, Uber, Instagram, Microsoft, Coursera — all of these firms, as well as the latest start-up firms, need economists."

Professor Athey went on to complete her PhD in economics at Stanford University and has since taught economics at the Massachusetts Institute of Technology (MIT), Stanford and Harvard University.

Professor Athey's reputation for dedication to her field is legendary. She once spent nearly a month holed up in her MIT office to complete a 40-page mathematical proof, leaving only to shower. According to Dr. Jonathan Levin, a Stanford economics professor who has witnessed Athey's work ethic, "She really cares about making sure you don't take short cuts and that everything is done incredibly carefully. She has a remarkable energy to get things done."

Prior to Professor Athey's research, economic researchers by and large considered auction bidders to be similar to one another, and they ignored decisions bidders made about whether to go to an auction at all. Professor Athey extended the theory to include the broader pool of potential bidders and applied that theory to data. Her research suggests that it's more important to design an auction "to attract bidders and make sure they're there to participate than to try to extract every last cent out of them once they get there." This is especially true, her work has shown, when smaller potential bidders expect to have difficulty competing: If those potential bidders don't show up at all, the auction will inevitably be less competitive and raise less revenue. This insight proved itself across a wide range of applications, including auctions for online advertising used by search engines like Bing and Google.

Her breakthrough findings also held major implications for governments. When British Columbia's Ministry of Forests needed help designing a new auction-based price system for their forestry auctions, they recruited Professor Athey. The Market Pricing System she developed has not only been used to price billions of dollars of timber for more than a decade, but also was instrumental in creating an agreement between the U.S. and Canada that helped avoid a trade war.

In 2007, Professor Athey became the first woman to earn the John Bates Clark Medal, one of the most prestigious awards in economics in the U.S., with roughly 40 percent of winners going on to win the Nobel Prize. That same year, Microsoft CEO Mr. Steve Ballmer asked Professor Athey to join the company as a long-term consultant and chief economist. At the time, Microsoft was seeking to make Bing as powerful and attractive as Google. Professor Athey believes that "it's indeed possible to have two competing search engines and that it's also incredibly important for the internet ecosystem." Her guiding force in the world's largest software company not only impacts the everyday interactions of internet users with search engines, but also has revolutionized the ability to predict user and advertiser behavior by analyzing massive amounts of data around internet searches and the position auctions they generate. "We've never had data on that scale before to study behavior. I want to help the economics field embrace those opportunities."

Professor Athey chose economics because of its ability to impact public policy. Economics continues to choose her because of her ability to move between the domains of theory and real-world applications. "There has never been a better time for young women to enter the field of economics. Google, Facebook, eBay, Pandora, Uber, Instagram, Microsoft, Coursera — all of these firms, as well as the latest start-up firms, need economists." ●

maria CHUDNOVSKY
Graph Theory Mathematician

One day, in a junior high school classroom in St. Petersburg, Russia, a passionate math teacher commented to his students that more than one kind of infinity exists. One of the students in the room, Professor Maria Chudnovsky, vowed at that moment that she would work hard to find out exactly what he meant.

Her pursuit of this answer and many others took her through two degrees at Technion - Israel Institute of Technology and a PhD at Princeton University before landing her an associate professorship in the Department of Industrial Engineering and Operations Research at Columbia University.

Professor Chudnovsky investigates abstract objects called graphs. Graph theory, which falls under the umbrella of combinatorics, is an area of mathematics that relates to many other branches, including linear programming, geometry and complexity theory. Graph theory also has real-world applications for molecular biology as well as for the design of complex networks, from transportation systems to computer networks, serving as shortcuts to more old-school mathematical methods. While graph theory problems use lines and points, Professor Chudnovsky explains, they have nothing to do with the *x*- and *y*- axes taught in school. "A graph consists of objects that are called vertices. Some vertices are in relationship and some are not. You can think of people in the world or think of computers: some computers can talk directly and some cannot. Same with people. So it's all about webs or connections. A graph and a network is the same thing. Think of social networks. We can abstract properties. We can ask questions like, 'if I want to talk to that guy, through how many vertices (people) must I pass to get an introduction?'"

While those real-world problems are important, they are not a central focus for Professor Chudnovsky. For her, she says, "It is not about applications. It's about internal beauty. My work is somewhere between solving a crossword puzzle and making a painting. It's about pure logic and pure aesthetics."

At the age of 25, Professor Chudnovsky was part of a team of four researchers who proved a mathematical theory called the Strong Perfect Graph Conjecture. The original notion, set forth by French mathematician Dr. Claude Berge, identified the factors required for a graph to fall into the "perfect" category. But proof of Dr. Berge's theory remained a mystery to the mathematical community for more than 40

"My work is somewhere between solving a crossword puzzle and making a painting. It's about pure logic and pure aesthetics."

years. Professor Chudnovsky learned of this mind-bending theory while studying at Technion. Compelled to find a solution, she worked on the proof with her advisor and two colleagues upon enrolling in the PhD math program at Princeton. Her team constructed a proof of the Strong Perfect Graph Conjecture by gaining in-depth understanding of the structure of perfect graphs. They were able to show that every perfect graph either falls into one of five basic classes, or "breaks apart" in a natural, predictable way, reducing the complexity of the problem.

For her groundbreaking contributions to this theorem and others, Professor Chudnovsky earned a series of awards, including the Ostrowki Foundation Research Stipend, the Fulkerson Prize, which is awarded for outstanding papers in the area of discrete mathematics, and the MacArthur Fellowship, otherwise known as the "Genius Grant," given to individuals who show extraordinary creativity in their research.

Professor Chudnovsky explains why she chose to specialize in combinatorics, as opposed to other fields of study within pure mathematics, by invoking the penetrating nature of proofs in this area. "Most of the problems are very easy to describe, but they do not have simple solutions. In fact, the reason for the answer being one way or another is often quite deep. In order to find the solution, one needs to uncover layers of phenomena that often seem to have nothing to do with the original question."

Professor Chudnovsky loves the clarity and logic behind mathematics. She knows she would not be where she is today without great math teachers who "made us, the students, believe that what we were learning in that class was the most interesting thing in the world." To this day, she is convinced there is nothing more worthwhile she could be doing than mathematics.

Her advice to young women who want to pursue math: "Don't fear doubt. Everybody doubts all the time, even after you've got all the prizes and the jobs. When I started graduate school at Princeton, the chair of the math department, Dr. Charles Fefferman, gave us a welcoming speech and in it, he said, 'A graduate student is just like any mathematician. The only difference is you're working on your first theorem.' So what he and I are trying to say is, there is always a feeling of 'what if I can't do this one?' You learn to live with it."

Through hard work and dedication, Professor Chudnovsky learned exactly what her junior high teacher meant by his off-handed remark all those years ago. She also discovered an entirely new world of mathematical questions that exists beyond infinity. ●

JEANNE GANG
Architect

Imagine walking along a street in the heart of downtown Chicago. Skyscrapers absorb the summer's heat and dish it back in the form of oven-like temperatures. You long for wildlife and shade, reminders of nature and what the world looked like before it resembled a concrete maze. Suddenly, an 82-story building above you sharpens into focus. From below, it reminds you of Lake Michigan's cool waves, swelling and rippling along with the wind. You can almost imagine yourself diving in headfirst.

Welcome to Aqua Tower.

In 2006, architect Ms. Jeanne Gang was at a post-lecture dinner when she found herself sitting beside noted Chicago-area architect and developer Mr. James R. Loewenberg. His preliminary design for a new building on North Columbus Drive needed something special, and he invited Ms. Gang to "make it sing." She and the firm she founded in 1997, Studio Gang, were awarded the project. At 869 feet, Aqua Tower is the tallest structure ever designed by a woman-led architecture team. In 2009, Aqua Tower received the prestigious Emporis Skyscraper Award for its captivating shape, changing visual appearance when viewed from alternate angles and sustainable, eco-friendly materials. Aqua Tower was also shortlisted in 2010 for the biannual International Highrise Award.

Despite its name, Aqua Tower's design is based upon terrestrial topography. It is a vertical landscape made up of hills, valleys and pools. Each of its 82 floor plates contains a slight variation. This modification allows for extra pockets of outdoor living space where residents can interact with each other and nature as they would on the ground, with the added perk of Chicago's spectacular skyline view.

In the architecture world, Ms. Gang's peers toss around words like *genius* and *starchitect* to describe her gifts. She has revolutionized the field by using scientific research to push the use of innovative materials harder and further than they've ever been pushed before. By incorporating her philosophy of connecting design to the culture and history of the local area, her buildings are the artful blend of the natural environment and urban life.

Ms. Gang grew up in the small town of Belvidere, Illinois, the third of four sisters. On road trips as a child, she bonded with her father, a civil engineer, over the feats of engineering and architecture expressed in roads and bridges. On those

Photo Credit: Jenny Hueston

"When you find something that really resonates with you, something that makes you stay up all night thinking about it, that's when you know you've found the right path for you."

trips, she was equally drawn to ancient feats of engineering in places like Colorado's Mesa Verde National Park, home to some of the world's best-preserved cliff dwellings. Her love of math, science and art drew her to study architecture; her interest in public spaces, nature and community foreshadowed the type of architect she would become. "When I started to look at architecture more seriously, there was no going back."

After earning a bachelor's degree in architecture from the University of Illinois at Urbana-Champaign, Ms. Gang went on to pursue a master's degree at Harvard University's Graduate School of Design. At Harvard, she met and worked with some of architecture's top educators and practitioners, including Professor Homa Farjadi, a pre-eminent architect based in London. Professor Farjadi encouraged her to think about the unique perspective women often bring to problem-solving (by thinking beyond one central position of power to a more inclusive view of stakeholders) and how she could apply this approach to architecture. Ms. Gang's unique point of view — as a woman, but more importantly as a driven, passionate and independent thinker — comes through in everything she designs today.

This perspective is evident in designs from her early days at the Office for Metropolitan Architecture (OMA), a leading international architectural firm based in Rotterdam, the Netherlands, where Ms. Gang worked with legendary Dutch architect Mr. Rem Koolhaas. After working on many exciting projects with OMA, such as a railroad station project in the Hague (the center of government for the Netherlands) and the Grand Palais, an iconic convention center in Lille, France, Ms. Gang moved back to the Chicago area and opened her own firm, building her architectural practice project by project. Today, she leads 80 architects, designers, planners and thinkers on projects throughout the world. In 2011, she

was awarded a rare MacArthur Fellowship, a $500,000 prize often known as the "Genius Grant," for setting new industry standards, creating striking designs and using environmentally friendly materials.

Architecture is, at its core, an artistic representation of math. The principles and language of mathematics have inspired architecture since ancient times, from the intricate tiling patterns of Islamic mosques to the geometry of modern geodesic domes. Ms. Gang knows this inspiration well. "Architecture is a way of life, a way of looking at the world. It makes it possible for someone who likes to make things, someone who likes to design, to have an impact on their immediate environment and then beyond to a larger context."

Ms. Gang's advice to those considering a career in architecture is beautifully simple. "It's important to expose yourself to different opportunities and ways of thinking, but you also have to follow your own interests. When you find something that really resonates with you, something that makes you stay up all night thinking about it, that's when you know you've found the right path for you."

And the Aqua Tower? Ms. Gang wanted to "reveal unexpected qualities, highlighting the different ways of seeing the world and the things around us." With its unique sightlines and meeting points, the interaction it fosters and the sense of community it creates, the tower stands as a powerful, tangible recognition of the individual and the communal.

Enjoy the view, Chicago. ●

Trachette Jackson
Cancer Modeling Mathematician

Each day, 4,500 Americans learn they have cancer. According to the American Cancer Society's Facts and Figures 2015 report, the current five-year survival rate stands at 68 percent, an improvement in the 49 percent survival rate from 1975-1977.

Internationally renowned mathematical biologist Professor Trachette Jackson won't be satisfied until that survival rate reaches 100 percent.

For years, math research has aided in the treatment of cancer, but it did not become a driving force in its diagnosis and treatment until dedicated researchers like Professor Jackson made computational cancer modeling their full-time job. A recipient of the James S. McDonnell 21st Century Scientist Award, Professor Jackson specializes in using mathematical models to describe tumor formation, progression and treatment. By producing innovative mathematical and computational modeling approaches, she is unifying math and natural sciences like never before. But her path to becoming the award-winning, cancer-fighting inspiration wasn't always obvious. Two pivotal moments in the early days of her undergraduate studies set the course for her life trajectory as a mathematician.

Before entering college, she says, "I was always good at math, but I never thought of pursuing it as a career. I just thought it was something that I liked and that I was good at." One day, a professor at Arizona State University (ASU), where she was pursuing an engineering degree, called her into his office. He had noticed her gift for the subject and encouraged her to consider mathematics as a career. She saw this as an invitation to explore the new possibilities math offered. "Once I found out math had the power and potential to address the world's most pressing problems, it made me vigorously pursue a career in math."

Another pivotal event early in college further focused the direction Professor Jackson's studies would take. It involved an unlikely source of inspiration: leopards. "I saw flyers around my math department walls saying that someone was coming to visit, and he was going to tell us how the leopards got their spots, using math. Every time I walked past these flyers, I would shake my head and think, there's no way math has anything to do with that! I had never been exposed to math combined with biology, so I decided to sit in on the talk." Though some of the concepts were beyond her grasp as an undergraduate, Professor Jackson walked away from the

"Once I found out math had the power and potential to address the world's most pressing problems, it made me vigorously pursue a career in math."

lecture with a firm belief in the power of math to advance scientific discovery. "Mr. William Butler Yates said that education is not the filling of a pail, but the lighting of a fire. That talk sparked a fire for mathematical biology that has been burning in me ever since. That was the 'aha' moment for me, that mathematical biology was going to be my field."

Professor Jackson was born in Monroe, Louisiana. For her, going to college and graduate school was a given. She credits her parents with instilling in her and her siblings the importance of education. "My father was also very interested in STEM. We always had the latest gadgets in our home, and he could take apart and rebuild every one of them. I remember watching him and asking all sorts of questions."

She graduated in the top 20 of her high school class and spent summers at a math-science honors program at ASU, where she developed her passion for math. After completing an honors degree from ASU, she earned both a master's and PhD from the University of Washington. She is now a full professor at the University of Michigan, whose robust medical research programs provided an ideal environment to test her mathematical applications. Her research focuses on the use of mathematical models to study cancerous tumors – how their blood vessels form and grow, and how cancer treatments can attack that growth with more efficiency and fewer side effects.

Professor Jackson is the second African-American woman to receive the prestigious Alfred P. Sloan Fellowship, an award that recognizes the outstanding research achievements of early-career scholars who possess exceptional potential to make great strides in their field of study. Other awards include the ASU Medallion of Merit and the 2010 Blackwell-Tapia prize for contributions to her field and efforts to bring awareness to minority populations who are underrepresented in mathematics. Since 2008, Professor Jackson has served as a senior editor for the academic journal *Cancer Research* and has reviewed articles for the *Journal of Mathematical Biology* and the *Proceedings of the National Academy of Sciences*.

She encourages young women "to be confident in your choice of science, engineering or mathematics and to rigorously pursue excellence in the field you've chosen. Take upper-level math courses and participate in STEM extracurricular programs. Enter into your future with a strategy to become the best you can be and then don't forget where you came from." ●

Bryna Kra
Dynamical Systems Mathematician

In 2012, the latest year for which figures are known, there were 26.2 billion credit card transactions in the U.S. With each and every swipe of plastic, we take for granted that these transactions will take place safely, thanks to encryption systems rooted in algorithms and complex number theory. But before they helped transform the world of finance, these systems were just that: theories that existed only in the world of the abstract, with absolutely no connection to the real world. That abstract world of numbers is where Professor Bryna Kra has made her mark and feels most at home.

Captivated by the world of concepts and theories, Professor Kra might have become a philosopher, examining cosmic questions about the nature of reality. But she came to realize that for her, probing deep questions wasn't enough. She also craved answers — concrete, provable, right-or-wrong answers. So she became a mathematician and expert on ergodic theory, an area of study that examines dynamical systems and the relationship between points in time and points in geometrical space. The movement of planets around the sun is a concrete example of a dynamical system, but Professor Kra's research is more abstract. "I try to make predictions about the long-term behavior of these systems — what will happen many, many iterations into the future and what kinds of things must show up inevitably." Her contributions have opened up new questions and techniques and cracked open an entirely new area of study into non-conventional ergodic averages, the subject of a dozen or more of her scientific publications. Through the highly abstract exploration of ergodic theory, Professor Kra got her answers. But it wasn't always clear that math would lead her on this path.

Her first year at Harvard University, she took a difficult math course. Midway through the class, she wanted to quit. Her professor encouraged her to work hard and finish the course. She stuck with it and passed the class before diving into a new line of study: philosophy. After a time, she returned to that very same professor and told him philosophy no longer excited her. With his encouragement, she recommitted herself to embracing math. "I returned to math because of the fuzziness of philosophy — that I couldn't prove anything definitively, that the arguments remained open and ultimately unprovable. That wasn't for

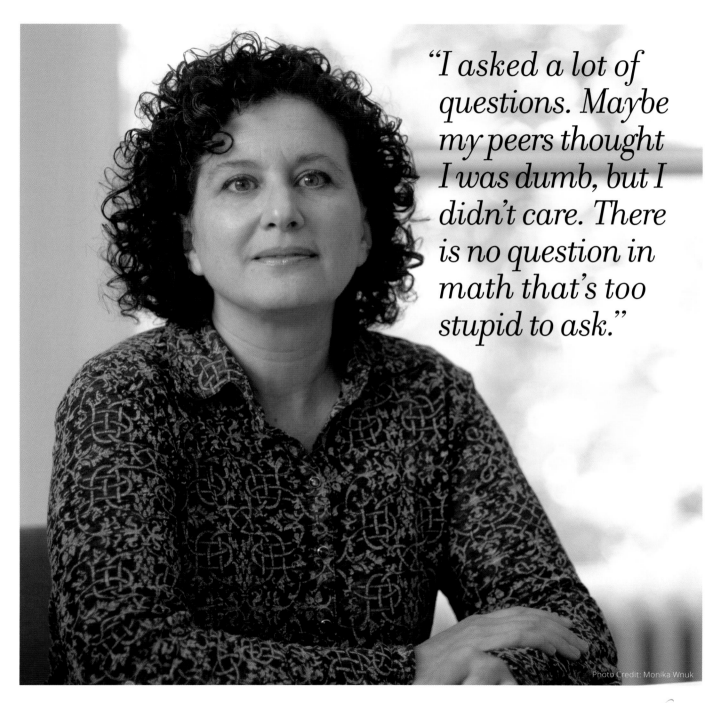

"I asked a lot of questions. Maybe my peers thought I was dumb, but I didn't care. There is no question in math that's too stupid to ask."

Photo Credit: Monika Wnuk

me. With math, unlike anything else in the world, once you've proven something, you know you've proven it. There's an absolute standard of truth."

Professor Kra's exposure to math came from her father, the world-renowned mathematician Dr. Irwin Kra. He, along with her teachers, encouraged her to explore and investigate beyond the classroom. As early as eight years old, she was sent to study math with older students, but did not seriously consider following her father into a STEM field until college. As a young adult, she filled her summers with reading and traveling, along with a fierce passion for creating music with her violin, viola and piano.

Professor Kra graduated with an honors math degree from Harvard before going on to earn master's and doctorate degrees in mathematics from Stanford University. After working on post-doctorate research at universities around the world — Hebrew University, the University of Michigan, Institut des Hautes Études Scientifiques in France and Ohio State University — Professor Kra became a math professor at Northwestern University. Of all her accomplishments, she is proudest of her endowed chair position at Northwestern and breakthroughs in ergodic theory that won her an American Mathematical Society Centennial Fellowship in 2006.

To pay forward the support she received in her pursuit of mathematics, Professor Kra has led elementary students in hands-on activities to encourage stronger math skills. She believes that improving the STEM workforce begins in the early stages of education, and that elementary schools should focus more on teaching math as a language, tailoring instruction to the needs of individual students just as literacy specialists modify text for children at all reading levels. Professor Kra also mentors college students, particularly women, to close the gender gap in mathematics.

She sees mathematics as a vital, core component of any scientific pursuit. "Mathematics provides a toolbox for the sciences. Models are used to explain and predict events around us, and rigorous mathematical thinking organizes ideas. Not every scientist needs a degree in mathematics, but every scientist needs the rigorous language and logic afforded by mathematics."

Her advice to young women thinking about a math career is to explore and ask questions. "I think the reason people get intimidated by math is that they're afraid to look a little bit silly or unknowledgeable so they don't ask questions. I asked a lot of questions. Maybe my peers thought I was dumb, but I didn't care. There is no question in math that's too stupid to ask. If you're asking, it just means that it hasn't been explained." She also believes that perseverance is the key to her success.

Professor Kra's current research focuses on predicting the long-term behavior of dynamical systems and using a portion of that information to say something meaningful about the whole system. Her findings don't always have applications for the real world — *yet*. But who knows what her work will make possible decades from now? ●

DEBBIE LAWRENCE
Geophysicist

Some superheroes need x-ray vision to see through granite mountain faces and detect secret, underground complexes where villains carry out their plans. But geophysicist Ms. Debbie Lawrence can see through rock without superhero vision.

How?

Ms. Lawrence has math.

To detect earthquakes or find oil-rich pockets deep beneath Earth's surface, seismologists and oil companies rely on instruments called seismic data sensors. To interpret the raw, messy, mega-amounts of data these sensors generate, they need geophysicists who can apply mathematics to create visual models of what lies underground. That's where Ms. Lawrence comes in.

Geophysics is the science of investigating what lies far beneath Earth's surface by measuring and analyzing data collected at or near its surface. Ms. Lawrence uses geophysical principles to process field-collected data and create pictures of an area's subsurface. She then passes her results on to geophysicists who specialize in interpreting her pictures to decide where to drill for water or hydrocarbons, such as coal or natural gas. Companies depend on the models she creates to determine where to drill. That means that in her

line of work, accuracy is everything. If the picture isn't just right, companies could lose an astonishing amount of money and time drilling in a dry space.

Ms. Lawrence compares her science to piecing together a puzzle. "To me, it's starting with something that's ugly and getting a solid product out. When I start with something that's a mess and in the end it all comes together correctly — because everything lines up as it is supposed to — it's very rewarding. I'm a problem-solver. It's like cracking a tough code."

She didn't always have her "x-ray vision" set on what lies beneath the earth's surface. Growing up, she adored math. Under the guidance of her father, a petroleum engineer who encouraged her to pursue her gift for numbers, she excelled in math and science in her Midland, Texas high school and graduated with honors. She earned a bachelor's degree in math from Angelo State University and began teaching algebra at her high school alma mater. Though she enjoyed teaching, she was eventually wooed away by a friend in the geophysics industry, who wanted her to

130

work with him because of her exceptional mathematics background. She has been a geophysicist ever since. "I loved it. It was the perfect match for me. I truly believe that God gives you gifts, and He expects you to use those gifts and enables you to use them."

In 1997, Ms. Lawrence co-founded Pinnacle Seismic, which specializes in crafting subsurface models taken from seismic data. She considers starting her own company a significant milestone. "That moment was huge — when I felt confident enough to go out on my own and take on the world."

To process the terabytes upon terabytes of data that are brought to the company, Pinnacle uses giant mega-computers — the equivalent of 60 linked computers. She jokes that hers is the

in these problem areas is just the kind of challenge she has always been driven to overcome. Another challenge is being a managing partner in Pinnacle Seismic. She considers herself a scientist at heart. Although the day to day responsibilities of running a successful business often pull her away from her first loves of math and science, the freedom to be her own boss and contribute to the field on her own terms is equally fulfilling.

When Ms. Lawrence considers the future of geophysics, she sees a need for new scientists to develop not only technology skills, but also problem-solving skills. "There are a lot of people coming out of college today who are trying to do what I do, and they've learned how to run the software but they don't know how to think it through themselves."

> *"Have integrity. Stay on top of technology. Once you've got your degree, it's only the beginning."*

"only industry that uses more computer power than the cartoon animation industry — like Disney."

In addition to the drive for accuracy, Ms. Lawrence's science has other challenges. Hard rock areas, such as the kind found in her region of West Texas, create static and signal noise that make the data among the toughest in the world to process. But that also makes it the most rewarding. Resolving issues

Her advice to young women considering entrepreneurship in a male-dominated STEM field? "You are a woman. Don't be intimidated. Be yourself and pursue your God-given talents. Have integrity. Stay on top of technology. Once you've got your degree, it's only the beginning."

Sounds like advice worthy of a superhero. ●

STACY LINDBORG
Biostatistician

When new pharmacy medications are developed, they must go through a series of rigorous clinical trials involving hundreds, often thousands, of volunteer patients to establish the effectiveness and safety of the medicine. With new treatments for stable diseases like diabetes, these studies often involve a crossover method: Some patients receive treatment A then B, and some patients receive treatment B then A. Which patients begin which sequence of medications, and when, is randomized to ensure the data's accuracy. Statisticians then compile the complex data and reach conclusions about the effectiveness of treatment A versus treatment B. But for decades, the crossover method has been problematic, for several reasons. Issues with measuring the effectiveness of a second treatment when the first is still active in the body, as well as unintended side effects in the first round of treatment, sometimes created data accuracy problems. As a result, researchers unsure about how to adjust their statistical models to account for these problems were often forced to toss much of the second round's data.

Dr. Stacy Lindborg was determined to solve this problem. As part of her dissertation, she created a new statistical model, a Bayesian method, that explicitly modeled the presence of a carryover effect and preserved the ability to use all data, instead of discarding *all* data after a drug carryover. By increasing the amount of valuable data that can be used in analyses, Dr. Lindborg's model allows for a bigger picture of a drug's effectiveness and safety and saves researchers valuable time — time that can be critical to patients anticipating new treatment options. Her methodological research was applied to data from an industry clinical trial early in her career and stimulated collaboration between industry and academia. This effective collaboration marked the beginning of a career that has increasingly influenced academia and pharmaceutical fields to join forces. Where good statistical data exists, patients and pharmaceutical companies benefit.

As with her path in healthcare research, math was a clear choice for Dr. Lindborg. It was a passion she shared with her engineer father, an early role model who requested the next year's math textbooks for her and her brother, and used long family road trips to help them work through the new concepts. "That experience set a foundation where math was easy for me and therefore fun. I attribute much of my excellence to him. We like the things we're good at and it sets our course." Though she began a course of study in computer science, her interests pulled her toward psychology. In a circular way, all roads for Dr. Lindborg eventually led her to the math she enjoyed during those early road trips.

So how did she find a STEM path that united her passion for human behavior with her love for math? Dr. Tom Bratcher, a mathematics professor at Baylor University where Dr. Lindborg

> *"I remember them looking at me and thinking that I was young and inept. They totally underestimated me. But it motivated me and turned up my juices to where I was like 'I'll prove you wrong.'"*

studied psychology, recruited her for a new program that blended many different areas of study with statistics. "He was the first person who began to translate my background and my strengths and what a statistics degree could do, even opening my eyes to the reality that because so few people pursue this degree, a full scholarship and stipend and a job was the standard. The field of statistics is about applications — solving real-world problems. That was a complete fit for me." So while other undergraduate seniors were traveling and enjoying their final days before getting their degrees, Dr. Lindborg loaded herself up with math courses in preparation for graduate school.

She went on to earn her master's and PhD in statistics at Baylor but again felt a desire to apply her knowledge to real-world situations. She was considering medical school when a pharmaceutical company, Eli Lilly and Company,

asked her to join their team. During her 16 years at Eli Lilly, Dr. Lindborg tackled statistical problems across all phases of development, focusing many years on treatments for schizophrenia and other psychiatric conditions. Her experience ultimately spanned a large and diverse range of illnesses, bringing statistical innovation and a multi-team approach to the company. While at Eli Lilly, she was nominated to serve on a Product's Presidential Council, an honor bestowed on her for the broad impact of her work. In 2012, she moved to Boston with her family and became head of Clinical Statistics and ultimately global VP of Biostatistics, Statistical Programming and Data Management for Biogen, a global biotech company that specializes in drugs for neurological disorders.

At Biogen, Dr. Lindborg focuses on using new statistical approaches to solve real-world problems. She has published more than 35 collaborative articles, served in numerous elected roles for the American Statistical Association (ASA) and the International Biometric Society and is the recipient of numerous awards, including a Development Sciences Innovation Award from Biogen Idec. In 2008, Dr. Lindborg was elected an ASA Fellow, an immense achievement because of the underrepresentation of statisticians from private industry in fellowships, and because the award is granted to less than one-third of 1% of all living ASA members.

Though Dr. Lindborg doesn't feel she has been judged for being a woman in a field largely dominated by men, she does recall a challenging moment in graduate school when she was asked to help a group of physicians develop and carry out a research problem. "I remember them looking at me and thinking that I was young and inept. They totally underestimated me. But it motivated me and turned up my juices to where I was like 'I'll prove you wrong.'"

And she's been proving them wrong ever since. ●

TOnya mannInG
Actuary

Ms. Tonya Manning calls her profession one of the most dynamic and in-demand careers out there. She is an actuary — and if you've never heard of actuaries, or don't know what they do, she says, you may be missing out on a path that is tailor-made for math lovers who like to solve real-world problems. That's because actuaries apply their skills to one of the oldest problems in the world of business: the financial risks that come with employing people.

So what is an actuary? Picture a weather forecaster, only instead of predicting snowstorms for commuters or rainfall for farmers, actuaries make highly complex mathematical forecasts for companies who need to understand financial risk to shape policies around health insurance and retirement pensions. As a pension actuary, Ms. Manning makes crucial mathematical predictions around how much money employees will need when they retire, what kind of pension plans companies should offer and how companies should pay for them — all questions that involve making multifaceted projections about how long employees are expected to live after retiring. The predictions have guided companies in ensuring that there will always be enough money to pay out in pensions when employees stop working.

It's no surprise then, that actuaries play a critical role in people's financial health. Imagine paying into a company's pension fund over a 35-year career. The fund promises to pay you monthly checks when you're a senior citizen and no longer work. Now imagine that same company telling you at age 70 that it does not have the money to send you checks so you can continue to live comfortably in your golden years. Ms. Manning, now serving as Chief Actuary for Buck Consultants, one of the largest retirement organizations in the U.S., wants to ensure nothing like that ever happens to anyone.

How does a girl go from asking for a calculator in elementary school so she can add along while watching *The Price is Right* to being an accomplished actuary? Not the way you might guess. As a child, Ms. Manning wanted to be a famous journalist. Her senior year English teacher thought differently, seeing her early aptitude for all things quantitative. Ms. Manning's mother had a "no excuses" policy that set high expectations for her two daughters, and her father laid out her future in words, not simply encouragement, but what he believed to be a fact: "If you really set your mind to something, you can accomplish anything."

Ms. Manning majored in mathematical science at the University of North Carolina at Chapel Hill. But her plans to

attend graduate school in a STEM field took a significant turn during her senior year of college. "My mother passed away, so I decided to go back home and live with my dad. That left me in search of a job in the suburbs of a relatively small city. I started scanning newspaper ads for a job. There was one that essentially read 'Will Hire Math Majors.' As it

women. You can be criticized for being too soft, or for being too tough. It's hard to find the right in-between. I observed other leaders in my profession — almost all men — and tried to emulate their style, but it just didn't work for me. My advice to other women? Don't try to copy someone else's style. Be who you are. That is what you will always be best at doing."

"Don't try to copy someone else's style. Be who you are. That is what you will always be best at doing."

turned out, they were looking for actuaries. I fell in love with the profession because it required doing math, but in so many different areas and with many applications: probability, consulting, programming and data management. It's been a rewarding and fulfilling career for me."

After 17 years rising through the company, Ms. Manning was named its U.S. Chief Actuary. In 2010, she took a position at the U.S. Department of Treasury as a policy actuary, overseeing thousands of government employee retirement plans before returning to private industry at Buck Consultants. Columbia University, recognizing her talents while she served as president of the Society of Actuaries (SOA), asked her to develop and teach an actuary course.

Ms. Manning attributes her success to three critical components: hard work, being true to herself and a sense of humor. "Humor is a great way to ease tension and get people to open up." Her career has not thrived without struggle. She considers her biggest challenge to be finding the style of leadership that best suits her. "It is tricky for

Because early success as an actuary is largely dependent on passing highly technical and challenging actuarial exams — an unbiased measurement of ability — it puts women on an equal playing field with men. Once an actuary, women frequently have an advantage over men because of their ability to be effective mathematical communicators to those in the business sector.

Closing STEM's gender gap, Ms. Manning believes, will happen with more visible female STEM role models. She wants girls to know they can excel in analytical fields while still being girls. "Our culture often puts these in two separate boxes. Not true! I like that I can be on a long flight and read both a fashion magazine and a report on mortality improvement. It's okay to do girly things (if that's what you like) and to also do math — they do not exclude each other."

How does Ms. Manning translate success? With spreadsheets, an affinity for teaching and a healthy dose of humor that all stem from her love of math. ●

anna nagurney
Network Systems Mathematician

Have you ever wondered how relief services like the Red Cross organize resources for recovery after hurricanes, wildfires and other natural disasters? How planners study the flow of city traffic to determine where to build new highways? How FedEx® manages to deliver all those packages on time during the holiday season? Or how blood banks get donated blood to networks of hospitals when they need it? These are all examples of vast and complex networks made more efficient by the use of applied mathematics.

Professor Anna Nagurney fell in love with networks as an undergraduate at Brown University. A mathematician who specializes in network systems, she has researched, published, taught and applied her way to super-network superstardom. "I love the fact that you can determine an optimal solution by setting up a mathematical model and then solve it using an algorithm. I love the applications, especially those of optimization, since I like to make our lives easier and make everything work well. I very much care about efficiency."

Born in Canada to Ukrainian refugees who fled Europe after World War II, Professor Nagurney moved to the U.S. as a young girl. Her father worked as an electrical engineer at the World Trade Center in New York, and her uncle, a hugely influential mentor, designed award-winning bridges, including the first cable-stayed bridge across the Mississippi River. In addition to her mother, who always encouraged her interest in STEM, a nurturing seventh-grade teacher also had a lasting

impact on Professor Nagurney, after inviting her and other students to her home to delve deeply into challenging math problems. This special teacher made a prediction in class one day that Professor Nagurney would become a calculus professor. "The confidence that Mrs. Fuller had in me gave me strength. It meant a lot to me that a teacher believed in me. As a professor, I try to instill confidence in my students and provide positive, enthusiastic support."

At Brown, Professor Nagurney earned bachelor's degrees in applied math and Russian language and literature. But her journey had its fair share of setbacks. Before college, she had never been exposed to calculus and did poorly on her first calculus test. Thankfully, she had a supportive professor who spent many office hours talking her through creative math modeling problems. She worked through every problem in her textbook, and in many other textbooks after that, and triumphed over calculus. "Math is like a sport — the more

> *"Math is like a sport — the more you use your muscles, the better you get at it."*

you use your muscles, the better you get at it," she says. "Hard work will get you where you want to be and discipline and focus are very important to success in STEM."

She went on to complete her PhD at Brown in applied math under the mentorship of the late Dr. Stella Dafermos, a renowned math scholar in networks and algorithms and the only female professor in either the applied math or engineering departments at Brown. Working with Dr. Dafermos was a particularly gratifying milestone for her because until then, she had never had a female professor in math or science.

While earning her master's degree, Professor Nagurney worked as a software developer for U.S. Navy submarines. After completing her PhD, she joined the University of Massachusetts Amherst faculty, where she is now the John F. Smith Memorial Professor. There she inspires students to cultivate the same passion she has for engineering, technology, operations research and management science. In 2001, Professor Nagurney founded the Virtual Center for Supernetworks at the university's business school, the Isenberg School of Management. The center, an academic facility dedicated to advancing knowledge about large-scale networks, has conducted award-winning research under Professor Nagurney's direction, and has been recognized by the AT&T Foundation, Rockefeller Foundation and National Science Foundation.

Professor Nagurney has authored or co-authored 11 books and countless journal publications. Her academic honors include 14 prestigious awards, a visiting professorship in Sweden and two Fulbright grants to teach and conduct research in Austria and Italy. An avid traveler, she considers meeting people from all over the globe one of the most exciting aspects of her work.

Her advice to young women considering a satisfying and rewarding STEM career is to love what you're doing and "practice, practice, practice, and you will do great." She also suggests learning computer coding. "You can do so much with it — design websites and apps and solve important problems that you really care about to make the world a better place." ●

rachel schutt
Data Scientist

The McKinsey Global Institute once predicted that U.S. companies would need four million data scientists in the workforce but would only have three million trained for the task — a shortfall of *one million* qualified workers. With skyrocketing job growth and salaries poised to surpass the average incomes of doctors and lawyers, the field of data science is hot. Think of a data scientist as the person fueling the engine of profitability in any company and you'll come close to understanding the reasons behind the high demand for these STEM leaders in the businesses of the future.

Meet Dr. Rachel Schutt. She wears many hats — mathematician, professor, researcher, analyst, statistician — but her expertise in the world of data has placed her at the forefront of data science in big business. In her current position as Chief Data Scientist at News Corp, a global corporation that owns many of the world's biggest media enterprises — publisher HarperCollins, the *New York Post* and *The Wall Street Journal* newspapers to name a few — Dr. Schutt supervises more than 100 employees on everything data: growing subscribers, advertising and bringing print journalism into the digital age. "Journalism is going through a transition as a result of the digital age," she explains. "Part of my job is to make sure we're using the data we have about what users are reading to build a sustainable business model for journalism. I also work with journalists to use data in the best ways possible to tell stories." And when Dr. Schutt heard from her peer data scientists that the subject could only be effectively studied in industry and could not be taught as an academic subject at the

university level, she took the challenge to become the one leading the charge to academia and Columbia University. "I wanted to test the hypothesis that it was possible to train awesome data scientists in the classroom. Data science has the potential to be a deep and profound research discipline impacting all aspects of our lives."

Was Dr. Schutt always into numbers? You bet. She recalls a difficult transitional period after her family moved from England to New Jersey, when math became a comfort to her. "I found middle school extremely painful but in eighth grade we all had to take this math test. I placed in the top four and was selected to participate in a team for MATHCOUNTS, an organization that strives to engage middle school students in fun, challenging math programs in order to expand their academic opportunities." Her team placed first in New Jersey and went on to compete nationally. "I enjoyed being part of the team and the competitive environment, and that shaped

"My father told me that I should study math even though it was hard, because it's the hard things we should tackle in life. That made sense to me."

some of my understanding of what makes me happy in terms of a working environment where we problem solve together."

Math didn't always come easily for Dr. Schutt, however. She attended the University of Michigan and recalls a conversation she had with her father, a Harvard-trained mathematician who had often bonded with his daughter over math puzzles. "At some point math started to be pretty hard for me. My father told me that I should study math even though it was hard, because it's the hard things we should tackle in life. That made sense to me." Her mother was also influential in her pursuit of a career in math. "My mother told me that the world needed people good at math to solve important problems and that I shouldn't waste that talent."

Dr. Schutt persevered and went on to graduate school. She wanted to pursue management science and engineering because she was passionate about tackling real-world problems. Stanford offered her the challenge she was seeking. After obtaining a master's degree at Stanford and taking some time away from studies to teach high school math, work as a Silicon Valley consultant and design math books for kids, Dr. Schutt landed at Columbia for her PhD in statistics. Her post-doctorate work found her engaged in a number of arenas, working as part of a Google Research team and writing a book, *Doing Data Science*.

Today, her research interests continue to be varied. In addition to statistical modeling and data analysis, areas traditional to her field, Dr. Schutt became fascinated by machine learning, which she describes as "writing computer programs that can help a machine learn the rules from the data. For example, a machine can look at digital photos of animals and the machine can start to isolate what makes a cat, a cat. It collects data on all the cat photos to get better at distinguishing a cat from a dog and other animals. So it's all about making machines smarter through smarter software. It can be applied to predict what story a user wants to read or what kind of shoes a user wants to buy."

At the same time, Dr. Schutt is also invested in the ethical dimensions of data science — who has access to consumer information and how can consumer privacy be protected? For example, data analytics today can make pretty solid predictions about a person's health, income level or religion based on purchases made from a credit or debit card. Cross-referencing that data with information from a person's internet browser history opens up a new level of access to personal information. Data science takes a close look at the benefits versus the drawbacks of such technology.

Dr. Schutt wants young women to know that "if you're sitting around, waiting for a teacher to tell you that you are special or have potential, stop! Believe in yourself. Ultimately, it comes down to taking your life in your own hands." She believes that "many girls and women, as well as boys and men, experience self doubt, and realizing that everyone faces it helps you learn to live with it. The more you push yourself past it, even though it's there, the more you can accomplish." She also advises young women to seek out female role models and peers to help stamp out the self-doubt that she, herself, has wrestled with from time to time. "Learn the practical things, take computer science classes, learn how to program, do machine learning, but also learn how to communicate your ideas clearly and figure out how to work with people across disciplines. Data is language, and if you can use technical language in human terms, you can solve very important problems."

Dr. Schutt envisions data science someday being used to solve problems of immense social value. With a passionate STEM crusader like Dr. Schutt leading her field, there is no doubt data science will grow in responsible ways that benefit us all. ●

STEFANI WILDHABER
Urban Planner and Designer

Hers was a youth of small-town farming — driving tractors, fixing machinery and caring for animals in rural Washington state. But an early love for math and art, fostered by influential teachers, set Ms. Stefani Wildhaber on a path toward big-city urban design.

Ms. Wildhaber is an urban planner and designer. Both of her passions require careful consideration of the surrounding environment, existing structures, infrastructure and most important, the communities that use and depend on those structures and infrastructure. From companies hoping to attract new business to city planners wanting to lead their communities into a better future, a wide range of clients seek out Ms. Wildhaber's design team at MAKERS architecture and urban design in Seattle, Washington, to turn their visions into reality. Whereas some larger architectural design firms assign each aspect of a project to different employees, her smaller, 16-employee firm encourages each individual to work across disciplines, enabling her to add skills like economics, engineering and even psychology to her architectural prowess. "All of our projects are done as teams, including close collaboration with our clients. A large part of my day is spent putting the project pieces together, working through the spatial relationships and making sure the solutions we come up with address and hopefully exceed project goals."

She credits several people with her choice to pursue a STEM field. First among them was her teacher in fourth and fifth grades, who "expected a lot from us as students and people. That period is really important for girls — to have really strong influences at the fourth and fifth grade age — and I had one." Ms. Wildhaber also recalls a family friend who encouraged her to dream in the direction of her talents. Like many others who choose urban planning, Ms. Wildhaber had natural talents in both math and art, which blended together seamlessly. She earned a degree in architecture from Washington State University in 1990. "I always enjoyed building things. I always had a project that involved creating something. I knew I wanted to contribute positively to my surroundings and community but I didn't know that was urban planning and designing. When I got to college, it clicked."

Ms. Wildhaber is working on several projects that seek to incorporate community values into aesthetically-minded urban design. She and her team are redesigning a Naval Air Station in California. Her master plan lays out a vision and

"I always enjoyed building things. I always had a project that involved creating something."

145

framework that will guide redevelopment to the base for the 12,000 people who live, work and train there. Fifty years ago, the base layout was dispersed and automobile-oriented. Together, Ms. Wildhaber and her clients envisioned an updated, modern, pedestrian-friendly base that brings together the community. She and her team developed recommendations that enhanced mission capabilities, provided multimodal transportation options, consolidated scattered facilities into walkable redevelopments and strengthened the sense of place and community, all while achieving a high level of sustainability. Back in Seattle, Ms. Wildhaber's firm is designing the framework for a streetcar that will run between historic Pioneer Square and Westlake Center in downtown. "We are looking at the street scape character to identify the key unique elements to ensure the street car complements and integrates with the unique pedestrian character that is treasured by many in Seattle. We will establish urban design principles to be used in the final design of the street car and the platforms."

Ms. Wildhaber embraces the responsibility that comes with being a partner in an urban design and planning firm. As a leader of a small business that mostly takes on public projects for local, state and federal clients, she must compete for nearly every project. "It is a daily challenge to balance my time between project work and getting projects lined up so that everyone stays busy and excited about what they are doing." An important part of her success is the ability to assemble a multi-disciplinary team that works together creatively to solve problems. She also relies on an intuitive ability to effectively knit together individual plan elements within a community-wide perspective for overall livability.

Ms. Wildhaber believes her rural upbringing gave her life skills that stretched far beyond her family's farm. "The farm work involved a lot of problem solving, a lot of mechanical abilities. I think it enhanced my spatial abilities but it also gave me a strong sense of community and a high value for teamwork." She believes young women need to have STEM role models. That includes "opportunities for girls to get out of their comfort zone and try things that fall outside of what they're normally used to and to be okay with that."

From downtown corridors to waterfront districts, from walkable neighborhoods to ports and military establishments, Ms. Wildhaber brings 24 years of master planning, urban design and STEM expertise to improve neighborhoods and communities in Seattle and the Northwest. ●

MELANIE MATCHETT WOOD
Number Theory Mathematician

Creativity drives everything Professor Melanie Matchett Wood does. It fueled her passion for theater as a college student at Duke University, where she produced and directed shows, including Shakespeare's *Macbeth*. But creativity is also at the heart of Professor Wood's love of math. It was there in high school, when she became the first female on a U.S. International Math Olympiad team. And it was there in college, when she became the first woman in history to win the prestigious Morgan Prize, an award given for superior mathematical research by an undergraduate. "People are used to the idea that to produce a great play or great piece of art that you need creativity as well as technical skill. But they don't realize that this is true of mathematics as well. Both mathematics and art require creativity and the ability to think in ways that others haven't been able to imagine."

Professor Wood's journey to being a mathematical prodigy began in Indianapolis, Indiana, when a middle school teacher asked if she would like to participate in a MATHCOUNTS competition. At the time, she was active in cheerleading and theater; while she had always liked math and reading and learning, she had never considered competing academically. MATHCOUNTS, a national math coaching and competitive program for middle schoolers, introduced her to fascinating, puzzle-like challenges — very different from the straightforward, formulaic problems she had always done in school. The competition connected her with other students who were excited about math and showed her that her favorite part of math was working on challenging problems with others. She was hooked. In ninth grade, she qualified for the U.S.A. Math Olympiad and was invited to train for the International Math Olympiad during summer breaks all four years of high school. When she turned 17, *Discover* magazine profiled her in an article titled simply, "The Girl Who Loved Math."

The title suggests that such a thing is rare and speaks to the longstanding gender biases in mathematics – biases that Professor Wood herself had internalized. Her math skills put her in the highest rung of students anywhere in the country, yet she was shocked when she won the U.S.A. Math Olympiad. "I thought, why am I so surprised? And then I realized that it was just that I had this image of the people who won this competition — and that image was of boys." At times, she has encountered colleagues who hold negative attitudes toward women in math. But she remains focused on the positive influences of female mathematicians who came before her, like Dr. Zvezdelina Stankova, a professor of Math at Mills College who, much like Professor Wood does today, mentors young women in university research programs.

Professor Wood emphasizes that she wasn't always a math star. Before she became invested in MATHCOUNTS, she was just a good student in math. She insists that it's absolutely

Photo Credit: Chris Frazee, UW Madison Media Solutions

"Math is something that you get better at by practicing and doing more and by hard work. It's not a matter of having a math brain or not having a math brain. It's not as if you can be a math person or not a math person. It's something that by working at and by practicing, you will get better at. The 'I'm not so good at it' excuse is a statement about how much work you've put in."

critical for young students to understand that "math is something that you get better at by practicing and doing more and by hard work. It's not a matter of having a math brain or not having a math brain. It's not as if you can be a math person or not a math person. It's something that by working at and by practicing, you will get better at. The 'I'm not so good at it' excuse is a statement about how much work you've put in. When I run into people, especially adults, they have this idea that it's a switch that's either on or off in their brain. But that's entirely untrue. It's something you can change."

After high school, she attended Duke and graduated with honors in 2003. Although she was drawn to neuroscience, her exceptional achievements attracted many coveted invitations to math graduate research programs, putting her on a definitive path toward a career in numbers. Today, she finds her passion in the "deep and beautiful connections" between the seemingly unrelated subjects of prime numbers and polynomial geometry: "I use tools from algebraic geometry to study things about primes and use primes to study the geometry of spaces." She adds, "primes, and even some algebraic geometry, are the heart of all encryption and security for what we do online. Mathematicians are interested in studying primes because you never know in 30 or 40 or even 50 years how they will be used. We try to

figure out everything we can so we're ready, not for the applications today but for the applications in the future."

After earning advanced degrees from the University of Cambridge and Princeton University, Professor Wood became an assistant professor at Stanford University and then at the University of Wisconsin-Madison. In between those milestones, she has blazed a trail of scholarships and fellowships that allow her to immerse herself in what she is best known for: solving problems few others can solve, and doing it creatively.

Professor Wood plans to continue her research and teaching, all while inspiring young women to pursue mathematics. To her, closing the gender gap in mathematics means "getting more girls excited about math and science starting at the middle school level, where people really start to develop images of themselves and who they are and what kind of person they are. One of the big tasks is to make it possible for more middle school girls to identify with being good at math." She adds, "Women do math as well as men!"

No longer simply "The Girl Who Loved Math," Professor Wood proves that hard work and dedication can transform any young woman into "The Mathematician Who Advanced Number Theory." ●

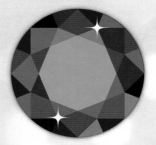

Crystals intro

There is a reason that gemstones are rare: They require a perfect storm of pressure and heat, of time and space and movement of tectonic plates, in order to form deep beneath the earth's surface. But even as rare as they are, gems are equally amazing in that they can form and be found anywhere in the world. Some places, like the Muzo region of the Colombian Andes, are hotbeds for emeralds. The Kudi Valley of northwestern India is famous for quality and rare sapphires. And on unassuming stretches of farmland in Arkansas, diamonds are known to crystallize and surface.

Not unlike mineral gems, a perfect storm of sorts is required to produce the rare crystals that eventually become STEM Gems. Every one of the women in these pages needed a particular combination of events to surface. Thankfully, when it comes to shining in the STEM fields, the process doesn't involve millions of years, and many of the conditions needed to get there are actually within your control.

This section takes the lessons of our 44 STEM Gems and translates them into actionable steps. If this book belongs to you, actively read, plan, doodle and make notes on these pages. If it is borrowed, start a journal and do the same. This section is *you* — about you, for you, celebrating you. Absorb its messages and strategies, put them into action, and you'll be amazed. Remember, a gemstone can form anywhere. Why not start mining it within you? ●

CHAPTER 1
Exceptional Teachers

Almost every adult has had that one teacher. The history teacher who hung hundreds of everyday artifacts from the ceiling, going above and beyond to make sure students connected with each item's historical significance. The first-grade teacher who turned a lesson on counting money into a student-run store for the school fundraiser. Or the junior high teacher who turned donated Barbie dolls into bungee-jumping experiments in physics. If we're fortunate, there are many such exceptional teachers in our past. Sometimes, it only takes one.

For our extraordinary STEM Gems, it was no different: Whether it was a parent exposing them to new worlds or an instructor making the world come alive in the classroom, exceptional teachers ignited the sparks of curiosity that would grow to become lifelong passions.

Consider two science teachers in a small town in Minnesota: Mrs. Warmka and Mrs. Challgren. In her elementary school class, Mrs. Warmka used cotton balls to teach cloud formation in physics and used cabbage juice as a pH indicator in chemistry. She taught statistics using M&Ms and forensic science using her students' fingerprints. With her middle-school students, Mrs. Challgren covered everything from insects to infectious diseases to reproduction with creativity, including a memorable lab using dental floss and a gel capsule to represent DNA in the nucleus of a cell.

What do Mrs. Warmka and Mrs. Challgren have in common besides instilling a love of learning in their students? They both taught STEM Gem Karen Olson, a forensic scientist whose work in cutting-edge technology has helped the Department of Defense solve crimes worldwide.

It's easy to trace Olson's path from a young girl diving into experiments with fingerprints and dental floss to a woman at the top of her field. Many of our STEM Gems credit their science and math teachers in their developmental years for their influence in sparking their passion, but any teacher who lays the groundwork for a lifetime pursuit of learning is indeed exceptional.

Parents as Teachers

Neuroscientists have determined that during the formative toddler years, before a child ever walks through the schoolhouse doors, parental involvement plays a huge role in language development. For many of our STEM Gems, one or both parents remained their most influential teacher throughout their education.

Thanks to Sara McAllister's mother, her first achievements in math started before she entered grade school. "My mom made it a point to teach me to read and do math when I was very young," says McAllister, now a mechanical and fire engineer. "She'd get the penny jar out, and we'd work through addition and subtraction problems and pick up a book and read every day. That really gave me a head start so that by the time I was in second grade, I was going to the third grade for math."

Stacy Lindborg, a biostatistician, remembers regular summer road trips. She sat in the back seat of her family's car with math books in her lap. "My father was an engineer. He would ask the teacher for next year's textbook and work through it with my brother and me. I attribute much of my academic excellence to him."

Trachette Jackson, a cancer modeling mathematician, says watching science fiction TV shows with her father marked her first scientific awakenings. "I recall watching *Star Trek* and being excited about all the 'advanced technology' and the science of space — black holes, wormholes. My father was also very interested in technology. We always had the latest gadgets in our home, and he could take apart and rebuild every one of them. I remember watching him and asking all sorts of questions."

Parents do not have to be gifted in STEM areas to raise exceptional STEM children. Simply instilling confidence in the formative years sets a child up for success. Caregivers who provide enriching life experiences and encourage children to engage actively in their world nurture the sense of wonder that lies at the foundation of all STEM careers. At this critical age, it's not about finessing word problems or breaking down an equation. It's all about the time, effort and encouragement to explore that let a child know: *I believe in you.*

Recognizing Exceptional Teachers

Have you heard the saying, "You don't know what you've got until it's gone?" It's one of the phrases that applies to the instrumental classroom teachers in our lives. Often, when we are in the presence of an exceptional teacher on a daily basis, we find ourselves immersed in the daily lessons, assignments and camaraderie of our classmates. We may sense the teacher is special, perhaps in a way that we can't quite put into words. Perhaps the mere thought of going to class makes us want to work harder or do more than what is required. But it is only with distance and time that we truly appreciate the impact of these individuals in our lives.

For Anna Nagurney, a network systems mathematician, this individual was her seventh-grade teacher, Mrs. Fuller. "She would invite us over to her home. She gave us a lot of math homework — algebra and tons of word problems. I'll never forget what she said to me in class: 'Anna, you will one day be a calculus professor!' The confidence that she had in me gave me strength."

Carol Espy-Wilson, an electrical engineer, encountered her exceptional teacher early in elementary school. "There was something I wasn't getting. I don't even remember what it was, but I do remember that this one teacher made me stay and do extra work. That was very important — that someone recognizes that you have a gap and that it can be fixed and they put the time in to close it."

Internet gaming technologist Holly Liu recalls two exceptional teachers. "The first teacher was Ms. Katlan. I had her for third, fourth and fifth grades. My parents teased me about being so attached to her. She was very approachable and firm about things, and I just thought she was really cool." Later, in high school, Mrs. Acianian taught Liu English. "Anyone who went through her curriculum passed the AP

English exam. I really looked up to her. She knew just the right amount of work to challenge us but not break us."

Where would these accomplished women be without exceptional teachers who inspired them? It's hard to say, but one thing we know for sure is that inspirational teachers share similar qualities:

- Possess a firm and strict, yet fair, mindset
- Encourage exploration
- Inspire confidence
- Believe in every student
- Understand how different students learn
- Set high expectations
- Establish a respectful learning environment

- Display passion and enthusiasm for their subject area
- Go above and beyond

Don't let the term "exceptional" fool you. The mere fact that teachers are exceptional does not necessarily mean they are the exception, or that they can only be found in certain schools. You can encounter exceptional teachers in a schoolhouse in the Alaskan wilderness or in an overcrowded urban school district. They might be fresh out of university or be experts who have taught two generations of families in the same classroom. They might even be members of your family — relatives who challenge you to be better, who model a sense of curiosity and determination and who ultimately inspire greatness.

When you find an exceptional teacher in your life, do everything you can to nurture that relationship. Return to visit. Tell that teacher how much he or she impacts you.

Ainissa Ramirez, a materials engineer, did just that after an inspirational year in Mrs. Howard's high school physics class. "When I was applying to colleges, she pointed a very skinny finger at me and said, 'Do me proud.'" It's easy to see why Ramirez grew up to find teaching such an important part of her legacy.

Give As Much As You Get

The role of a teacher is to teach. Your role, as a student, is to challenge.

Surprised? Doesn't learning mean accepting and repeating what the teachers and textbooks have to say? Learning can be difficult to measure. Homework, quizzes and tests are tools used to gauge learning, but assessments often come long after concepts are introduced. And those conventional tools don't always capture the full picture of how much learning is happening in the classroom. In fact, for every lesson, teachers must write concrete, observable verbs that they expect their students to emulate before concluding that learning has taken place. Verbs such as *measure, create* and *recite* are active responses to the invisible process of learning.

Without active engagement on your part, the teacher is a bit like a tour bus driver. She has a destination in mind, perhaps even a few stops along the way. But without questions and requests to get out, stretch your legs and take a look around, her tour is a bit one-sided. As the tourist, the knowledge being shared tends to wash over you; you may end up absorbing it or you may not.

So how do you get the classroom learning *you* want? You challenge.

Let's be clear. Challenge isn't an invitation to prove you know more about a topic or even a license to be disrespectful. The tour bus challenge is simple: engage in class discussions, ask questions and complete assignments. Sounds simple, right? For some, this is easier said than done.

Paula Hammond, a chemical engineer, attended a Catholic school run by the Oblate Sisters of Providence, an African-American order of nuns known to be very strict. She considers her experience a gift that fostered a love of learning, discipline and curiosity. "Going to an all-girls school did provide a particular environment in which there was no fear in asking questions. I think there's a dynamic that sets in during the tween years where you don't want to open your mouth and ask questions because there's a sense of evaluation by your peers. This anxiety can become more marked when you're in a mixed classroom, gender-wise. In an all-girls school, that goes away. There's no very strong social tension or gender tension, and there's no sense of who's expected to know the answer. It frees you up to dive in and ask questions and get involved in class. That provides a level of confidence that is unique to women."

If you find yourself hesitant to raise your hand during class, talk to your teacher privately. He or she may be unaware of your anxiety. Find out if there is a time when you can ask questions one-on-one, such as before or after class or during the teacher's planning time. Suggest a system of communication, such as in the space at the top of assignments or via message to a digital class board, where you feel comfortable asking questions.

Bryna Kra, a dynamical systems mathematician, gives great advice about asking a question in your math class: "I asked a lot of questions. Maybe my peers thought I was dumb, but I didn't care. There is no question in math that's too stupid to ask. If you're asking, it just means that it hasn't been explained."

Lastly, if you are reluctant to ask questions during class, you can bet other students are as well. They might be looking to you to be that leader. Even astronomer Edwin Hubble, of Hubble Space Telescope fame, must have been laughed at to suggest Albert Einstein's theory of a fixed universe was wrong. But turns out he was right — so right that a new law of physics was named after him, Hubble's Law, which proves that the universe is expanding at a rate of roughly 70 kilometers per second. So, it was great that he wasn't afraid to speak up and ask questions.

Fill The Void

What happens if you find yourself in a classroom situation that doesn't challenge you? Are there resources available to ensure you become an actively engaged learner? Absolutely.

Before we head down that path, stop, take a deep breath and consider this: Every teacher has something to offer. It may not be the lesson you think you need, but you can bet every classroom experience will teach you something about the most important lesson you will ever learn: yourself.

Make every effort to build relationships with teachers, even when you don't feel a strong connection. Ask what sparked their love for the subject matters they teach or which teachers influenced them. Seek out your teachers' perspectives, whatever they may be. Sometimes, a simple act of appreciation for their time is all that is needed to forge deep bonds.

Another idea is to ask for extra work or independent study. Good teachers know that different students have different styles and with some extra time, teachers can tailor the material to a style that will catalyze your success. Some students, for example, learn better with visuals; others are more verbal, and still others are physical and learn through models. Andrea Luecke's middle-school teacher allowed students to pitch ideas for independent learning. "I jumped at the opportunity to escape the rote syllabi," says Luecke, now a solar energy technologist. Self-guided learning is a strength all successful STEM professionals must develop. Why not use the opportunity of a classroom void to develop this vital muscle?

There may come a time when, despite your best efforts, you want more — more challenge, more experimentation, more engagement with the subject matter. School counselors are a great resource for supplemental learning opportunities. They can put you in touch with educational and community institutions that offer programs like online distance learning, summer opportunities at science museums or nature preserves, or dual enrollment opportunities at local colleges that offer school credit for college-level courses. These more advanced opportunities are ideal for students who have extra time to devote to coursework, have a genuine interest in the subject matter or need a little help deciding on a future path of study.

Outside of formal institutions, there are organizations and clubs in your local community and online that may offer that challenge you're seeking. Melanie Matchett Wood, a number theory mathematician, found her passion through a middle-school math competition. "MATHCOUNTS is the first time I was really drawn into math — the problems were way more interesting than the formulaic school problems. For the first time, I actually had to solve math problems like puzzles."

Find out how you can become involved or start a club in your area. Not only will these extracurricular opportunities fill the void, but they also look fantastic on college applications and often lead to contacts, scholarships and network of mentors and role models as you work toward higher education. ●

Every profession has individuals who excel. Teachers are no exception. You can view exceptional teachers as a rare phenomenon or you can recognize your role in helping to make all teachers the best they can be.

- Acknowledge your parents and caregivers as your first teachers.
- Identify the qualities of exceptional teachers so you can recognize them and maximize your learning experience while you're in their classrooms.
- Reflect on your own exceptional teachers. Thank them and stay in touch.
- Give as much as you get. Ask questions. Take the learning tour in unexpected directions.
- Seek out opportunities to fill the void.

CHAPTER 2
Active Summers

Summer. Break.

Put these two words together, and they instantly evoke visions of long, lazy days without homework, nights spent staying up late and afternoons spent relaxing poolside. Summer break is a much-needed sigh from the pressures of school, tucked conveniently into a season when outdoor activities take center stage. But what if summer break meant more? More fun. More life experiences. More friends. More of everything that makes you, you.

It's true that major factors like family plans and finances often dictate how you end up spending *some* of your vacation from school. But a larger portion than you might think is up to you.

The average summer break falls somewhere between 42 and 84 days. Over an entire K-12 career, that's 770 days — essentially two years. If you get eight hours of sleep each night, you already spend one-third of your life sleeping. Do you really need to add to that snooze-fest? Let's not even count the hours binge-watching reality TV or playing video games. Two years is an associate's degree. Two years is 350 novels read, 75 Habitat for Humanity houses built or enough tennis matches to make you the next Serena Williams. And while it's safe to say you won't be doing any of those things the summer after kindergarten, every experience sets the foundation for what comes next. It's never too early to start building your launch pad to greatness.

Pay attention to the childhoods of our amazing STEM Gems. Notice anything? They didn't view their summers as time off from learning; they saw them as crucial periods for ramping up their learning and engagement. During these summer breaks, they sought new challenges, played sports, volunteered and dedicated themselves to the craft of music or the art of exploration. Some stuck close to home and worked for the family business; others traveled to the far reaches of the globe for cultural experiences. Their summers weren't just gaps between academic years. Their summers were filled with intention, curiosity and wonder.

Just because school is out doesn't mean learning has to be.

Everyone needs downtime. Spend a few days indulging in the things your parents might view as a waste of time, and then get out there. Your future is calling.

Sports

A recent study commissioned by the Los Angeles Unified School District examined the connection between academic performance and athletics. Compared to non-athletes, student athletes in the district attended, on average, 21 more days of school and maintained .55 to .74 higher grade point averages than non-athletes. These findings confirm what has long been suspected: Participating in sports improves academic progress.

Experts attribute the difference to two factors. Neurologists believe the increased blood flow triggered by chemicals released during exercise improves cognitive brain activity, possibly even triggering the creation of new neurons. At the same time, a network of coaches provide a level of involvement and mentorship that can prove invaluable to student athletes in other realms of their school lives. Participation in sports also improves self-discipline and sharpens the competitive edge necessary to excel.

Because students are often involved in multiple other activities during their formative years, it can be difficult to isolate sports as a contributing factor to school achievement, but a joint study from the University of South Carolina and Pennsylvania State University aimed to do just that: uncover the direct correlation between sports and academics. Researchers analyzed a data pool of 9,700 high school students aged 14-18. The students represented a mix of rural, urban and suburban areas and participated in a diverse array of extracurricular activities, including academic clubs, performing arts clubs such as drama and team sports. Findings indicated that although many students benefitted academically from other after-school clubs, sports was the only activity to have "a consistent and significant effect on students' grades across all schools." And according to the study's lead researcher Matthew Irvin, assistant professor at the University of South Carolina's Department of Educational Studies, "Team sport is significantly related to higher grade-point averages and a higher likelihood of completing high school and enrolling in college. [Sports] help socialize you

into being more focused on school and may help develop time-management skills, initiative and an ability to work with others."

Andrea Luecke, a solar energy technologist, is a prime example of the impact sports can have on achievement in other areas. Her year-round sports regimen growing up, which included basketball, softball and volleyball, transitioned into ultra-active summers spent swimming, hiking and horseback riding on the family's country farm. "We have very good weather in Wisconsin, so we stayed outside during the summer. Sports were a major factor for me." The skills she honed in her physical activities leave little doubt that sports shaped Luecke into a leader, both in academics and in the solar energy industry.

Consider a 2013 survey on sports and leadership commissioned by global audit firm Ernst & Young that included high-ranking female political leaders, such as former Secretaries of State Hillary Clinton and Condoleezza Rice, Brazilian President Dilma Rousseff and women on the board of directors at major corporations, such as PepsiCo CEO Indra Nooyi and Dupont CEO Ellen Kullman. A staggering 96 percent of political leaders and senior executives, the survey showed, had participated in sports in school. Ernst & Young's Women Athletes Global Leadership Network advisor and Olympic swimming champion Donna de Varona believes the survey "confirms to the world [that] what we've been doing for the last 40 years on the field of play for women has helped change the landscape around the world for business women, which has an impact on the economy, which helps everyone."

Leading broadcast journalists and co-authors Katty Kay and Claire Shipman cited the link between sports and achievement in their *The New York Times* best-selling book *Womenomics*

and in Kay's current guide for women to achieve confidence in their careers, *The Confidence Code*. Kay explains, "We both realized very clearly during the course of our research and numerous interviews with neurologists, psychologists and educators that something happens when girls play sports. Playing competitive sports embodies the experience of not just winning, but the experience of losing. The losing is almost as critical; when you're playing sports and you do badly and you lose, you have no choice but to pick yourself up and carry on. It's that process of carrying on and clearing hurdles that really builds confidence. It's an incredibly useful proving ground for business and leadership."

Whether it's the physiological impact of healthy activity on a growing brain or the expanded skill set a team-oriented activity brings to young students, sports enhance academics.

Music

As with sports, music education is widely recognized as a secret weapon that spurs academic achievement. According to The College Board's Profile of College-Bound Seniors National Report for 2001, students with music backgrounds scored 60 points higher on the verbal section and 45 points higher on the math section of the SAT than their non-musical peers. Data suggests that the longer students are immersed in music study, the greater the positive impact on their scores.

Until recently, much of the research into the link between music and academic achievement has focused on middle- to high-income children, whose caregivers could afford private music lessons. In 2015, Northwestern University researchers published the first documented study to focus on the brains of low-income children receiving music education. The study focused on Los Angeles students aged six to nine who received music instruction through the non-profit organization Harmony Project, dedicated to offering music education to low-income children. Neural probes were hooked up to the students' brains to record changes in their ability to distinguish between similar speech sounds, a skill fundamental to language and reading skills. Researchers found that while music education did not alter this portion of a child's brain much after year one, two years offered a definitive impact — a clear testament to the value of continuing and ongoing music education for all.

Music makes a positive impact on learning in many ways. Often, a student's level of involvement in the school experience increases with music, as does their self-esteem. Socially, music develops listening and collaborative skills. Mentally, music requires creativity, sharpened focus, the ability to multitask and problem solve. The discipline required to master any aspect of music also proves an excellent training ground for tackling many different kinds of life challenges.

The direct connection between STEM fields and music is often debated. Although there is no significant brain research to support the conclusion that learning music makes a student better at math and science, students who engage in music are better able to recognize patterns and search for a creative way to circumvent problems. Microsoft's billionaire Co-founder Paul Allen found that at the end of a marathon day of programming in the early days of his company, picking up his guitar rebooted his creativity in a new way. Robert Taub, a renowned concert pianist and founder of a music software company, MuseAmi, believes strongly in the connection between music and math. He perceives patterns in three dimensions and can "visualize all the notes and their interrelationship." This allows him to make "multiple connections in multiple spheres."

Likewise, several of our STEM Gems cite music as critical to their development. Bryna Kra, a dynamical systems mathematician, spent her summers immersed in music. She played the violin, piano and viola and attended either day or sleep-away music camps each summer. Sara McAllister's mother was a piano teacher, so McAllister, now a mechanical and fire engineer, spent her summers practicing at the keys. Trachette Jackson, a cancer modeling mathematician, also dedicated substantial portions of her childhood summers to music.

Music opens up rich pathways to critical thinking and enhances our ability to communicate and express ourselves, either in solo or as part of an ensemble. Music can also provide a counterbalance to academic performance, often serving as a pleasurable diversion and joy away from the rigors of academics. Either way, music has the capacity to enrich a young achiever's life experience.

Academic

Often the rigors of classwork leave little time to explore more deeply the subjects students love most. Summer is the perfect time to explore those passions. Seek out enrichment camps that will engage you in finding answers to the questions that keep you up at night, or at least keep you after class longer than most students. You'll be surrounded by people who share those same passions and who want to learn more. Academic enrichment can take many forms, from recreation center classes to day or sleep-away camps to internships at local companies. Expect the cost of enrichment activities to run the spectrum from high tuition to free, but many offer scholarships, discounts and payment plans. Universities and companies offering summer programs want to fill their camps and will work with you to make it happen.

Melanie Matchett Wood, a number theory mathematician, recalls looking forward to thumbing through her school district's summer enrichment catalog in elementary and middle school and picking out classes of interest to her. "My mother was a teacher so she really inspired a love of learning in me. Once I was in high school, I did trainings for a month for the Math Olympiad and other math programs. By then, enrichment classes were very specialized."

Ainissa Ramirez, a materials engineer, spent her high school summers boosting her mathematical skills. "There was a program called STEP (Stevens Technical Enrichment Program) and it recruited minority students from New York and New Jersey. We took college-level classes. It wasn't just during the summer; it was on Saturdays during the school year, too. So I took calculus during the summer, and it was much harder than what I was doing in high school. It gave me a wake-up call that college would be difficult and that I better prepare."

Carol Espy-Wilson, an electrical engineer, found that summer programs at Bennett College and a 10-week pre-engineering program at University of Wisconsin-Madison (UWM) provided a tremendous boost to her confidence. "I did so well in the UWM program that they didn't want me to return to high school. They wanted me to enroll as a freshman. The summer programs that I did in engineering really helped me."

Structured academic programs and classes aren't the only ways to gain valuable experience in an area of interest. In middle school, Lorrie Faith Cranor, an online security expert, worked with engineers and college students at a government research lab, an experience that had a lasting impact on her interest in engineering. "I mostly helped with data collection. I worked on one project where they were working on acoustics for the navy, on submarines, and they needed to understand the acoustical properties. So they had me lower microphones into the pool to gather data. That was really cool."

Erika Ebbel Angle, a bio-technologist, loved her hands-on, science-oriented summer camps. Sometimes these camps spawned projects that she continued into the school year. Her greatest summer memories, however, involved another immersive aspect of learning: travel.

Exploration

Angle says her parents had an abiding belief in travel as an experience in learning and self-discovery. "It was important to my parents to show me the world and impress upon me how fortunate I was — to open my eyes and expose me to what was happening internationally."

Holly Liu's parents wanted her to stay close to her Chinese heritage. Chinese camps when she was a young girl gave way to summers abroad in Asia as she grew older. "I highly recommend traveling when you're younger," says Liu, now an internet gaming technologist. "You learn so many different ways of doing things, and it opens up so many opportunities."

Travel doesn't have to be international to be life-impacting. Anna Nagurney, a network systems mathematician, spent summers in a rented bungalow in eastern Pennsylvania. "There were several families that would regularly spend the summer there, and as children and middle schoolers, and even as high schoolers for a few years, we were free to roam through the woods and nature. We had a great freedom to explore. I think this helped me to develop a curiosity about the beauty of nature and the wonders of the world. The experiences in the countryside also taught us a lot of independence and even survival skills."

Laurie Glimcher, an immunologist, was profoundly shaped by childhood summers on Martha's Vineyard, an island off the coast of Massachusetts. "I dissected frogs outside our home during the summer I was six, and I also tried to revive dying flowers with potions I concocted."

Road trips offer a special kind of adventure no airline terminal can match. In addition to reconnecting in an extended way with important people in our lives, heading out on the open highway personalizes what we know intellectually about a place or a region. It's one thing to read about the Battle of Gettysburg in your history textbook. It's quite another to sink your shoes into the same grassy Pennsylvania field where Civil War soldiers lost their lives. Roadside diners become an adventure in different cuisines and everywhere you look is a life lived differently than yours.

Paula Hammond, a chemical engineer, is well acquainted with the magic of road trips. Her explorations took her all over the country with her father as he attended annual conventions for the American Association for Clinical Chemistry. "From Detroit, we drove to San Francisco, stopped in Yellowstone National Park. There was a Houston, Texas trip. My father liked to drive a lot." Her childhood trips didn't only represent thousands of miles. They represented thousands of new perspectives that helped shape her into the STEM Gem she is today.

Summer trips to the Jersey Shore made a huge impact on one little girl from Philadelphia. See if you can figure out which of our STEM Gems began as a beach-comber:

"I was always interested in digging for things and metal-detecting and looking for creatures in the rocks along the beach. At an early age I was exposed to beach combing, and the process of just discovering and examining and looking closely at the life along the beach fascinated me. Those summers were very formative for my decision to pursue anthropology. Being out in nature and being curious about what was happening around me and the possibility of finding something always motivated me."

You guessed it: archaeologist Michele Koons. From childhood explorer to professional explorer, she discovered her life's passion by immersing herself in summer activities that engaged her curiosity and fostered her love for learning.

One other form of travel deserves mention: reading. Where else can you attend a magical boarding school in a castle, become the heroine in a post-apocalyptic world or hang out on Long Island, N.Y. in 1929 with Jay Gatsby and his ultra-rich friends? Maybe code diving or getting inside the mind of one of your favorite role models makes non-fiction more your thing. No matter your interests, books can take you places that are impossible in real life. The majority of our STEM Gems cite reading as part of their active summers. Not only does reading enhance vocabulary and brain connectivity (even as long as a few days after finishing a book!), it remains the best kind of "armchair travel" in the world — all for the low, low cost of a free library card.

Whether you travel to London in person or through the mind of Sherlock Holmes, whether you set off in an RV with your family or pitch a backyard tent and gaze at the stars through a telescope, exploration opens the mind and frees the soul.

Your Backyard

Some of our STEM Gems discovered that the greatest exploration required no travel at all. It's easy to see how Christine Goforth became an entomologist: "I spent my summers largely in the mountains collecting minerals, fishing and camping. When we weren't doing that, my sister and I spent a good part of our time flinging ourselves down the hill we lived on in Colorado on any wheeled contraption we could get our hands on with all the other neighborhood kids. We also had a lot of water balloon wars, played catch and football and climbed trees. And I collected insects. I *loved* collecting insects. Basically, I lived outside." Karen Olson, now a forensic scientist, spent time at her aunt's cabin swimming, fishing and making sand castles. Pilar Molina Lopez, an animation technologist, developed an early love of playing video games with her brother and cousins, but also struck a healthy balance of playing outside and working through math workbooks her parents bought her each summer.

Summer enrichment activities such as camps and travel can be costly. Pardis Sabeti, a computational biologist and geneticist, knows well the struggles some families face when trying to provide a learning environment over the summer. "We were immigrants so we'd recently come to America. We didn't have much money. We didn't know about summer programs. My mom was a creative person so she would get us these books where you problem solve — math and English problems. She would give us a huge stack of those and tell us to work through them. We had book reports we would have to write regularly. My mom told my sister when she was older to develop a course and teach me stuff that she learned in school so I got to learn things in advance. And my sister was very thorough. We even had PE and music."

Helene Gayle, a global health scientist, discovered that spending summers working in her father's store, a retail business that focused on barber and beauty supplies, gave her life experience she could not have learned anywhere else. "You saw a lot of different people coming through. It instilled an ability to work with a wide range of people and cultivated a sense of responsibility. It also made us hone arithmetic skills and helped with understanding basic numeracy and the practical realities of running a business."

Sylvia Lee, an environmental engineer, began volunteering in middle school as a way to "give something back." Planting that seed of public service in her own community set her on a course to use her education to tackle some of the world's biggest social challenges.

Exploring in your backyard means being resourceful and looking at familiar surroundings in a new way. Stefani Wildhaber, an urban planner and designer, is convinced that being raised on a rural farm in Washington gave her the tools to succeed in STEM. "Farm work involved a lot of problem solving, a lot of mechanical abilities. I think it enhanced my spatial abilities and it showed me that I liked working with my hands." Build a treehouse. Plant a garden. Seek out the thousand and one things you can do without ever packing a suitcase. ●

Idle moments, especially in our fast-paced digital world, offer an important time for us to reconnect with ourselves, to be creative, to stretch our minds in ways that appeal to us. There is abundant value in the stillness you experience when you watch a hawk soar overhead or grab your yoga mat and find a spot under your favorite tree for an hour.

But it's easy to become lulled into a passive summer. The days are long and hot. Friends and other social temptations are plentiful. Active summers mean getting more out of your break once you're recharged. Consider your future. Do some of your summer activities coincide with your existing plans? When considering an activity, ask yourself: *Is what I'm doing going to matter in a day? A week? A month? A year?* If you can't see your major summer activities mattering much beyond dinnertime, you may need to rethink your summer game plan.

Two *years*.

How will you spend yours?

- Plan ahead. Summer camps and programs sometimes begin registration the moment the program is over the previous fall. Planning ahead will also provide time to save if financial resources are necessary.

- Express to family and friends your desire to learn, travel and explore.

- Look for opportunities to meet with mentors in your area of interest.

- Consider volunteering for a local organization.

- If you have an interest in sports or music, nurture it.

- Get lost in books. Make your library card your best summer companion.

- Grab a subject area workbook to avoid inactivity.

- Live summer with purpose.

- Reject boredom. Remember the saying: Boredom doesn't exist — boring people do.

CHAPTER 3
Go Beyond

Albert Einstein once said, "I have no special talents. I am only passionately curious." Imagine that. One of the greatest minds in human history attributed his success to mere curiosity. Einstein must have been outrageously curious in 1905, his so-called "miracle year," when he revolutionized the way that scientists, and then the entire world, thought about fundamental elements and forces of nature: gravity, energy and matter.

Curiosity is the hunger that drives those to reach beyond — to challenge convention, to reject established theories (including those of Einstein), to explore and keep exploring, discover and innovate. Reaching beyond is what comes after you've absorbed the science explained in textbooks and, at some point, realized that those explanations aren't entirely satisfying. In different ways — sometimes in quiet moments of observation, sometimes in moments of frenetic exploration — many of our STEM Gems came to this exact turning point in their scientific lives. Over and over, they describe reaching a certain place, where they stopped learning just to ace the test, where the standard science fair projects wouldn't cut it, where they refused to be knocked down by failed experiments or negative voices. Let's call it Beyond. It's not a place you can find on a map. It has no geographic boundary, no color, no national language. Think of Beyond as a state of mind, a resolve that allowed them to reach new heights, to see old problems with totally new eyes and more than anything, to look in the mirror and say: Scientist. Tech innovator. Engineer. Math pioneer.

At some point in their lives, these STEM Gems all remember getting to Beyond, even if they didn't always know they were headed there. More often than not, their curiosity began with their own daily surroundings.

Sarah Kovaleski, a nuclear engineer, remembers her father casually dropping deeply abstract brain teasers into dinner conversation. "'What do you think would happen if you walked halfway to the wall, then halfway again, and again and again?' I puzzled over that question for days, unaware I was learning about asymptotes and infinity."

When Sara McAllister turned 16, she inherited her family's Volkswagen Beetle. "I drove that car every day throughout high school and college. By the time I graduated college, I was obsessed," says McAllister, now a mechanical and fire engineer. "I went from being the little girl handing my dad tools while he was under the car to *being* the one under the car. When I went off to graduate school, I really wanted to know more about combustion because, well, that's what makes the car work. Combustion is a core piece of fire, so when the opportunity came to do research on fire, it made sense."

For Pardis Sabeti, a computational biologist and geneticist, the entire existence of her lab is built around pushing beyond

what is known. "We're going to discover phenomena. That's what we're here for." She and her team are explorers in uncharted territory, developing tools designed to uncover and combat complex and deadly viruses. Relentlessly curious about how viruses evolve, Sabeti decided at the age of 21 to innovate new tools for assessing the genetic markers of viral diseases instead of tinkering with the old ones. Those new tools became the biggest breakthroughs in computational biology of the 21st century.

These women allowed their curiosity and determination — their ability to think beyond that which is easy and comfortable — to take them to new understandings and opportunities.

To take them to Beyond.

Ask Beyond

What do you do when you want to push beyond and come up against an obstacle?

You ask. And ask and ask and continue asking.

Though they may seem like they've been around forever, scientific fields of study did not fall from the sky fully formed, like sacred texts from the ancients. Every aspect of STEM — or any field of study — can be traced back to a body of questions. And those very subjects remain relevant and current based solely upon the production of new questions. Asking drives the future.

At age four, network scientist Jennifer Chayes wanted to know more about math. She witnessed her neighbors having a blast while engaged in math puzzles. "I started knocking on their door and asking for math. They seemed to enjoy it so much. That's when my love of math started."

Bryna Kra, a dynamical systems mathematician, sees the beauty in questioning everything, especially when it comes to math. "With math, unlike anything else in the world, once you've proven something, you know you've proven it. In math, a proof can be solid, an acceptable established proof because there is a standard that we hold things to. It's not a fuzzy standard. There's an absolute standard of truth." Math makes sense because it builds on your knowledge. If you don't ask and explore the concepts you don't understand during those early stages, it can be difficult to fill in the learning gaps.

Kra's best advice is to "keep exploring and ask, ask, ask! There's no question in math that's too stupid to ask. If you're asking, it just means that it hasn't been explained." She believes that people who are intimidated by mathematics are the ones who don't ask questions because they are afraid to look silly or unknowledgeable.

Barbara Liskov's greatest career achievements were based upon one fundamental question she asked herself: *How can I build software in a more efficient way?* Pursuing that answer led the computer scientist and engineer to the idea of modularity — breaking software into smaller, independent pieces called modules — which in turn became the key to better organized software. By asking questions and pushing beyond existing programming methods, Liskov transformed the field of computer science forever.

All worthwhile pursuits of knowledge begin with a question. Asking beyond takes you beyond. Ask questions for which there is no answer — yet — then drive the future.

Learn Beyond

Learning beyond means striking out in new directions, cultivating new interests and examining new possibilities — not always in your primary area of interest, and not necessarily during the confines of the school day. You may have biology class for only an hour a day. That leaves 15 waking hours to go beyond the curriculum to what *you* find exciting in biology. Through her social work in the Buffalo, New York area, Helene Gayle's mother exposed Gayle, now a global health scientist, to many international students while she was young. By paying attention to the world around her, Gayle became interested in South Africa's anti-apartheid movement and liberation struggles globally. She started thinking about what could be done to improve the lives of historically oppressed groups in the United States. She pursued psychology, a discipline she felt would enable her to impact the self-esteem and behavior that led to struggles in the African-American community, and she went on to become a physician and the leader of one of the world's largest humanitarian organizations in the world. Her eagerness to realize her own potential by incorporating social justice into her science shaped her career in ways that helped her to realize her potential.

Environmental engineer Sylvia Lee can still remember hearing about a dispute in her Great Lakes community that fascinated her. "It was big at the time, or at least, seemed big to me. There was rhetoric about how the Americans were stealing the Canadian's water. It was an issue that somehow touches on all the things that interest me. There's a huge technical and public component. It's something that really spoke to me and intrigued me." So much so that Lee took courses on water issues at school to learn more. The more she immersed herself in the material, the more she realized that she wanted water and water rights to be her life's work.

Erika Ebbel Angle, a bio-technologist, took her learning beyond when she went from learning about crocodiles to conducting her own experiments inspired by their behavior. "During my April vacation in Cancun, Mexico, we visited a crocodile farm. I learned that when crocodiles are mortally wounded they can flip over onto their backs, slip into a coma and die. For some reason that really affected me, and I remembered this fact about the crocodiles' mortality when it was time to do a science fair project when I returned from vacation. I wondered if cells commit suicide when they are infected by viruses similar to what happens with crocodiles in order to avoid a horrible death. From there my science fair hypothesis was born."

With practice, learning beyond becomes second nature. You'll find you are no longer satisfied with the basics of subjects. Your curiosity will push you to ask more and expect more from yourself and those around you. Learning becomes an appetite difficult to satisfy.

Work Beyond

Often, going beyond means blazing a new trail and choosing not to walk the well-worn path. The good news is, you don't have to be Einstein to achieve this. For some of our STEM Gems, blazing a new trail started with coming up with an original experiment for the local science fair.

Immunologist Laurie Glimcher's most memorable science fair project, dating back to when she was eight years old, explored the molting cycle of crayfish. "One of my father's colleagues loved marine biology, and she took me out to the river to catch crayfish early one morning. When I got home, I put them in a large bowl filled with water and went to bed. The next morning, I was horrified to see crayfish all over the floor. They had managed to climb on top of each other and jump out of the bowl." She could have chosen any number of projects that had already been tried, but Glimcher allowed her curiosity about the natural environment and the inspiration of others around her to drive her further.

The curiosity that burned in Lee took her from mastering how to build water systems to thinking about when, where and why they should be built. "I was an engineer for seven years — building and designing things — but what got me frustrated was that I wasn't in a position to contribute to the decision-making process. I became more interested in public policy and raising awareness, a bit more upstream than just the building of things." Her desire to see what lay beyond took her to the World Economic Forum, a non-profit organization where she became an integral part of the decisions surrounding water systems.

Likewise, Angle blazed her own trail by achieving an unusual trifecta in STEM: PhD scientist, CEO and winner of the Miss Massachusetts beauty pageant. In doing so, she in turn has empowered young women to think beyond stereotypes about who they can be as women in STEM.

Number theory mathematician Melanie Matchett Wood could have rested on her school achievements in math, but her seventh-grade teacher saw a tremendous work ethic in her. To join MATHCOUNTS, a competition-based middle school organization that engages students in fun, challenging math programs, Wood had to work beyond school hours to compete at a high level. "Before that I'd done fine in math, but when I first did MATHCOUNTS, I was really drawn into math. The problems were way more interesting than what we did in school. For the first time, I actually had to solve math problems like puzzles."

Working beyond helped Wood with another aspect of the Go Beyond motto. Through MATHCOUNTS, Wood found her "tribe."

Find Your Tribe

The word "tribe" describes a group of people with similar interests, knowledge or values. They are kindreds — the folks you like to spend time with, the peers who have similar ambitions and drive, the people who not only inspire you, but *get* you in a way few others do.

Wood found that the MATHCOUNTS competitions she entered "put her in touch with other students that were really excited about math." The love of numbers pulled her in, but it was the relationships that gave her a sense of belonging and community.

Sheryl Sandberg, Chief Operations Officer of Facebook, co-wrote a 2013 best-seller entitled *Lean In: Women, Work and the Will to Lead*. The book's philosophy is simple: Together, women can accomplish more. Since its publication, *Lean In* has inspired the creation of online communities of women offering peer support and strong networks. "The more women help one another," Sandberg writes, "the more we help ourselves. Acting like a coalition truly does produce results. Any coalition of support must also include men, many of whom care about gender inequality as much as women do."

Materials engineer Ainissa Ramirez champions the idea of tribe. Finding it, she says, starts with finding the question that you're passionate about. "Let that be your compass. That will push you past all the barriers that seem to be there. You'll be willing to work hard and stretch, and it will propel you past bias and stereotypes and upbringing. Find the thing you're excited about and then you'll find your tribe."

Finding your tribe takes time. To seek out those who think beyond and ask beyond and work beyond, you must first know yourself. Some girls find their STEM tribe in middle school. Others may not find it until they reach college and suddenly find themselves surrounded by others pursuing the same passions. Be patient, open yourself up to meeting new friends and you will find *your people*. ●

These 44 STEM Gems, all citizens of Beyond, share a core trait that catalyzed their success as STEM pioneers: curiosity. As girls and young women, they had to know more, about the how crayfish reproduce, why some molecules attract and others repel, or when the cosmos came into being. As they chased the questions that fascinated them, they sought out environments where that questioning was celebrated and where they would be further challenged. These women choose every day to live beyond.

- Go beyond. Don't settle.

- Keep a journal or list of things that pique your curiosity.

- Ask, ask, ask. Then ask some more.

- Engage in your STEM passion broadly and deeply.

- Don't just do a job. Do a job differently and well.

- Seek out your tribe.

CHAPTER 4
Set Sail

Let's assume you've started out on what many would consider "the right path," even though you're smart enough to know there isn't simply one path that can take you where you wish to go. Still, your path *feels* right. You work hard at everything you do, you nurture your curiosity, you're ambitious and you want to contribute to society. Let's assume you're asking lots of questions, you're finding your way to your passion and you're determined to take that passion into Beyond. You might have even found your tribe. From all indications, you're finally on your way.

Then comes the hard part: real life. Life as a promising STEM Gem isn't all stars and sunshine. Life is, well, *life*. In all its glory and sloppiness, it is filled with moments that will test you, sometimes disappoint you and occasionally threaten to derail you. What you do and think and believe in those moments will shape the course for your success.

Our STEM Gems have all had these moments. Some may have drifted — and even felt deeply lost — but never for too long. Use their words and experiences as your compass.

Preparing Your Route

Many high achievers did not know who they wanted to become or what their ideal lives looked like at your age. Ask yourself the following questions:

- What are my interests?
- What do I already do well?
- What would I like to do better?
- What gets me excited?

Several of our STEM Gems did not find their way until well into their adult lives. Atmospheric scientist Inez Fung did not know where her path would lead until graduate school. At the recommendation of her mentor, Fung shifted from hurricane studies to climate modeling. Similarly, chemical engineer Paula Hammond reached a major turning point in her career when she took a sabbatical (a year-long break) from the daily demands of her work as a university professor. "I had already been involved in working with materials but had never directed my knowledge at biometrics. So I used my sabbatical to explore more applications, to move into biomaterials and materials for health. That process transformed my group."

Even when their paths weren't clear, Fung and Hammond had something almost as valuable in their grasp: a sense of direction.

Self-starters who don't yet know what they want to become still strive to fulfill underlying values: excellence, integrity, a desire to better the world in some way. Those values can be as important as the destination itself — sometimes more important — as it can help set the stage for multiple opportunities down the road.

It's easy to see the way when calm waters prevail. But what happens when the wind shifts? Setbacks can quickly send us swirling and toss our best-laid plans around in circles. Often, these setbacks are things we can't control. But how we react to them *is* within our control.

Staying grounded in your goals and your own sense of direction is sometimes all that's needed to get back on course. Write them down, and write them down often — in a journal, on your bathroom mirror, in an email you schedule to send yourself each year on your birthday. Organize your goals into short and long-term lists. Include the mantras and values you want your life to reflect: courage, tenacity, self-assurance. Perhaps more important than *what* you hope to accomplish is *why*. The *why* is the passion that drives you toward your goals.

Inevitable Self-doubt

Of all the adversities you may encounter in your STEM journey, self-doubt may be your biggest foe. At best, it slows your progress; at worst, it can cripple you and throw you off your path. It's one thing to tune out others who say you can't accomplish your goals; tuning out the doubting voices inside yourself is another thing entirely.

The important thing to know about self-doubt is that no one is immune. Ironically, often the higher people climb in their prospective fields, the greater the self-doubt. For many of our STEM Gems, success in their fields has meant recognizing the self-doubting voices, understanding where they're coming from and finding a way to move pas them.

Despite all her accolades, prizes and job promotions, graph theory mathematician Maria Chudnovsky has battled self-doubt many times. As a graduate student at Princeton University, she recalls a math department chairperson's welcome speech. "In it, he said, 'a graduate student is just like any other mathematician. The only difference is you're working on your first theorem.' There is always a feeling of 'what if I can't do this?' You learn to live with it." Doubt is something we must learn to acknowledge quickly when it arises and then set aside in order to forge ahead.

Sometimes the discouragement of others sows the seeds of doubt in ourselves. When computational biologist and geneticist Pardis Sabeti worked on her PhD research at the University of Oxford, some of her colleagues and mentors doubted that she would be able to innovate the new computational tools that she imagined. "Many people thought what I was trying to find in my research was a distraction," Sabeti recalls. "It seemed as if I was just going to go nowhere. My research was going in a new direction, and I had a lot of failures that made it seem like I was flailing. Though I was pursuing something I believed in, I understood that society will judge you until you're proven. And perhaps if you're a woman, the judgment is even more severe." She understood her self-doubt was rooted in what others believed — not in what she believed and not in reality.

For Sabeti and many other STEM Gems like her, pushing past the skeptics offered a valuable lesson: Determination is one of the best weapons against self-doubt. Determination comes from a place of choice inside you. It allows you to choose positive thoughts and take self-affirming action, like taking a needed break, seeking out a mentor, or connecting with supportive peers. It might be just the thing you need to remember that they, too, have moments of self-doubt.

Society or Me?

Sometimes doubt comes to us in the form of expectations that are placed on us by our culture. Society tells us that women are supposed to be caregivers of children, not career astrophysicists. Supermodels, not engineers who create super models.

All the messages about gender norms, which shape us so early in life — the pink versus blue, the dolls versus trucks — create a wall of noise and static that can also take us off course. Static can come from a classmate who frowns on you joining an after-school activity dominated by boys, a well-meaning relative who focuses on your appearance more than your ideas, or a mixed-gender study group where girls are put in the role of organizing ideas but never presenting them. Our STEM Gems have learned how to recognize the static and more importantly, how to tune it out. The first step is awareness.

Research indicates that girls pick up on gender stereotypes in math and science as early as elementary school. In 2007, French researchers placed third graders into two groups assigned to take a math test. Prior to the test, one group was asked to color gender-specific pictures (a girl with a doll and a boy with a ball). The other group was asked to color pictures of a landscape. Girls who had colored the landscape performed in a similar manner to boys on the most difficult math problems, while girls who had colored the doll picture scored worse. In other words, when girls and young women were reminded of gender stereotypes before taking a math test, they were more likely to perform in a way that tended to confirm gender stereotypes. This powerful phenomenon, known as stereotype threat, has been repeated numerous times in various ways, consistently pointing to the same finding: though girls and young women may not be conscious of it, the anxiety and self-doubt that gender stereotypes produce can undermine their ability to perform and excel in STEM.

Given the persistence of these studies, it's clear that long-held stereotypes about women in STEM won't change overnight. But being aware of them can help you tune out the noise and stay focused on your journey.

Among our STEM Gems, network scientist Jennifer Chayes' unconventional path to STEM success proves that challenging the authority and expectations of others is a crucial part of finding success. "If you're going to be a scientist, you have to challenge the norm." She encourages women to question whether insecurity comes from within or from outside pressures. "Not giving up is important. Just say to yourself, 'If I'm feeling insecure, it might not correspond to reality. It may just be that society has put into my head false ideas about what I can do, and I just need to ignore them.' Women must tell themselves that in order to succeed in STEM."

Chemical engineer Paula Hammond agrees that determination in STEM sometimes means tuning out society's messages about traditional female roles. "The key is to try your best

not to take cues from outside. When your environment pushes on you, you can push on it, too. Some will be surprised to see you at the table, but you can't allow that to intimidate you. Turn it into an opportunity for you to engage and instruct. Prove them wrong."

Barbara Liskov knows, perhaps more than most, how to navigate gender expectations. She entered into STEM in a decade when women had few career options besides nursing or teaching. This pioneering computer scientist and engineer challenged the norm in a profound way. Her sage advice is to "just go for it. Do what you're interested in. It's good to not pay too much attention to the expectations of society. My mantra is 'Don't be intimidated. Just do it.'"

"A" Is For Assertive

If the lives of our STEM Gems tell us anything, it's that determination goes hand in hand with assertiveness. Being assertive doesn't mean being aggressive. It simply means being direct and confident in expressing your views or needs.

Solar energy technologist Andrea Luecke credits much of her success to an assertive mindset. "My natural tendency to be assertive and direct has been advantageous. If you're not assertive, you'll get run over. In leadership, you must be very assertive." Like Luecke, online security expert Lorrie Faith Cranor knows that assertiveness is part of the STEM game. "Sometimes I'm at meetings and the men are all talking and I have to speak up extra loud to be heard." When her university department consistently scheduled weekly meetings at 5 p.m., she was assertive in requesting an alternate time so that she could meet her family obligations. Similarly, electrical engineer Carol Espy-Wilson has also had to assert herself and her presence in her field. "People just don't think of women, particularly minority women, when it comes time to put people forward for awards. I've really had to advocate for myself. That's a hard thing to do, and it requires energy. Some people never get what they deserve because they won't advocate for themselves."

Becoming an assertive communicator takes practice, and it can take different forms in different situations. Sometimes the best (and only) time to advocate for yourself assertively is in the moment. At other times, there can be big advantages to stepping back, reflecting and composing a thoughtful response. It is never too late to speak your mind.

For many of us, being assertive requires overcoming some degree of fear. We may worry how others will perceive us, and it can be hard to step outside ourselves and find perspective. The next time you feel you need to advocate for yourself, think about what you want the outcome to be *before* you enter the situation. Try to visualize yourself succeeding and what that might look like. Afterward, reflect on what happened. If you realized the outcome you wanted, how were you able to achieve that goal? If you didn't, consider how you can adjust your style for the next situation. Sometimes it is helpful to rely on a trusted peer to share some honest feedback about your communication style. Always approach situations with good intentions and stay true to yourself. ●

You've set off for STEM success, and you've got a strong compass to guide you when things go awry. As Hammond reminds us, "Difficulty is a fact of life. Accept it." Then, holding true to your values and your vision, do more than accept it. Learn from it. Adjust with it. And steer back toward your goals with purpose.

- Know your direction. Write down your goals and know the whys behind them.
- Recognize society's stereotypes, so that you can avoid absorbing them. Make it a game with your friends to spot examples of old-fashioned gender roles on television and in movies.
- Practice being assertive. Learn to recognize situations where advocating for yourself is important.
- Accept that there are no straight paths to success, that you will face obstacles and that you might lose your way. Believe in yourself enough to know that when those things happen, you can fall back on core values to steady you so that you can begin to move forward again.

CHAPTER 5
Work Hard

Americans have always worked hard, and we have always innovated. Our drive and idealism have carried us as a nation through revolution, one civil and two world wars, a Great Depression, the Dust Bowl, the Civil Rights movement and countless other adversities that tested our country's resolve. Likewise, our future promises daunting challenges: an exploding aging population, skyrocketing education costs, global competition for jobs, the threat of terrorism and, most disheartening, deepening fears that our nation is in decline and our planet in peril. And as before, it will fall to a new generation of thinkers and doers to meet those challenges head-on.

Your generation has yet to be named. Members of the generation ahead of you are known as Millennials. Generation X came before that and the legendary, post-World War II Baby Boomers before that. Labels like *selfie generation*, *digital natives*, *generation Z* and the *9/11 generation* have been tossed around for today's youth, but nothing yet has taken hold. The upcoming generation is still shaping its identity.

That's where you come in.

As part of this yet-to-be-named generation, you have the power to shape that legacy. The trials facing your generation are no less difficult than those of earlier times — simply different. These challenges will require a generation that embraces diversity of experience, develops pioneering new technology and holds tight to the belief that the best is yet to come.

More than any previous generation of STEM leaders, yours will be defined by the need to collaborate, working together across many disciplines and from diverse perspectives to tackle complex problems. In other words, it's time to debunk the notion of the lone STEM genius, gifted since birth and toiling away on formulas or equations. As it turns out, the capacity for genius lies in each one of us.

Debunking the Genius Myth

In movies and storybooks, in the posters that line your classroom walls, we still pay tribute to legendary figures of genius, from Isaac Newton to Marie Curie to Albert Einstein to Stephen Hawking. Though they were all patient observers with bottomless curiosity and the determination to persist through failure, we remember them as naturally brilliant, with a genius that was fully formed practically from the womb.

Neuroscientists now suspect that genius is related not to any kind of native intelligence, but to a person's ability to approach problems creatively and learn from failure. In this way, genius can be understood more as a frame of mind, or perhaps a series

of steps on a ladder in which the climbing lies in the effort. Does that make genius more environmental than genetic? Some of the most innovative, groundbreaking STEM Gems in these pages believe the answer is a resounding YES.

Melanie Matchett Wood is a number theory mathematician. The number of people in the world who truly understand her expanding theories could probably fit in your bedroom. But her perspective on math achievement is no different than her view of achievement in sports. "Math is something that you get better at by practicing and doing more and by hard work. It's not a matter of having a math brain or not having a math brain. It's not as if you can be a math person or not a math person. The 'I'm not so good at it' excuse is a statement about how much work you've put in. When I run into people, especially adults, they have this idea that it's a switch that's either on or off in their brain. That's entirely untrue. It's the result of hard work."

For some of our STEM Gems, the very subjects that helped them achieve greatness proved a struggle at first. Internet gaming technologist Holly Liu learned the basics of the Java programming language from books the summer before graduate school. It wasn't until she began pair programming — working alongside other programmers — that her talents soared. And midway through a difficult first-year math course at Harvard, dynamical systems mathematician Bryna Kra wanted to quit.

Kra might have doubted her path, taking her early performance as a sign she wasn't meant to pursue her passion. Instead, she voiced her concerns to her professor, who encouraged her to work hard and finish the course. She stuck with it, passed the class and dabbled in a new line of study: philosophy. After a time, she returned to that very same professor and told him philosophy didn't excite her. He encouraged her to embrace math again and she recommitted herself to STEM.

From an outside perspective, Wood, Liu and Kra may look like born STEM geniuses. When you look closer, though, what becomes clear is that they all shared a burning passion, a stick-to-it determination and an ability to propel themselves through failures to achieve their goals.

Could it be that that's all genius really is? And if it is, how will you be a genius today?

Work Ethic

What exactly is a work ethic? Is work ethic something we are born with, something that is rooted deeply in our personalities, or do we hone the discipline and focus associated with hard work along the way to adulthood? To help us shape a good definition, let's examine six characteristics often associated with work ethic:

- Integrity — honesty, trustworthiness
- Responsibility — how you work and how *much* you work
- Dedication (with an emphasis on quality) — not simply getting it done but getting it done *right*
- Discipline — staying on task and completing tasks
- Persistence — rising above adversity
- Teamwork — meeting goals together helps everyone

A strong, positive work ethic is evident in each one of our STEM Gems. According to network scientist Jennifer Chayes, "A lot of it is just *work*, and not getting bummed out and just the nerve to keep working." In different ways, all of the women in these pages reflect the core principles associated with work ethic.

Hard work demands integrity. While others in her profession run software to create visual models of an area of the earth's subsurface, geophysicist Debbie Lawrence achieves a higher level of precision by applying razor-sharp critical thinking and problem-solving skills to create even more accurate models, knowing that some parts of the earth's subsurface aren't handled well by the software. Companies who rely on such models to set up million-dollar drilling operations can count on experts with integrity like Lawrence to ensure that their operations are successful.

Another strong component of work ethic is responsibility. Many of our STEM Gems became employees at a young age, including global health scientist Helene Gayle. She recalls, "My summers growing up I spent working in my father's store. It instilled an ability to work with a wide range of people. It also cultivated a sense of responsibility. It felt like a thing we had a stake in and were responsible for."

Economist Susan Athey once spent nearly a month at her MIT office completing a math problem. Her dedication — a critical component of work ethic — paid off when she emerged victorious at the end of that work marathon with a 40-page mathematical proof. According to Jonathan Levin, a Stanford economics professor who has witnessed Athey's work ethic, her 75- hour work weeks are well-known to her peers. "She really cares about making sure you don't take short cuts and that everything is done incredibly carefully. She has a remarkable energy to get things done."

Anna Nagurney, a network systems mathematician, knows how critical discipline is to success. She worked through every problem in her calculus textbook and then sought other textbooks and worked through those problems as well in order to master the fundamentals of advanced math. Nagurney believes that "hard work will get you to where you want to be and that discipline and focus are very important to success in STEM. The hard-working tortoise beats the fast-talking hare every day."

Hard work requires not just discipline and dedication, but also persistence through setbacks. When math got tough in college, data scientist Rachel Schutt leaned in. "At some point math started to be pretty hard for me. My father told me that I should study math even though it was hard, because it's the hard things we should tackle in life. That made sense to me."

Lastly, skilled teamwork is an all-essential component to work ethic. Companies are increasingly moving away from old-fashioned boss-employee models to leadership-team dynamics. For Liu, thinking creatively about the best use of people in her 1,000-employee company, Kabam, is just as challenging and rewarding as designing games. "A company of this size involves communication nodes and feedback loops."

To facilitate team work, Liu fosters that communication. "I try to reduce the space between Kabam-ers, because the smaller the space, the more trust there is, and the more trust, the more information sharing. I really enjoy getting people together and getting them excited about the product."

It's important to remember that hard work is not without sacrifice. Because biostatistician Stacy Lindborg found her way to statistics initially through her engineering and psychology majors, she had some academic catching up to do. "For the last year of my undergraduate, every elective was a math course to try to prepare for graduate school. I was in the library taking 18 hours of credits in math while my friends were taking trips."

A strong work ethic also means never reaching a point where you believe you know everything about a subject. STEM fields are dynamic and constantly evolving. Nurture that love of learning. Embrace new methods, ideas and research, and you'll go further than you ever thought possible.

Is work ethic, then, something within our control? Without a doubt. Each day presents challenges. How we handle that adversity defines how others perceive us and how we see ourselves. To develop a healthy, balanced work ethic, incorporate these tips into whatever challenge you find yourself facing:

- Rock a positive attitude.
- Be on time.
- Keep a task list and cross items off as you accomplish them.
- Improve daily.
- Know your weaknesses. Set a plan in motion to improve on those weaknesses.
- Never stop learning.

Support

As any adventurer knows, good support starts at the foundation. Just as cushioned insoles provide your body with the proper support for a physical trek, emotional insoles are needed for any journey of the mind and heart. Look to these individuals to provide you with a boost of energy and encouragement when yours runs low:

- Friends
- Parents
- Siblings/Extended Family
- Teachers/Role Models/Mentors
- Libraries/Clubs/Organizations

Forensic scientist Karen Olson recalls a time when she considered quitting graduate school. "Encouragement from my parents, peers and finally seeing my work pay off after my first paper was accepted kept me going."

As the mother of three children for much of her career, immunologist Laurie Glimcher says she could not have risen to the top of her field without the support of her parents.

"My parents lived nearby and were an enormous help to me. They provided constant and tireless support. On weekends, when my husband was on call, I remember packing up the kids and literally moving into my parents' house. I would be able to grab a few hours to run to the lab, while my parents took the kids to the playground. I know my children appreciated developing such a close bond with their grandparents. I don't know how I would have gotten through that extremely busy time in my life without my parents helping me to balance work and family."

Bio-technologist Erika Ebbel Angle offers advice that could apply to any point in a person's STEM career: Simply put, mentors matter. "Find mentors who can support you. There's no way you can do it alone. Find people who can help you. It means being proactive. You're not expected to know how to do it all yourself. None of us were born with all of this knowledge." ●

Success in STEM isn't about being perfect. It's about effort. Let your work ethic propel you forward and inspire others to do the same. Who knows? Your impact might help to shape a generation.

- Redefine genius in your mind. Recognize that potential in yourself.
- Practice a strong work ethic now. Your adult self will thank you.
- Find your support. Ask for help. Recognize that everyone needs help sometimes.
- Learn to balance by cultivating and developing hobbies.
- Never stop learning.

chapter 6
Take Risks

Reaching to go beyond is an endeavor filled with risk. And no matter what your personal threshold for risk happens to be — it could be jumping out of a plane with a parachute, or it could be choosing a tough class knowing your GPA might take a dip — there is no escaping the fact that taking chances is frightening.

But like the huge leaps involved in skydiving, taking risks in your STEM path doesn't have to mean walking into a situation haphazardly. When we picture skydivers, we picture bodies in free fall. What we don't see is the preparation, the training, the information gathering, back-up plans and support behind the jump. A skydive is a well-planned, calculated risk, with exhilarating results. The same holds true in STEM.

Ainissa Ramirez, a materials engineer, took the kind of risk few people in academia could imagine taking: She walked away from a position of rare achievement and prestige as a tenured college professor. While teaching at Yale University, she began *Science Saturdays*, an original and free science education program for middle-school kids. When the program launched in 2004, she crossed her fingers hoping to get 50 kids. She got 100. "Aristotle says that your calling lies at the intersections of the world's needs and your talents. I was at a decision-making point where I could have continued along the same path, or I could do something that was really scary but could satisfy me far more than anything else had." Soon after Ramirez took the leap, others started to recognize her

passion, innovative work and talent for communicating science to wide audiences. She was asked to present a talk for TED, a global series of conferences viewed by millions of people online each year.

As she followed her passion more deeply, her high-stakes risk continued to pay dividends: Shortly after giving the TED talk, Ramirez was recognized with the Massachusetts Institute of Technology's (MIT) TR100 Award, an honor recognizing the top 100 innovators under the age of 35.

Ramirez packed her parachute when she made the jump from academia to science communication. She prepared for her decision by transitioning slowly, getting *Science Saturdays* off the ground while still teaching at the college level. She let the new project grow organically and contemplated that intersection between her talents and the world's needs.

For Debbie Sterling, a product designer and mechanical engineer, it was the toy industry that marked a new frontier for risk-taking. As she walked across the stage at Stanford

University to receive her engineering degree, she developed "an obsession with changing the status quo and tackling the staggering gender gap in engineering." Sterling knew that meant tapping into the science and math know-how of young girls. Using materials from the hardware store, she built a prototype of her engineering toy, GoldieBlox, and showcased the creation at the New York Toy Fair — where toy industry veterans discouraged her from pursuing her dreams or ignored her altogether. To get her toy into production, she took a risk and launched an online fundraising Kickstarter campaign: raise $150,000 in 30 days to create construction sets and books for girls. "Thirty days to prove those toy industry veterans wrong. Thirty days to prove that I wasn't the only one who wanted more for our girls. I hit my goal in five days."

Sterling's journey illuminates the importance of preparation in risk-taking. Before she struck out on her own and challenged conventional thinking, she did her homework on the industry she was up against. "[Some members] escorted me up and down the aisles of glittery princesses and busty dolls to show me what success looks like. One man set up appointments for me to meet with struggling toy companies to give me a 'dose of reality.'" When the time came to take a risk, she designed something that filled a huge void in the toy market for girls. Her calculated risk led to greater rewards than she could have imagined.

Ultimately, new frontiers demand that you take a leap of faith in yourself. Ramirez and Sterling both believed they had something unique to offer the world and had the courage to take that leap.

Overcoming Fears, Leaping with Faith

Another benefit to risk taking is that it conditions you to face your fears — especially that of failure — so fears are minimized the next time around. Carol Espy-Wilson's fear of failure almost held her back from pursuing her PhD at MIT, the best school for her area of specialization within electrical engineering. "I just sat with myself and realized that I was intimidated by MIT. I was afraid. Once I realized that, there was no choice. I had to go. I promised myself when I was a child that I would never allow fear to guide my decisions."

Espy-Wilson went on to become the first African-American woman to earn a PhD in electrical engineering at MIT. Her accolades include awards from the National Science Foundation and the National Institutes of Health.

With her work ethic and determination, there's no doubt she would have been successful no matter the school she had chosen. What makes her an inspiration is that she faced her own fears. Facing fear means you are on the right path. No matter what the outcome is, you are bound to learn something important about who you are, what you can achieve and how to get there.

In the world of science and technology, the most dramatic advances often take place where risk meets reward.

From a young age, immunologist Laurie Glimcher learned to embrace risk. "My father taught me to never be afraid to try something new and to be stubborn as a bull. Those lessons have stayed with me throughout my life and have dramatically influenced my career. I give young women the same advice. To be successful as a scientist, you can't be afraid to take risks. Laboratory breakthroughs are never made by being cautious. There are so many talented and smart young women, but they lack the same self-confidence that a lot of men have."

Pardis Sabeti, a Harvard computational biologist and geneticist, needed tremendous confidence when she approached universities to begin research programs for deadly viruses, starting with Lasso fever. The risks she took on not only involved her own young career and reputation, but also the liability of an entire university, which would need to house samples of the pathogens. "Starting as a junior faculty member and trying to go into a research area where there are a lot of safety and other issues that you have to deal with, and having

an administration that's risk-averse...there are exceptional challenges in trying to start a program involving deadly viruses."

Now, as a lead investigator, Sabeti stands at the forefront of research on Ebola, a disease few facilities in the U.S. are bold enough to research.

Failing Forward

Risk taking also has the potential to teach us one of the most valuable lessons in life: how to learn from failure and persevere beyond it. Although we rarely think of famously successful people as failures, all of them have stumbled and faltered along the way. Abraham Lincoln failed politically and professionally ten times before being elected to the presidency in 1860. The first cartoon production company that Walt Disney launched from his home garage went bankrupt. Before he founded the Ford Motor Company, one of the largest carmakers in the world, Henry Ford's first two automotive companies failed abysmally. Michael Jordan, arguably the most talented player to ever walk onto a basketball court sums it up best: "I have missed more than 9,000 shots in my career. I have lost almost 300 games. On 26 occasions I have been entrusted to take the game-winning shot, and I missed. I have failed over and over and over again in my life. And that is why I succeed."

Failure is the soil from which new ideas take seed. That's true in life, and it's especially true in science and technology, where random mishaps can spur major discoveries, and where experiments and inventions repeatedly fail — until one day they don't. The 1928 discovery of the antibiotic penicillin, one of the greatest advances in medicine, came about when a British scientist who could never keep his lab space clean noticed a curious mold in his petri dish. The invention of gunpowder, a mixture of salt peter, sulfur and charcoal, happened when ninth-century Chinese alchemists tried to make an elixir for immortality.

And in 1964, two astronomers in New Jersey famously convinced themselves they had failed, trying to build a radio telescope to map signals from the Milky Way. They were frustrated at every turn by an annoying background static that kept coming in. Was it coming from the nearby Manhattan skyline? Was it the droppings from pigeons that would nest in the antenna? Was it the seasons? For more than a year, Arno Penzias and Robert Wilson tested all the possibilities (and cleaned a lot of bird poop), trying to silence the noise interfering with their experiments.

It turned out that the static wasn't actually getting in the way of their science: It *was* the science. The astronomers had stumbled onto Cosmic Microwave Background Radiation, the first convincing evidence of the Big Bang theory of the cosmos. Years later, in 1978, the two scientists would go on to win the Nobel Prize in physics for their discovery. ●

We don't necessarily have to look to science to know that failure and risk lead to greatness and change. The Former First Lady and women's rights advocate Eleanor Roosevelt once famously said, "Do one thing every day that scares you." She also lived by those words, whether facing crowds of angry protestors to meet with leaders of the Civil Rights Movement, or holding female-only press conferences to pressure newspapers to hire female journalists. She took calculated risks, confronted fear and risked embarrassing failure so that future generations could reap the rewards. If you're willing to step out of your comfort zone, you can, too.

Break the mold. Overcome your fear. Take a risk. Or 20. Sail into unchartered waters.

- When taking risks, let your passion be your guide.

- Pack a parachute. Do not leap unprepared.

- Look for the new opportunities that risk brings.

- Take a leap of faith in yourself. Show your confidence.

- Learn from failure. Use it to propel you higher.

- Do one thing every day that scares you.

CHAPTER 7
Refine Your Vision

Successful people tend to have something in common: a vision. They project themselves into the future, taking into account all aspects of their lives that matter to them: family, friends, finances, career, achievements, hobbies. They take stock of what they value and what fulfills them, they consider what steps are needed to get where they want to be and they plan.

To get beyond the stage of daydreams, your hopes need to become plans. That plan can start with a powerful tool: a vision statement.

Think of a vision statement as a commitment to yourself, an intention to follow through that grounds your dreams in specific actions. A vision statement doesn't set your dreams in stone. Your vision will likely change — and probably should change — as you acquire more life experiences and knowledge. But writing down what you want and how to get there will bring those dreams into real focus, above the noise and distractions of everyday life. Use language as if you are already living the life you envision. Write a few sentences or dive deep into your vision and fill pages. Share your vision statement with those closest to you or keep it private.

The goal-setting described in Chapter Four is part of this statement, but it is more concrete and focused compared to a vision statement. It is the difference between trekking through a lush forest with a detailed map and seeing it in all its glory from 30,000 feet in the air, stretched out beneath you.

Role Models

Developing a vision for yourself — your ability to see the big picture — is one of the most important tasks you will have as you make your way along your STEM path. Like any young person trying to understand the big picture, you are bound to need some help and inspiration along the way. That's where role models come in.

Role models are an essential component to supporting, challenging and directing your vision. A role model can be your senator or your neighbor, a famous athlete or your grandmother. Anyone who has a quality or qualities you aspire to for yourself can be a role model. Here's the challenge: On any given day, you might meet or read about people you *don't* want to emulate. The media glare often shines the brightest on public figures who make really poor choices. It isn't hard to see why young some women struggle to find positive role models.

The best way to find the role model that is right for you is to start with you. Your values, beliefs and passions will

be powerful guides as you seek to surround yourself with inspirational people.

Trying Out Role Models

A recent university study asked 42 college students to recall the people who inspired them in childhood and adolescence. Researchers distilled the participants' feedback into five qualities that all good role models share:

- Passion
- Values
- Determination
- Fairness
- Selflessness

Do you agree with this list? What qualities would you add? Remove? Write down qualities you think are essential in a role model, then ask yourself the following questions:

- Who is leading the life I would like to lead?
- Who is doing work that I want to do?
- Who has characteristics that I value (but that I may not yet have)?
- How are my strengths similar?
- What sets me apart from this role model? How am I unique?

From the perspectives of our 44 STEM Gems, increasing the number of female role models and their visibility is critical to making sure young women thrive in STEM. From a single life-changing female mentor, like the one who inspired architect Jeanne Gang to radically re-think her approach to architecture, to a nurturing community of peers like Women 2.0, the network of startup entrepreneurs launched by startup champion and entrepreneur Shaherose Charania, our STEM Gems fully recognize how important role models

have been in supporting and advancing their professional and personal lives.

Erika Ebbel Angle, a bio-technologist, believes role models are key to getting more girls into fields that aren't as well represented, such as physics and computer science. "There are a lot of female doctors and biologists. But there are way fewer women in computer science and in tech. We need young women to know that they can pursue these fields and still be feminine." Karen Olson, a forensic scientist, echoes that thought, saying that "if girls are shown that they can have any career they want, and have role models in their life that prove it, it will help close the gender gap."

Laurie Glimcher, an immunologist, believes this intervention should start when girls are toddlers. "We need to expose girls to the wonders of science when they're in kindergarten and support and mentor them to go into STEM fields throughout middle and high school. Part of the problem is a lack of self-confidence, and we need family members, teachers and other mentors to act as role models and tell girls that it's okay to go into STEM as a career."

American heroes like Abraham Lincoln and Rosa Parks are often touted as role models, and much has been written about their lives. But it's important to keep in mind that extraordinary role models may be hiding among the ordinary people you come into contact with everyday — your parents, your teachers, community leaders and dedicated volunteers — not just in individuals enshrined in history books or prominent on magazine covers and TV screens.

Once you discover the role models who are right in your midst, the next question is a no-brainer: Why not ask him or her to mentor you?

A Mentor: The Special Kind of Role Model

A recent survey of 1,000 female executives conducted by the networking site LinkedIn found that only one in five women have a mentor. These results support an earlier, similar survey by *Harvard Business Review*. Respondents stated several reasons for not pursuing mentorship, including the belief that hard work and long hours alone are enough to accomplish their goals. Hard work and dedication are important components to success, but these women are missing the intellectual boost, emotional support and all-important professional network a mentor can provide. As a result they are alone in doing the hardest work of all — finding and fulfilling their vision. But you don't have to be.

Mentors are role models who take a special interest in your success. If great role models inspire from afar, then mentors nourish and sustain you with day-to-day inspiration. Mentors share their experiences, struggles and triumphs with you so that you may benefit from their journeys. They challenge you to do better, they eagerly follow your progresss and they can open critical doors of opportunity.

Angle believes that finding a mentor is all about being proactive. "If you're interested in something, find someone who can sit down and talk with you about it. If someone told me at age 11 that I would start a biotech company, I would have said, 'Whatever. How do you expect me to do that?' So it happens over time. And you never do it alone."

Many of our STEM Gems name educators as the primary mentors who helped shape their vision of themselves. One of network systems mathematician Anna Nagurney's mentors was the late Stella Dafermos, a Brown University professor who reviewed Nagurney's application to the doctoral program there. "I was drawn to her because she was the only female professor in both applied math and engineering." Archaeologist Michele Koons's mentor at the University of Denver supported her in reaching her goal of attending Harvard University for an advanced degree. Nuclear engineer Sarah Kovaleski's high school calculus teacher opened her eyes to all the possibilities awaiting her in a STEM field. "She also happened to be a young woman and quickly became one of my role models."

Planetary scientist Carolyn Porco's mentor, the famous astronomer and cosmologist Carl Sagan, had a profound impact on her career. Porco interacted with Sagan over many years, first when she was a graduate student, then later as a peer and collaborator on the iconic 1990 photograph of Earth *Pale Blue Dot*, and again in 1994 as a character consultant for his movie, *Contact*. Sagan wrote a glowing letter of recommendation for Porco to receive full professorship two weeks before he passed away in December 1996. Her beloved mentor had received a bone marrow transplant shortly before writing it. "He couldn't have been feeling very

well. But knowing how important this letter would be to me, he wrote it anyway. So if you want to know how I feel about Carl Sagan and why, you need look no further than this infinite kindness, because it says it all. I remember the times when he felt someone had been particularly vicious or disrespectful to me and either actively came to my defense or took me aside to shore me up. I came to feel that the man had my back."

When you find mentors like these, be sure to value their time. Volunteer to help in ways that benefit you both. Show them that you're willing to work hard and earn their advice and guidance. Whether you learned from them in grade school or a college seminar, stay in touch, let them know how your vision is developing and always acknowledge the role they've played in shaping it.

Forty-Four Women, Two Lists, One Living, Breathing Vision

By reading this book, you've got a pretty good head start in finding the role models and mentors that can help you shape your own vision. Our STEM Gems come from big cities and small towns, from every region of the country, from every economic class and from wide-ranging ethnicities. They are currently doing extraordinary things, some traditional, some decidedly non-traditional, at institutions in 17 U.S. states and Canada. Perhaps one or more of these inspirational 44 will plant the seeds of possibility and greatness within you.

Some of these careers, like urban planner or biostatistician or actuary, may be unfamiliar to you. But no doubt some thing or things will spark your imagination and might even spark a new vision.

As you explore their careers, go back to that original vision statement. Revisit and revise it. And as you do, it may help to make two lists, side by side.

On one side, list all the qualities you think are essential in a role model or mentor. On the other, list possible candidates. Consider all the people with whom you come into contact with in a day, a week, a month. Start with teachers — past and present — and family and branch out in unexpected directions from there.

As these lists grow, draw lines connecting those all-important qualities to the people you've identified as possible role models. Some may have one quality in particular, others may have more than one. Doing this mapping technique is bound to give you more insight and generate new ideas about mentors and role models who can help you shape your own vision. ●

It may seem daunting at first — committing your vision to paper, approaching mentors, imagining yourself as one of the 44 role models in these pages. But as you'll read, all 44 STEM Gems began in the same place, at the same age, with the same passions but also the same doubts. As your vision starts to take shape and become something real, you will find yourself doing just what these women had to do at one point or another: living out their own unique vision in the real world.

Your future awaits.

- Write your vision statement. Consider sharing it with others. Revisit as needed.
- Complete the Two Lists activity to brainstorm possible role models and mentors in your life.
- Consider our 44 STEM Gems as role models. Consult their stories for wisdom and guidance.
- Live your vision.

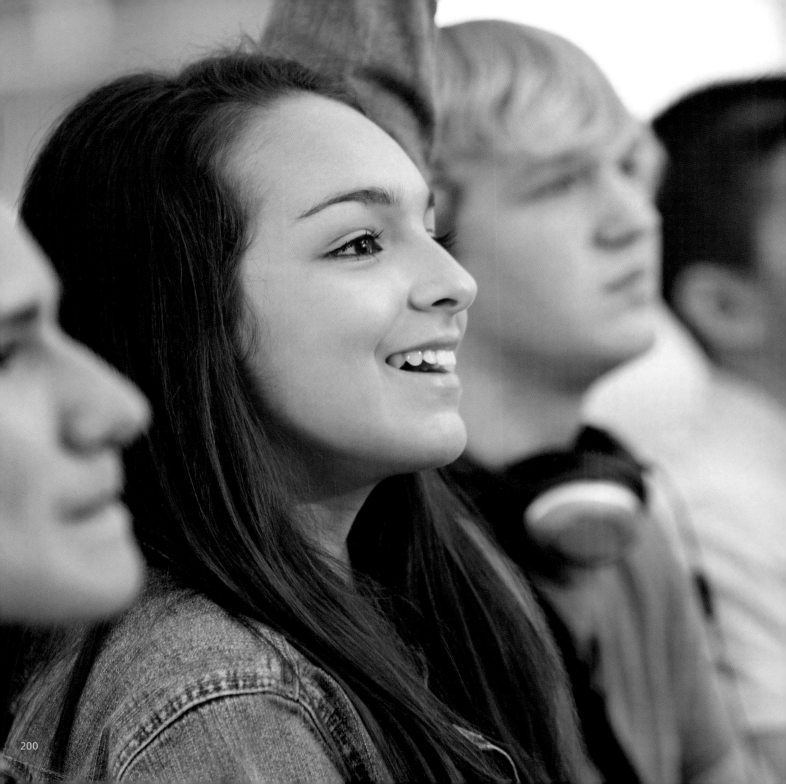

CHAPTER 8
The Gender Gap

Gather 100 middle school girls together in a gymnasium and ask to see a show of hands: How many have an interest in science, technology, engineering or mathematics? The most recent statistics put the number of raised hands at about 74. Awesome, right?

Get those same 100 girls together between high school and college and again ask how many would consider a STEM career. This time, 28 might raise their hands. Biology fields? Eleven hands. Math and physical science fields? Two or three hands. Computer science? *Maybe* one hand. Statistically speaking, it would take a group of 300 young women to find one willing to major in computer science.

What explains this drastic drop in STEM interest during those critical years between middle school and high school graduation? Are young women moving through an educational system plagued by gender bias? Are there too few visible, celebrated women currently in STEM fields to serve as role models? Does our society derail or limit young women's ambitions with old-fashioned stereotypes and misinformation?

These questions and more haunt those in education and industry who are trying to eliminate the gender gap in STEM careers. Most agree that it is not attributable to any *one* factor but to a combination of missteps, industry practices and societal influences that must be addressed to turn things around.

The Gender Gap in Schools

According to a 2009 report published by the American Association of University Women (AAUW), *Why So Few Women in Stem?*, male and female high school students on average are taking the same number of STEM courses. This marks an improvement from 1990, when the STEM course load for boys was slightly higher. The report also found that both boys and girls in today's STEM classes are earning better grades and are better prepared for STEM majors in college.

If these trends held beyond high school, women would fill half of the seats in all STEM courses in college and graduate with half of all STEM degrees. Women would comprise half of the STEM industry workforce. Half of the people interviewed in the media as experts in their field would be women. Women, who make up half of the population, would make up half of the STEM population. But it isn't half. Not even close.

Researchers are looking closely at that critical transition period between high school and college, when the gender gap in STEM education starts to grow from a crack to a canyon.

At the same time, there is increasing awareness that empowering young women for success in a STEM field begins much earlier in their education.

Research over the past two decades makes a strong case that boys and girls can sit in the same classrooms with the same teachers and still receive a much different education. A 1994 study on gender bias by Myra Sadker and David Sadker, education advocates and authors of *Failing at Fairness: How America's Schools Cheat Girls*, found that boys in elementary and middle school classrooms called out answers eight times more frequently than girls. In response, the study found teachers were far more likely to indulge the outbursts from boys and reprimand girls for the same behavior. Other studies have found that classroom textbooks often minimize or ignore the contributions of women and minorities in core subject areas.

In 1992, the AAUW issued recommendations for change to combat and reduce gender bias. They included teacher training to recognize and avoid bias when evaluating and interacting with students. The recommendations also called for school curricula to better reflect the contributions of women throughout history and "dispel myths about math and science being 'inappropriate' for women." The AAUW also recommended showcasing "women role models in scientific and technological fields, disseminating career information and offering 'hands-on' experiences and work groups in science and math classes."

Melanie Matchett Wood, a number theory mathematician, advocates a critical emphasis on math and science for girls in middle school, when students "really start to develop an image of themselves and who they are. One of the big tasks is to make it possible for more middle school girls to identify with being good at math."

Holly Liu, an internet gaming technologist, believes that presenting STEM in a way that appeals to larger numbers of women can also have a huge impact. "A great example of this is a programming class at the University of California, Berkeley that was re-imagined to be more project-based. This increased the ratio of women to men — for the first time, ever, more women enrolled in that class. It didn't lower the bar. The quality was the same. Women are more likely to join project-based programming classes than more theoretically-based programming classes. We have to ask ourselves, are we introducing science that favors men over women? How can we present STEM so that it reaches more women?"

The Gender Gap in Industry

In 1979, Sharon Sassler, a professor of policy analysis and management at Cornell University, began the first comprehensive study comparing women in STEM and non-STEM professions. She and her team tracked 258 female STEM professionals and 842 non-STEM professionals through mid-life to determine how many remained in their prospective fields. After 12 years, half of all STEM-career women had switched to other careers, while only 20 percent of non-STEM-career women changed careers. This is a puzzling statistic, considering that most STEM jobs offer significantly higher pay than non-STEM jobs.

"A lot of people still think it's having children that leads to STEM women's exits," notes Sassler. "It's not the family. Women leave before they have children or even get married. Our findings suggest that there is something unique about the STEM climate that results in women leaving."

Pardis Sabeti, a computational biologist and geneticist, has a theory about why that climate is problematic. "The culture of science needs to change. The way we do science is not effective, and it's not good for young people. It's often toxic and there is a lot of bad behavior going on. A lot of young women look at this field and say it's not for me because of the cutthroat environment. The work of science does not exhaust me — it energizes me — but the politics and culture of science sometimes makes me feel as if it's not worth it. We need to create a positive, ethical environment. We'll be able to retain more women once we do this."

Wood supports more family-friendly policies to support women in academia, where conferences and networking are critical to sharing ideas and launching collaborative projects. "Traveling and speaking on your research is a big part of what mathematicians do," she says. More funding to support researchers with families to attend conferences would level the playing field and allow women to advance in their careers while also raising children.

Andrea Luecke, a solar energy technologist, is passionate about exposing the gender gap within her own industry. "We need people to be vocal and stand up and say we need to be more diverse because it makes business sense and it's the right thing to do. We also need more racial and cultural and socioeconomic diversity as well. Everyone needs to be at the table."

Ainissa Ramirez, a materials engineer, believes industry and academia will change once conscientious individuals and groups pressure the government to make science funding for universities conditional on closing the gender gap. "We need a ground swell of litigation to fix the enterprise of science. It's mostly funded by government agencies… They need to say: if you want this funding, change your practices. If these government agencies really wanted to close the gender gap in academia, they could easily say, 'Look, you're not getting money because you haven't hired X-number of tenure-track female faculty in engineering.'"

From academia to industry, a closer look at the reasons women in STEM choose to leave their professions is warranted. If starting a family is a factor, what policies can be implemented to attract and retain women so they don't lose valuable research time while rearing children? If women who have shown consistent achievement in STEM are largely ignored for promotions and tenure, who is making these decisions? How can private industry foster real equity in STEM fields so that research benefits from having all talented professionals participating?

The Gender Gap in Society

Erika Ebbel Angle, a bio-technologist, would love to see women pioneers in STEM celebrated in the same way we celebrate women pioneers in entertainment. "Imagine Sally Ride on the cover of *Vogue*. Why aren't female STEM leaders on the covers of *Vogue* magazine? How can we make STEM — and education, in general — more glamorous? How do we make education that cool, sexy thing that people want to pursue?"

Barbara Liskov, a computer scientist and engineer, speaks specifically to the perceived "nerd culture" that surrounds STEM fields. "Think about the programs on TV. How many women scientists do you see? How are they depicted? How are the men in technology depicted? Is it something that you think might make women want to do that stuff?"

To some degree, this "nerd culture" is changing. In our digitally dependent society, techies are now the ones we rely on to keep things humming. There is a new respect inherent to being part of technology, and in a larger scope, part of STEM. But it's unclear whether that new badge of cool extends to women in the same way it does to men. A Google search for "female nerds" and "female geeks," for example, tends to produce commentary on women's appearance, not their intelligence or accomplishments.

It can take generations to shift social attitudes or change a particular culture, including the culture of STEM. But as any societal shift has shown us, culture works both ways: It can resist change, but it is also susceptible to big changes, influenced by the people who make up the culture. Think about the tremendous power you have to change the culture of STEM just by entering it and sticking around. As Mahatma Gandhi said, "Be the change that you wish to see in the world."

Closing the Gender Gap

Our culture has come a long way since Liskov became one of the first women to earn a PhD in computer science.

Women are now at the helm of top internet gaming sites, serve as experts in robotics, build models to solve age-old math theorems and fight cancer in exciting new ways. Women are leading debates on global issues like climate change, water rights and local concerns that impact ordinary people on a daily basis. Women are conquering everything from nanotechnology to astrophysics. Women are scientists and techies and engineers and mathematicians. Women are here, celebrated in these pages, and they are eagerly awaiting your arrival, the next generation of STEM Gems. ●

What can you do to close the gender gap? Let's look at some proactive steps you can take to make a difference at your school, at your job and in your social circles:

School
- Be on the lookout for gender bias in the classroom. If you see it, discuss it privately with your teacher. He/She may be unaware this is taking place.
- Ask your STEM teachers if they can implement more group and project-based activities. Discuss the possibility of reaching out to role models in the community.
- If your school doesn't have a STEM-oriented club, start one. Search online for helpful resources and enlist your principal and teachers along the way.

Industry/Workplace
- Seek out opportunities to demonstrate your range of skills, even if it isn't in your job description. Go beyond and be a team member.
- Foster a positive work environment that celebrates and respects everyone's contributions.
- Seek out more responsibilities (and more pay) once you have proven yourself as an employee that goes beyond.

Society
- Recognize the influence you have on your peers and younger girls. Use that power to make a positive difference.
- Support your friends and peers, especially in STEM classes. Encourage them to think beyond what society tells them about themselves.
- Ask for support when you need it, and accept support when it is offered.
- Learn to listen to your own instincts about what interests you. Learn to question others who think certain interests are only for boys or only for girls.
- Celebrate being a girl. Then go out and conquer the world.

Bibliography

Science

Jennifer Chayes

"A Chat With Jennifer Chayes, 2013 Catalyst Award Nominee," Science Club for Girls, accessed August 19, 2014. http://scienceclubforgirls.org/news-events-2/blog/jennifer-chayes-2013-science-club-for-girls-catalyst-award-honoree.

Gregory T. Huang, "Microsoft Research's Jennifer Chayes: 5 Projects for the Future of Computing," Xconomy, April 9, 2012, accessed August 19, 2014. http://www.xconomy.com/boston/2012/04/09/microsoft-researchs-jennifer-chayes-5-projects-for-the-future-of-computing/.

Jennifer Chayes, interview via phone, August 11, 2014.

"Jennifer Tour Chayes," Microsoft Research, accessed August 19, 2014. http://research.microsoft.com/en-us/um/people/jchayes/.

Inez Fung

Inez Fung, feedback via email, September 22, 2014.

"Inez Fung," Our Environment at Berkeley, Department of Environmental Science, Policy and Management, accessed June 2, 2014. http://ourenvironment.berkeley.edu/people_profiles/inez-fung/.

"Inez Fung, The Climate Modeler," National Academy of Sciences, accessed June 2, 2014. http://www.iwaswondering.com/inez_homepage.html.

"InterViews Series: Inez Fung." National Academy of Sciences, 2011. http://www.nasonline.org/news-and-multimedia/podcasts/interviews/inez-fung.html.

Helene Gayle

Erin Carlyle, "Power Woman Helene Gayle: How to Make the Greatest Impact on the Most People," *Forbes*, May 22, 2013, accessed July 11, 2014. http://www.forbes.com/sites/erincarlyle/2013/05/22/power-woman-helene-gayle-how-to-make-the-greatest-impact-on-the-most-people/.

Helene Gayle, interview via phone, July 10, 2014.

Saporta, Maria, "CARE's Helene Gayle to Lead New Global Non-Profit for McKinsey & Co.," *Atlanta Business Chronicle*, March 19, 2015, accessed December 14, 2015. http://www.bizjournals.com/atlanta/news/2015/03/19/care-s-helene-gayle-to-lead-new-global-nonprofit.html.

Sheena McKenzie and Isha Sesay, "Helene Gayle: Meet the CEO Feeding the World," CNN, September 17, 2013, accessed May 22, 2013. http://edition.cnn.com/2013/09/17/business/helene-gayle-meet-the-ceo/.

"Spotlight on CARE USA President & CEO Helene D. Gayle, MD, MPH," Care.org, October 9, 2013, accessed May 22, 2013. http://www.care.org/about/people/helene-gayle.

Laurie Glimcher

"Breaking down barriers to clinical translation: an interview with Laurie Glimcher," *Disease Models & Mechanisms*, The Company of Biologists, Ltd. Jan 2012; 5(1): 6–8, accessed July 1, 2014. doi: 10.1242/dmm.009191.

"Dean Laurie H. Glimcher, MD," Weill Cornell Medical College, accessed July 1, 2014. http://weill.cornell.edu/about-us/dean/dean-laurie-glimcher.html.

Laurie Glimcher, interview via email, June 30, 2014.

"Laurie H. Glimcher," Lean In.org, accessed July 1, 2014. http://leanin.org/stories/laurie-h-glimcher/.

Peter DeMarco, "Science is in the Bones for Dad, Daughter," *The Boston Globe*, August 21, 2006. http://www.boston.com/yourlife/health/diseases/articles/2006/08/21/science_is_in_the_bones_for_dad_daughter/?page=full.

Christine Goforth

Christine Goforth, interview via email, June 13, 2014.

"Studying Dragonfly Swarms With Citizen Science," Christine Goforth, guest blogger, SciStarterBlog, July 11, 2011. http://www.scienceforcitizens

Janet Jansson

"Biological Sciences Staff Information," Pacific Northwest National Laboratory, accessed March 7, 2015, http://www.pnnl.gov/biology/staff/staff_info.asp?staff_num=8138.

"Global Warming to Awaken Soil Microorganisms." Hosted by Robyn Williams. The Science Show. *Australian Broadcasting Company*, March 3, 2012. http://www.abc.net.au/radionational/programs/scienceshow/global-warming-to-awaken-soil-microorganisms/3862170.

Janet Jansson, interview via email, March 3, 2015.

Michele Koons

Michele Koons, interview via phone, June 23, 2014.

"Michele Koons, PhD," Denver Museum of Nature and Science, accessed June 1, 2014. http://www.dmns.org/science/museum-scientists/michele-koons/.

Marcia Kemper McNutt

"About USGS," United States Geological Survey, accessed June 9, 2014. http://www.usgs.gov/aboutusgs/organized/bios/mcnutt.asp.

Anthony B. Watts and Marcia McNutt, "McNutt Receives 2007 Maurice Ewing Medal," Eos, Transactions American Geophysical Union, Vol. 89, No. 5, accessed June 9, 2014, doi: 10.1029/2008EO050004.

Carolyn Gramling, "Marcia McNutt, Bringing Her 'Intellectual Energy' to Science," Science Insider, AAAS, April 2, 2013, accessed May 26, 2015. http://news.sciencemag.org/2013/04/marcia-mcnutt-bringing-her-intellectual-energy-science.

Marcia Kemper McNutt, feedback via email, September 2, 2014.

"Marcia Kemper McNutt," National Science Foundation Graduate Research Fellowship Program, accessed June 9, 2014. http://www.nsfgrfp.org/pdfs/60th_anniversary/Marcia%20K%20McNutt.pdf.

"Marcia McNutt, Director, U.S. Geological Survey," United States Geological Survey, accessed June 9, 2014. http://www.usgs.gov/aboutusgs/organized/bios/mcnutt.asp.

"Marcia McNutt, Ph.D., Editor-in-Chief of Science Magazine, Ocean Exploration 2020 Executive Chair," The Report of Ocean Exploration2020: A National Forum, National Oceanic and Atmospheric Administration (NOAA), accessed June 9, 2014. http://oceanexplorer.noaa.gov/oceanexploration2020/speakers/mcnutt.html.

"Officials, Marcia K. McNutt," Allgov.com, accessed June 9, 2014. http://www.allgov.com/officials/mdnutt-marcia?officialid=29154.

Karen Olson

Karen Olson, interview via email, June 15, 2014.

Carolyn Porco

"Carolyn Porco," Carolyn Porco, About, accessed on November 15, 2014. http://carolynporco.com/about/biography/.

Carolyn Porco, interview via email, September 28, 2014.

Erin Allen, "Portraits of the Solar System: Talking With Carolyn Porco About Carl Sagan," Library of Congress blog, November 14, 2013, accessed November 15, 2014. http://blogs.loc.gov/loc/2013/11/portraits-of-the-solar-system-talking-with-carolyn-porco-about-carl-sagan/.

Joel Achebach, "To Go Boldly (and on Budget)," The Washington Post, December 25, 2013, accessed on November 15, 2014. http://www.washingtonpost.com/sf/national/2013/12/25/to-go-boldly-and-on-budget/.

Maggie Koerth-Baker, "Women Scientists on the Debate Over Women in Science," Boing Boing blog, June 11, 2010, accessed November 15, 2014, http://boingboing.net/2010/06/11/women-scientists-on.html.

Lisa Randall

Adrian J. Smith, "Supersymmetry and Parallel Dimensions, Harvard Physicist Among World's Leading String Theorists," The Harvard Crimson, January 6, 2006, accessed May 26, 2014, http://www.thecrimson.com/article/2006/1/6/supersymmetry-and-parallel-dimensions-professor-of/.

Corey S. Powell, "The Discover Interview: Lisa Randall," Discover, July 2006, accessed May 26, 2014, http://discovermagazine.com/2006/jul/interview-randall/.

John Crace, "Lisa Randall: Warped View of the Universe," The Guardian, June 20, 2005, accessed May 26, 2014, http://www.theguardian.com/education/2005/jun/21/highereducation.highereducationprofile.

Lisa Randall, feedback via email, February 27, 2015.

Robert Sullivan, "A Beautiful Mind," Vogue, August 2007, 212-275, accessed May 26, 2014, http://randall.physics.harvard.edu/RandallCV/Vogue_08_07l.pdf.

Pardis Sabeti

"Pardis Sabeti," FAS Center for Systems Biology, accessed May 24, 2014. http://sysbio.harvard.edu/csb/research/sabeti.html.

Pardis Sabeti, interview via phone, June 12, 2014.

"Pardis Sabeti," Sabeti Lab, accessed May 24, 2014. http://sabetilab.org/people/pardis-sabeti.

Seth Mnookin, "Pardis Sabeti, The Rollerblading Rock Star Scientist of Harvard," Smithsonian Magazine, December 2012, accessed May 24, 2014. http://www.smithsonianmag.com/science-nature/pardis-sabeti-the-rollerblading-rock-star-scientist-of-harvard-135532753/?no-ist=&fb_locale=sv_SE&page=2.

Technology

Mireille Akilian

Mireille Akilian, interview via email, August 14, 2014.

"Mireille Akilian," Resume, Massachusetts Institute of Technology, accessed August 20, 2014. http://web.mit.edu/makilian/www/resume.pdf.

Shaherose Charania
"10 to Watch – Shaherose Charania, Entrepreneur," Fast Company, Republic of Brown, accessed June 27, 2014. http://republicofbrown.com/10-to-watch-shaherose-charania/.

"About Us," Women 2.0, accessed June 27, 2014. http://women2.com/about/.

Jen Chien, "Women in STEM: Interview With Shaherose Charania of Women 2.0," KALW Public Radio, San Francisco, February 13, 2014, accessed June 27, 2014. http://kalw.org/post/women-stem-interview-shaherose-charania-women-20.

Jessica Stillman, "Young and Female in Start-Up Central," Inc., April 15, 2012, accessed June 27, 2014. http://www.inc.com/jessica-stillman/young-female-networking-in-start-up-central.html.

Shaherose Charania, feedback via email, May 11, 2015.

Lorrie Faith Cranor
"EPP Faculty: Lorrie Faith Cranor," Engineering and Public Policy, Carnegie Mellon University, accessed June 24, 2014. http://www.epp.cmu.edu/people/bios/cranor.html.

"Honorable Mention: Security Blanket," *Science*, February 7, 2014, accessed June 24, 2014. http://www.sciencemag.org/content/343/6171/600.full.

Lorrie Faith Cranor, interview via phone, June 23, 2014.

Scott M. Fulton, "Dr. Cranor on 'Do Not Track' & the Improbability of Complete Privacy," ReadWrite, February 24, 2012, accessed June 24, 2014. http://readwrite.com/2012/02/24/dr-cranor-on-do-not-track-and#awesm=oI7E3V3cPxo5HB.

"What's Wrong With Your Password," Lorrie Faith Cranor, TEDxCMU Talk transcript, June 2014, accessed June 24, 2014. http://www.ted.com/talks/lorrie_faith_cranor_what_s_wrong_with_your_pa_w0rd/transcript?language=en.

Erika Ebbel Angle
"Cool Things Happen at the Edges: Erika Ebbel Angle at TEDxBeaconStreet," YouTube, December 6, 2013, accessed June 19, 2014. https://www.youtube.com/watch?v=WodbEFlIFMM.

Danielle Caldwell, "Dr. Erika Ebbel Angle, Biochemist, Educator, CEO," Stemworks, December 10, 2012, accessed June 19, 2014. http://stem-works.com/subjects/17-medical-innovations/cool_jobs/224.

Erika Ebbel Angle, interview via phone, June 13, 2014.

Mary Lou Jepsen
"Could Future Devices Read Images From Our Brain?" Mary Lou Jepsen, TED Talk, March 2014, accessed May 21, 2014. https://www.ted.com/speakers/mary_lou_jepsen.

"Dr. Mary Lou Jepsen, Resume," MaryLouJepsen.com, accessed May 21, 2014. http://www.maryloujepsen.com/#!resume/c46c.

J. O'Dell, "What Hardware is Google Making After Glass? Mary Lou Jepsen Knows," Venture Beat, May 16, 2013, accessed May 21, 2014. http://venturebeat.com/2013/05/16/what-hardware-is-google-making-after-glass-mary-lou-jepsen-knows/.

Mary Lou Jepsen, feedback via email, February 23, 2015.

Mary Lou Jepsen, "Bringing Back My Real Self With Hormones," *The New York Times*, November 23, 2013, accessed May 21, 2014. http://www.nytimes.com/2013/11/24/opinion/sunday/bringing-back-my-real-self-with-hormones.html?pagewanted=all&_r=0.

"Mary Lou Jepsen," Wikipedia, accessed May 21, 2014. http://en.wikipedia.org/wiki/Mary_Lou_Jepsen.

Holly Liu

Cassie Phillips, "Kabam Co-founder Holly Liu Talks Early Startup Failures," *Forbes*, October 17, 2011, accessed July 8, 2014. http://www.forbes.com/sites/women2/2011/10/17/kabam-co-founder-holly-liu-talks-early-startup-failures/.

Holly Liu, interview via phone, July 10, 2014.

Pranati Reddy, "Holly Liu: Co-founder & Chief of Staff at Kabam," Insight Berkeley, March 12, 2014, accessed July 8, 2014. http://insightberkeley.com/tag/holly-liu/.

"The HR Star – Holly Liu, Co-founder & Chief of Staff, Kabam," Womenetics, May 12, 2014, accessed July 8, 2014. https://www.womenetics.com/Article/ArtMID/2681/ArticleID/3660/Holly-Liu-Kabam.

Andrea Luecke

Andrea Luecke, interview via phone, July 3, 2014.

"Live From WREF Denver: A Conversation with Andrea Luecke," Narrated by Frank Andorka, Solar Power World, May 16, 2012, accessed July 7, 2014. http://www.solarpowerworldonline.com/2012/05/live-from-wref-denver-an-interview-with-andrea-luecke/.

"Staff," The Solar Foundation, accessed July 7, 2014. http://thesolarfoundation.org/aboutus/staff.

Pilar Molina Lopez

Pilar Molina Lopez, interview via phone, August 20, 2014.

"Pilar Molina Lopez," LinkedIn, accessed June 26, 2014. https://www.linkedin.com/in/pilarmolinalopez/en.

Heather Payne

"About," Heather Payne website, accessed March 19, 2015. http://heatherpayne.ca/about/.

Erin Bury, "Beating the Code Barrier," Financial Post, June 11, 2012, accessed March 19, 2015, http://business.financialpost.com/2012/06/11/beating-the-coding-barrier/?__lsa=8dcf-4c33.

Heather Payne, interview via email, March 16, 2015.

Igor Bonifacic, "Movers and Starters: Heather Payne," Toronto Standard," March 7, 2013, accessed March 19, 2015, http://www.torontostandard.com/industry/movers-and-starters-heather-payne/.

Russ Martin, "HackerYou Aims to Disrupt Tech Education," O.Canada.com, June 6, 2012, accessed March 19, 2015, http://o.canada.com/technology/hackeryou-aims-to-disrupt-tech-education.

Zoe McKnight, "Ladies Learning Code Seeks to Close Gender Tech Gap," thestar.com, November 4, 2011, accessed March 19, 2015, http://www.thestar.com/life/2011/11/04/ladies_learning_code_seeks_to_close_gender_tech_gap.html.

Kaliya Young

"Bio," Identity Woman, accessed November 3, 2014. http://www.identitywoman.net/about-kaliya/bio.

Chris O'Brien, "Kaliya Hamlin Tackles Our Online Identities," *Mercury News*, March 6, 2012, accessed November 3, 2014. http://www.mercurynews.com/ci_20116258/obrien-kaliya-identity-woman-hamlin-hopes-international-recognition.

"Kaliya Hamlin, Biography," O'Reilly Community, accessed November 3, 2014. http://www.oreilly.com/pub/au/2418.

Kaliya Hamlin, interview via email, October 22, 2014.

"Kaliya Hamilin," LinkedIn, accessed November 3, 2014. http://www.linkedin.com/in/kaliya.

"Kaliya Hamlin," Unconference.net, accessed November 3, 2014. http://www.unconference.net/kaliya-hamlin/.

Engineering

Cynthia Breazeal

Adam Cohen, "Cynthia Breazeal," *Time*, December 3, 2000, accessed June 12, 2014, http://content.time.com/time/magazine/article/0,9171,90515,00.html.

Claudia Dreifus, "A Conversation With: Cynthia Breazeal; A Passion to Build a Better Robot, One With Social Skills and a Smile," *The New York Times*, June 10, 2003, accessed June 12, 2014. http://www.nytimes.com/2003/06/10/science/conversation-with-cynthia-breazeal-passion-build-better-robot-one-with-social.html.

Cynthia Breazeal, feedback via email, October 30, 2014.

"Cynthia Breazeal," MIT Media Lab, accessed June 12, 2014. http://www.media.mit.edu/people/cynthiab.

"Cynthia Breazeal, Robot Designer," National Academy of Sciences, accessed June 12, 2014, http://www.iwaswondering.org/cynthia_homepage.html.

"Robot Pals: A Conversation With Cynthia Breazeal," Scientific American Frontiers, PBS, accessed June 12, 2014. http://www.pbs.org/saf/1510/features/breazeal.htm.

"Welcome to Cynthia Breazeal's Website," Massachusetts Institute of Technology, accessed June 12, 2014. http://web.media.mit.edu/~cynthiab/index.html.

Carol Espy-Wilson

Carol Espy-Wilson, interview via phone, July 13, 2014.

"Espy-Wilson, Carol," The Institute for Systems Research, University of Maryland, accessed June 2, 2014. http://www.isr.umd.edu/faculty/espy-wilson.

Steven Overly, "With Little Business Experience, Professor Shows Promise in Developing Tech Firm," *The Washington Post*, August 2, 2010, accessed June 2, 2014. http://www.washingtonpost.com/wp-dyn/content/article/2010/07/30/AR2010073005671.html.

Yoder, Brian L., PhD, "Engineering by the Numbers," American Society for Engineering Education (ASEE), 2011, accessed June 2, 2014. http://www.asee.org/papers-and-publications/publications/college-profiles/2011-profile-engineering-statistics.pdf.

Paula Hammond

"Paula Hammond: The Possibilities of Polymers," The Catalyst Series: Women in Chemistry, Chemical Heritage Foundation, transcript August 2012, accessed June 26, 2014. http://www.chemheritage.org/discover/online-resources/women-in-chemistry/paula-hammond-transcript.aspx.

Paula Hammond, interview via phone, June 2, 2014.

Sarah Kovaleski

"FAQ About Nuclear Energy," Nuclear Energy Institute, accessed July 30,2015. http://www.nei.org/Knowledge-Center/FAQ-About-Nuclear-Energy.

Sarah Kovaleski, interview via email, July 9, 2014.

Sarah Kovaleski, "Life As a Wife, Mother and Nuclear Engineer," *The Independent*, May 6, 2014, accessed July 13, 2014. http://www.independent.co.uk/news/business/analysis-and-features/life-as-a-wife-mother-and-nuclear-engineer-9324408.html.

Sylvia Lee

Sylvia Lee, interview via phone, June 5, 2014.

Sylvia Lee, "Water as a Catalyst for Peace," Skoll World Forum, Debates and Series, March 22, 2013, accessed June 21, 2014. http://skollworldforum.org/2013/03/22/water-as-a-catalyst-for-peace/.

"Water, Water Everywhere: The Paradox of the 21st Century," Skoll World Forum video session, April 11, 2014, accessed June 21, 2014. http://skollworldforum.org/session/skoll-world-forum-2013/water-water-everywhere-the-paradox-of-the-21st-century/.

Barbara Liskov

"Computer Wiz Barbara Liskov Wins Turing Award," *NPR*, March 13, 2009, accessed May 28, 2014. http://www.npr.org/templates/story/story.php?storyId=101868293.

"Barbara Liskov," A.M. Turing Award, Association for Computing Machinery, accessed May 28, 2014. http://amturing.acm.org/award_winners/liskov_1108679.cfm.

Barbara Liskov, interview via phone, June 11, 2014.

"Barbara Liskov," Wikipedia, accessed May 28, 2014. http://en.wikipedia.org/wiki/Barbara_Liskov.

Kimber Lockhart

"Board of Directors, Kimber Lockhart," Circus Center, San Francisco, accessed June 11, 2014. http://circuscenter.org/board-of-directors/.

"From Entrepreneur to Engineering Powerhouse: Kimber Lockhart, Director of Engineering, Box," July 2, 2014, accessed June 11, 2014. http://blog.hackbrightacademy.com/2013/07/box-director-engineering-kimber-lockhart/.

Kimber Lockhart, interview via phone, June 17, 2014.

Lynne Nolan, "Box Clever," Dublin Journalist, May 27, 2003, accessed June 11, 2014. http://dublinjournalist.com/2013/05/27/innovating-inside-the-box/

Mike Cassidy, "Box's Kimber Lockhart Says Women Who Start Late in Computer Science Catch Up Quickly," *San Jose Mercury News*, February 25, 2014, accessed June 11, 2014. http://www.mercurynews.com/mike-cassidy/ci_25224486/boxs-kimber-lockhart-says-women-who-start-late.

"Statistics: State of Girls and Women in STEM," National Girls Collaborative Project, accessed June 11, 2014. http://www.ngcproject.org/statistics.

"The Millenial – Kimber Lockhart, Vice President of Engineering, One Medical Group: Tech Star Tells All About Confidence," Womenetics.com, August 4, 2014, accessed May 7, 2015. https://www.womenetics.com/Spotlight/Conversations/ConversationArticle/ArtMID/2741/ArticleID/3751/CategoryID/48/Kimber-Lockhart-Box-Engineering.

Sara McAllister

"Fire, Fuel and Smoke Science Program," Rocky Mountain Research Station, accessed August 7, 2014. http://www.firelab.org/profile/mcallister-sara.

Nancy Bronstein, "Fire in Space: A Berkeley Lab Group is Focused on How to Prevent Disasters," Berkeley Graduate Division News, February 10, 2009, accessed August 7, 2014. http://grad.berkeley.edu/news/profiles/fire-in-space/.

Sara McAllister, interview via email, June 6, 2014.

"Sara McAllister," United States Department of Agriculture, Forest Service, accessed August 7, 2014. http://www.fs.fed.us/research/people/profile.php?alias=smcallister.

"Scientists Find Signs of Ancient Man-Made Fire," Lightyears blog, *CNN*, April 2, 2012, accessed August 7, 2014. http://lightyears.blogs.cnn.com/2012/04/02/scientists-find-signs-of-ancient-man-made-fire/.

Ainissa Ramirez

Ainissa Ramirez, interview via email, July 1, 2014.

Ainissa Ramirez, "Periodic Tables, Gender Bias and Stereotypes," Big Think, April 1, 2013, accessed June 22, 2014. http://bigthink.com/experts-corner/periodic-tables-gender-bias-and-stereotypes.

"Ainissa Ramirez, Science Evangelist," Ainissa Ramirez, accessed June 22, 2014. http://www.ainissaramirez.com/bio.html.

Barrett H. Ripin, editor, "High School Physics Enrollments Hit Post-War High: Undergrad and Grad Enrollments at a Low." APS Physics, November 1999, Volume 8, Number 10, accessed May 15, 2015. http://www.aps.org/publications/apsnews/199911/.

Jen Matteis, "The Science Evangelist: Ainissa Ramirez, PhD," Byron Academy, accessed June 22, 2014. http://www.byronacademy.org/women-in-STEM/id/9/The-Science/Evangelist:-Ainissa-Ramirez.

Jessica Ruby, "Ainissa Ramirez on Women in STEM," TED blog, September 18, 2010, accessed June 22, 2014. http://blog.ed.ted.com/2013/09/18/ainissa-ramirez-on-women-in-stem/.

Rachel Lehmann-Haupt, "Let's Fix Science Education: A Q & A With 'Save Our Science' Author Ainissa Ramirez," TED blog, February 6, 2013, accessed June 22, 2014. http://blog.ted.com/2013/02/06/lets-fix-science-education-a-qa-with-save-our-science-author-ainissa-ramirez/.

"Revenge of the Nerds: The Best Jobs," *CNN*, Schools of Thought Blog, June 19, 2012, accessed June 22, 2014. http://schoolsofthought.blogs.cnn.com/2012/06/19/revenge-of-the-nerds-the-best-jobs/.

Debbie Sterling

"About," GoldieBlox, accessed June 23, 2014. http://www.goldieblox.com/pages/about#pink.

Brenae Leary, Sunshine Sachs, feedback via email, January 22, 2016.

"Debbie Sterling," Engineer Girl, National Academy of Engineering, accessed June 23, 2014. http://www.engineergirl.org/Engineers/Directory/13512.aspx.

"Debbie Sterling's Mission to Inspire the Next Generation of Female Engineers," *KatieCouric.com*, March 11, 2013, accessed June 23, 2014. http://katiecouric.com/features/debra-sterlings-mission-to-inspire-the-next-generation-of-female-engineers/.

Elizabeth Lindsay, Derris & Company, feedback via email, September 24, 2014.

James H. Burnett III, "Debbie Sterling Builds New Play Patterns," *The Boston Globe*, January 9, 2013, accessed June 23, 2014. http://www.bostonglobe.com/lifestyle/style/2013/01/09/rhode-island-debbie-sterling-focuses-creating-toy-for-young-girls-build/DvO0TD9YwbSX932EVl7n0L/story.html.

Jinny Gudmundsen, "New Toys and Apps for Girls Present Strong Role Models," *USA Today*, March 10, 2013, accessed June 23, 2014. http://www.usatoday.com/story/tech/columnist/gudmundsen/2013/03/10/girls-toys-apps-games-parents-daughters/1962735/.

Kristen Nicole, "Beauty, Brains and Business: Engineering Girls for a Man's World," *Forbes*, October 15, 2012, accessed June 23, 2014. http://www.forbes.com/sites/siliconangle/2012/10/15/women-engineers/.

Lorena Ruiz, "Meet Debbie Sterling, Building Toys and Women," *MSNBC.com*, July 27, 2013, accessed June 23, 2014. http://www.msnbc.com/melissa-harris-perry/meet-debbie-sterling-building-toys-and-women.

Robin Wilkey, "GoldieBlox 'We Are the Champions' Video Features Girls Who Crush Gender Stereotypes," *The Huffington Post*, July 3, 2013, accessed June 23, 2014. http://www.huffingtonpost.com/2013/07/03/goldieblox-video_n_3541690.html.

Mathematics

Susan Athey

Clement, Douglas. "Interview with Susan Athey." *The Region*, a publication of The Federal Reserve Bank of Minneapolis. June 10, 2013.

Ito, Aki, "Stanford Economist Musters Big Data to Shape Web Future," *Bloomberg*, June 26, 2013, accessed June 5, 2014. http://www.bloomberg.com/news/2013-06-26/stanford-economist-musters-big-data-to-shape-web-future.html.

Susan Athey, feedback via email, March 2, 2015.

"Susan Athey," Stanford Graduate School of Business, accessed June 5, 2014.

Maria Chudnovsky

Maria Chudnovsky, interview via phone, May 30, 2014.

Unknown, "Interview With Research Fellow Maria Chudnovsky," CMI Annual Report, University of Oxford, 2005, accessed May 30, 2014. http://www2.maths.ox.ac.uk/cmi/library/annual_report/ar2005/05report_chud.pdf.

Jeanne Gang

Amy Schellenbaum, "Seven Fascinating Facts About 'Genius' Architect Jeanne Gang," Curbed, May 13, 2014, accessed June 9, 2014. http://curbed.com/archives/2014/05/13/seven-fascinating-facts-about-genius-architect-jeanne-gang.php.

Glancey, Jonathan, "Aqua Tower – The Tower That Jeanne Gang Built," *The Guardian*, October 20, 2009.

"Jeanne Gang, Founder and Principal," Studio Gang/Architects, accessed June 9, 2014. http://studiogang.net/people/jeannegang.

"Jeanne Gang/Studio Gang Architects." ArchDaily Interviews. April 8, 2014. http://www.archdaily.com/493927/ad-interviews-jeanne-gang-studio-gang-architects/

Lynn Becker, "Jeanne Gang: Before Aqua – An Early Portrait," Repeat, accessed June 9, 2014. http://www.lynnbecker.com/repeat/studiogang/gangprofile2004.htm.

Sarah Kramer, Publications Director for Studio Gang, feedback via email, September 15, 2014.

Stott, Rory. "MAD Architects + Studio Gang Selected for Chicago's George Lucas Museum" July 28, 2014. ArchDaily, accessed June 9, 2014. http://www.archdaily.com/531945/mad-architects-studio-gang-selected-for-chicago-s-george-lucas-museum/.

Trachette Jackson

Trachette Jackson, interview via email, June 10, 2014.

Evelyn Lamb, "Mathematics, Live: A Conversation with Victoria Booth and Trachette Jackson," *Scientific American*, October 9, 2013, accessed May 31, 2014. http://blogs.scientificamerican.com/roots-of-unity/2013/10/09/mathematics-live-booth-jackson/

Bryna Kra

Bryna Kra, interview via phone, May 29, 2014.

"Bryna Kra, Northwestern University," Association for Women in Mathematics, accessed June 4, 2014. https://sites.google.com/site/awmmath/home/awm-2013-elections/bryna-kra.

Bryna Kra, "Mathematics: 1,000 Years Old, and Still Hot," The Chronicle of Higher Education, June 24, 2013, accessed June 4, 2014. http://chronicle.com/article/Mathematics-1000-Years-Old/139943/.

Gerdes, Geoffrey R., May X. Liu, Jason P. Berkenpas, Matthew C. Chen, Matthew C. Hayward, James M. McKee, Scott Dake, Patrick Dyer, Dave Brangaccio, Nancy Donahue and others, "The 2013 Federal Reserve Payments Study, Recent and Long-Term Payment Trends in the United States: 2003-2012." *2013 Federal Reserve Payments Study*, Summary Report and Initial Data Release, December 2013.

Debbie Lawrence

"About Pinnacle Seismic, Ltd.," Pinnacle Seismic, accessed June 5, 2014. http://pinnacleseismic.com/about.

Debbie Lawrence, interview via phone, June 4, 2014.

Stacy Lindborg

Stacy Lindborg, interview via phone, July 1, 2014.

"Stacy Lindborg," LinkedIn, accessed July 6, 2014. https://www.linkedin.com/pub/stacy-lindborg/14/228/a67.

Tonya B. Manning

"Tonya B. Manning, FSA, MAAA, EA, FCA," Society of Actuaries, accessed November 12, 2014. https://www.soa.org/about/bios-and-photos/about-tonya-manning.aspx.

"Tonya Manning," Actuarial Science Faculty, Columbia University, accessed November 12, 2014. http://ce.columbia.edu/actuarial-science/faculty-advisors/tonya-manning.

Tonya Manning, interview via email, November 2, 2014.

Anna Nagurney

Anna Nagurney, interview via email, June 6, 2014.

"Anna Nagurney," Isenberg School of Management, Operations and Information Management, accessed June 6, 2014. https://www.isenberg.umass.edu/oim/Faculty/Profiles/Anna_Nagurney/.

Rachel Schutt

Interview, Rachel Schutt, Google Research, October 25, 2012, accessed August 22, 2014. https://plus.google.com/+ResearchatGoogle/posts/e7qgT37kd7j.

Rachel Schutt, interview via phone, August 20, 2014.

Stefani Wildhaber

Stefani Wildhaber, interview via email, September 5, 2014.

"Stefani Wildhaber," LinkedIn, accessed June 11, 2014. https://www.linkedin.com/pub/stefani-wildhaber/5/789/352.

"Partners," Makers, accessed June 11, 2014. http://www.makersarch.com/about-us/our-team/.

Melanie Matchett Wood

"April 2010-Melanie Machett Wood," Sock It To Me, April 2, 2010, accessed June 12, 2014. http://www.sockittome.com/coolgirl/2010/04/april-2010-melanie-matchett-wood/.

Deepti Scharf, "Melanie Wood: The Making of a Mathematician," *Duke Today*, May 8, 2003, accessed June 12, 2014. http://today.duke.edu/2003/05/melaniewood0503.html.

Gallian, Joseph A., "A Conversation With Melanie Wood," Math Horizons, University of Minnesota Duluth, September 14, 2004.

Niki Denison, "Math, Mentoring and Motherhood," *On Wisconsin Magazine*, accessed August 2, 2014. http://onwisconsin.uwalumni.com/uncategorized/math-mentoring-and-motherhood/.

Melanie Wood, interview via phone, June 11, 2014.

Other

Linda Becerra and Ron Barnes, "Measuring Women's Progress in Mathematics," Math Horizon's Aftermath, September 1, 2014, accessed September 12, 2014. http://horizonsaftermath.blogspot.com/2012/08/measuring-womens-progress-in-mathematics.html.

Amanda Chapman, "Gender Bias in Education" Critical Multicultural Pavilion, EdChange, accessed October 5, 2015. http://www.edchange.org/multicultural/papers/genderbias.html.

Joseph F. Coates, "Engineering and the Future of Technology," National Academy of Engineering, 1997, accessed September 21, 2014. https://www.nae.edu/Publications/Bridge/EngineeringEvolving/EngineeringandtheFutureofTechnology.aspx.

"Empirically Dancing Your Way to the Top: How Nicole Dubilier Does It!" Ashley Campbell, guest blogger, *Scientific American*, April 18, 2012. http://blogs.scientificamerican.com/guest-blog/2012/04/18/empirically-dancing-your-way-to-the-top-how-nicole-dubilier-does-it/.

Adam Frank, "I Was Promised Flying Cars," *The New York Times*, June 6, 2014, accessed September 15, 2014. http://www.nytimes.com/2014/06/08/opinion/sunday/i-was-promised-flying-cars.html.

"Gender Equality in Education: A Data Snapshot," U.S. Department of Education, Office for Civil Rights, June 2012.

Elizabeth Green, "Why Do Americans Stink at Math?" *The New York Times*, July 23, 2014, accessed September 21, 2014. http://www.nytimes.com/2014/07/27/magazine/why-do-americans-stink-at-math.html.

"How Confidence Can Help Women Athletes in Business," Women Athletes Business Network, EY (Ernst & Young)-Brasil, accessed July 7, 2015. http://www.ey.com/BR/pt/About-us/Our-sponsorships-and-programs/Women-Athletes-Global-Leadership-Network---QandA---Katty-Kay-and-Claire-Shipman.

Janet S. Hyde, Sara M. Lindberg, Marcia C. Lynn, Amy B. Ellis, Caroline C. Williams, "Gender Similarities Characterize Math Performance," *Science*, July 25, 2008, Vol. 321, 494-495.

Kevin Kelly, "Speculations on the Future of Science," Edge, April 6, 2006, accessed September 17, 2014. https://edge.org/conversation/speculations-on-the-future-of-science.

Rebecca Klein, "Study: Music Education Could Help Close the Achievement Gap Between Poor and Affluent Students," Huffington Post, September 2, 2014, accessed September 7, 2014. http://www.huffingtonpost.com/2014/09/02/harmony-project-music-study_n_5755448.html.

Joanne Lipman, "Is Music the Key to Success?" *The New York Times*, October 12, 2013, accessed September 7, 2014. http://www.nytimes.com/2013/10/13/opinion/sunday/is-music-the-key-to-success.html?pagewanted=all.

Alyson Shontell, "Why More Startups Succeed in Silicon Valley: 22 Fascinating Research Findings," Business Insider, April 13, 2012, accessed April 22, 2015. http://www.businessinsider.com/silicon-valley-vs-new-york-startup-genome-findings-2012-4#.

"Amy Smith," D-Lab, Massachusetts Institute of Technology, accessed on September 20, 2014. http://d-lab.mit.edu/people/amy_smith.

"The Future of Engineering," Raise the Bar for Engineering, accessed September 6, 2014. http://www.raisethebarforengineering.org/future-engineer.

"The Nobel Prize in Physics 1978 – Speed Read." *Nobelprize.org*. Nobel Media AB 2014. November 17, 2015. http://www.nobelprize.org/nobel_prizes/physics/laureates/1978/speedread.html.

"Women in STEM: A Gender Gap to Innovation," U.S. Department of Commerce, Economics and Statistics Administration, August 2011.

"Women in STEM," Office of Science and Technology Policy," Whitehouse.gov, June 2013, accessed September 2, 2014. http://www.whitehouse.gov/administration/eop/ostp/women.

#GiveGirlsRoleModels